PYTHAGOREAN PALACES

Magic and Architecture in
the Italian Renaissance

Pythagorean Palaces

MAGIC AND ARCHITECTURE IN THE ITALIAN RENAISSANCE

G. L. HERSEY

CORNELL UNIVERSITY PRESS
ITHACA AND LONDON

First published 1976 by Cornell University Press.
Published in the United Kingdom by Cornell University Press Ltd.,
2–4 Brook Street, London W1Y 1AA.

International Standard Book Number 0–8014–0998–5
Library of Congress Catalog Card Number 76-13661
Printed in the United States of America by Vail-Ballou Press, Inc.
*Librarians: Library of Congress cataloging information appears
on the last page of the book.*

Walton J. Lord

FOR MY MOTHER AND FATHER
AND IN MEMORY OF
VINCENT F. HOPPER

Preface

I have written this book to establish the hitherto neglected fact that Italian Renaissance domestic architecture was largely ruled by Pythagorean principles. In recent generations of scholars, from Stegmann and Geymüller in 1885 to Heydenreich and Lotz in 1974, the historiography of Renaissance architecture has been in the hands of positivists—those who believe that knowledge is based only on physical objects empirically studied, and that meanings must be sought within the objects themselves. Their approach goes back to the nineteenth-century work of Auguste Choisy, who treated the history of architecture as an analogue to comparative zoology. From such a viewpoint there is little room for magic; rather, the achievement of this positivist school has been to classify styles of, and to reveal processes of, revival and influence.

However, another movement among contemporary scholars really is more relevant to my topic. This movement is almost solely the creation of one man—Rudolf Wittkower. In his epochal book, *Architectural Principles in the Age of Humanism* (1949), Wittkower established the importance of numerical proportion in the design of buildings, both real and ideal, from Alberti to Palladio. With Wittkower the importance of number in Italian Renaissance architecture began to be perceived.

But number, for Wittkower, was a question of proportion and of proportion only. He ignored dimensions and distributions. He ignored the five orders. And numbers, for Wittkower, were modern numbers; they were abstract quantities and nothing more, as in modern mathematics. Wittkower will say, for example, that an 8:6 proportion is really 4:3, or that a room with dimensions of 7.4, 10, and 15 represents a harmonic ratio. When he has established such facts, perhaps also investigating their analogies with music, Wittkower moves on to his next analysis. And so on to the end of the book.

What he does not at all emphasize, however, is the basic assumption of Pythagorean mathematics—that numbers are *not* mere quantities, and that they are not abstract. To the Pythagoreans, who were essentially number magicians, numbers were not only quantities, they were qualities as well. They had fixed or predictable geometric, psychological, moral, and even personal natures. The relation of one number to others was perceived according to cultural and social models. There were, as we shall see, temples, cities, worlds, heavens of numbers. In such constructs lay their magic. The proportion 8:6 is therefore *reducible,* in Wittkower's sense, to 4:3. But it is not the same as 4:3, because 8 and 6 have all sorts of characteristics, together and independently, that 4 and 3 do not have. The Pythagorean would say that the expression 8:6::4:3 makes 4 and 3 the "children" of the "marriage" between 8 and 6. The reductive process is conceived as a genealogy, a procreation of social entities.

Not only does this view affect proportion in architecture—the subject that Wittkower and his followers almost exclusively treat—it also affects the dimensions and distributions of a building as well. It affects, that is, the size of a volume in braccia or feet, the number of doors, windows, and columns it possesses, and the decoration of those doors, windows, and columns.

I will show in the following pages that Renaissance architectural "philosophers" from Alberti to Vincenzo Scamozzi understood number, and therefore proportion, dimension, and distribution, in this sense. In other words, the mathematical tradition that was imparted to these writers, whether in shop, *scuola d'abacco,* or university, was Pythagorean. My book therefore applies, to architectural history, material that has been used for the writing of intellectual history by such authors as Eugenio Garin, Frances Yates, and D. P. Walker. More precisely, the book belongs with the work of such art historians as Manfredo Tafuri, Robert Klein, Marco Rosci, Günter Bandmann, and Georg Weise. I have chosen to concentrate on palaces rather than, say, churches, because a palace, much more than a church, constitutes the sort of omnidirectional cubic grid that Pythagorean mathematics implies. But one could—and I hope this will happen—go on to apply the ensuing ideas to other types of buildings besides palaces.

In writing this book I have been greatly helped by friends and colleagues, especially Susan Ryan, Heinrich Klotz, Judith Colton, Sheldon Nodelman, Donald Preziosi, Chiara Passanti, George Kubler, Larry Lowic, Douglas Lewis, Philip Foster, Humberto Rodriguez-Camilloni, Brenda Preyer, David Cast, Janet Smith, Thomas Cole, Hisao Koyama, and James Ackerman. I have a particular debt to Rab Hatfield for his careful criticism of an early draft of Chapter 5, and I also wish to thank Vincent Scully, Samuel Y. Edgerton, Jr., and Carroll W. Westfall for their comments on the manuscript as a whole. Finally, I am very grateful to my courteously vigilant editor, Daniel R. Snodderly of Cornell University Press. All translations into English are my own.

G. L. H.

New Haven, Connecticut

Contents

Illustrations

Tables

Abbreviations for Works Cited

Agrippa: Henricus Cornelius Agrippa von Nettesheim. *De occulta philosophia sive de magia libri tres.* [Cologne]: n.p., 1553. Facsmile ed. K. A. Nowotny, Graz: Akademische Druck- und Verlagsanstalt, 1967.

Alberti: Leone Battista Alberti. *De re aedificatoria,* ed. G. Orlandi and P. Portoghesi. 2 vols. Milan: Polifilo, 1966.

Barbaro: Daniele Barbaro, ed. *M. Vitruvii Pollionis: De architectura libri decem.* . . . Venice: F. Franciscum Senensem, 1567. Corrected Latin edition of first edition (in Italian, 1556), with commentary.

Cataneo: Pietro Cataneo. *I quattro primi libri di architettura.* . . . Venice: Aldus, 1554. Facsimile, Ridgewood, N.J.: Gregg, 1964.

Cesariano: Cesare Cesariano, ed. *D. Lucio Pollione: De architectura libri dece* [sic] *traducti de latino in vulgare affigurati.* Como: Gotardus de Ponte [1521]. Like Barbaro, an edition of Vitruvius with commentary.

Colonna: Francesco Colonna. *Hypnerotomachia Poliphili* [1499], in E. Carrara, ed., *Opere di Jacopo Sannazaro.* Turin: UTET [1952].

Diels: *Die Fragmente der Vorsokratiker . . . von Hermann Diels,* ed. Walther Kranz. 6th ed. 3 vols. Berlin: Weidmann, 1951.

Ficino: Marsilio Ficino. *Opera omnia.* Basel: Officina Henricpetrina, 1576. Facsimile, 2 vols. in 4, Turin: Bottega d'Erasmo, 1959.

Filarete: *Filarete's Treatise on Architecture,* ed. and trans. J. R. Spencer. Vol. 2, facsimile of Magliabecchiana ms. New Haven and London: Yale University Press, 1965.

Francesco di Giorgio: Francesco di Giorgio Martini. *Trattati* [I and II] *di architettura ingegneria e arte militare,* ed. C. Maltese. 2 vols. Milan: Polifilo, 1967.

Leonardo: *The Literary Works of Leonardo da Vinci,* ed. J. P. Richter. 3d ed. 2 vols. London: Phaidon, 1970.

Lomazzo, *Idea:* Giovanni Paolo Lomazzo. *Idea del tempio della pittura* [1590]. Rome: Colombo, 1947.

Lomazzo, *Trat.:* Ibid., *Trattato dell'arte de la pittura.* Milan: Paolo Gottardo Pontio, 1584.

Manetti: Antonio di Tuccio Manetti. *The Life of Brunelleschi,* intro. and notes by H.

Saalman, trans. C. Enggass. University Park and London: Pennsylvania State University Press [1970].

Martianus Capella: Martianus Capella. *De nuptiis philologiae et mercurii,* ed. Adolphus Dick. Leipzig: Teubner, 1925.

Palladio: Andrea Palladio. *I quattro libri dell'architettura.* . . . Venice: De'Franceschi, 1570.

Scamozzi: Vincenzo Scamozzi. *L'idea della architettura universale.* . . . 2 vols. Venice: Author, 1615. Facsimile, Ridgewood, N.J.: Gregg, 1964.

Serlio: Sebastiano Serlio. *Tutte l'opere d'architettura, et prospetiva.* . . . Venice: De'Franceschi, 5th reprinting of 1575 ed., 1619. Facsimile, Ridgewood, N.J.: Gregg, 1964.

Vitruvius: *Vitruvio (dai libri I–VII),* trans. and ed. Silvio Ferri. Rome: Palombi, 1960.

PYTHAGOREAN PALACES

Magic and Architecture in
the Italian Renaissance

Introduction

0.1 The Cube as Procreator. It was held in ancient times that the cube was the source of all number and form. "The god is adored in all temples with cubic solidity," says Martianus Capella (7.31). Renaissance Pythagoreans and Platonists repeated or elaborated the idea, saying for example that the cube generates numbers because its root is 1 (Alberti 831). And the number 1 is not itself a true number. It is more stable than such a number, for when multiplied by itself it does not increase. The number 1 is thus called "the First of Cubes"; and its stability, its quality of being a father among children or a god in his creation, is shared in Renaissance geometry by its plane and solid forms, the square and the geometrical cube.

The notion of the cube-as-father has a mystical side. The Pre-Socratics, and Plato in the *Timaeus,* had equated the cube with Earth (Diels 1.345, 403). It was held that each planet corresponded to an ideal solid—Mars to the pyramid, Jupiter to the octahedron, and so forth—and that the most stable of these solids pervaded the motionless planet on which man resides and builds. In the Renaissance, Earth was said to "*contain* [my italics] the first cube of eight solid corners, twenty-four planes [that is, twelve edges] and six bases" (Agrippa 2.23.155). Thus our planet is both a visible sphere and an invisible cube—a round earth with imagined corners as John Donne would say. And this cube creates other cubes, they in turn being the sources of what were thus called cubic numbers, such as the already mentioned 6, 8, and 12.

If Earth could be cubic so could space. Again, for Pythagoreans, 1 is the procrea-

Table 1. Basic Pythagorean hierarchy of number and form

Number	Form
1	point
2	line
3	plane
4	solid

tor. But this time the numerical cube procreates because of its role in a sequence. Putting the idea in this tabular form is no mere convention. It makes the number series 1 2 3 4 *produce* a series of geometric entities (Diels 1.400–406). It portrays affinities, rather like cousins or parents, horizontally, while vertically it portrays issue. It shows how solids and volumes ultimately derive from points, and how certain numbers "marry" geometric entities. It implies that, as the solid is the ultimate state of point, so 4 is the ultimate state or goal of 1, or vice versa. It also shows that, in addition to 1, 6, 8, and 12, 3 is cubic because it is the number of the third power while 4 is cubic because it marks the creation of solid out of plane. In a related sense, according to the Pythagoreans, *any* sequence of odd numbers makes a square or cube-base, while *any* sequence of even numbers makes an oblong (Diels 1.225; Fig. 0.1).

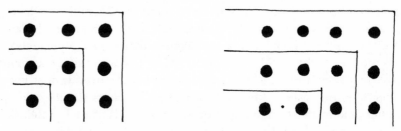

0.1 Pythagorean numberforms: nine-"column" square (left) and twelve-"column" rectangle (right)

Hence a given number can be cubic in several ways. All odd numbers are at least tinged with cubism. And the notion that a number can have a cubic tinge in turn suggests that some numbers are more cubic than others. Indeed, in most cases it is not so much that a given number is cubic in the absolute sense, but rather that it is part of a progression from a less stable to a more stable, that is more cubic, number. Ultimately the stablest, most cubic of all numbers, and the origin and destination of all cubic sequences, is the "point," 1.

Closely allied to the cubic numbers are the "perfect" numbers. Vitruvius mentions 6 and 10. Six is perfect because the ideal human body is six feet high and because ⅙, ⅓, ½, ⅔, and ⅚ of its height are respectively one, two, three, four, and five feet (Vitruvius 3.1.7). The denominators of these fractions in turn form a palindromic sequence: 6 3 2 3 6. In these and other ways 6 is both cubic *and* perfect. Ten is perfect, says Vitruvius, because it represents the number of our fingers and toes (our *digits*) and because it is the sum of $1+2+3+4$. In both these cases the perfect number, like a cubic number, is the goal of a progression that achieves a stable value lying outside the progression itself.

In antiquity the notions of the perfect and of the cubic tended to fuse. The quality of being cubic therefore partook of the divine. To Platonists the cubic procreator 1 was a principle like God or Idea. For Pythagoreans the cosmos was constructed from an array of ten binary components—that is 10 2s (the product of a perfect number and 2, which represented the principle of duity)—of a stable versus a "mobile" quantity. The pairs were: the limited vs. the unlimited, the odd vs. the even, the one vs. the many, the right vs. the left, the male vs. the female, rest vs. motion, the straight vs. the curved, light vs. darkness, good vs. evil, and square vs. oblong (Diels 1.449). Note that the square is on that side of things which is limited, odd, one, right, male, at rest, straight, light, and good.

0.2   Cubices Rationes and Greek Temple Descriptions. Such notions had applications to architecture, and to the description of architecture. Vitruvius was a Pythagorean and called the cube divine. More specifically he saw it as a privileged mode of description and memory:

Those who followed Pythagoras and his teachings liked to write their precepts in volumes according to the principles of the cube [*cubices rationes*]. And they established that 216 lines of words formed a cube, and thought there ought to be no more than three [of these cubes] in any single piece of writing. Now a cube is a square-sided body formed of six equal sides. After being thrown, if it is not touched, it remains motionlessly solid no matter what side it landed on [*incubuit*]. So that cubes are used for the dice that players toss on hollowed gaming boards. The parallel between the cube and the written work seems to be drawn from this, that the unit of [216] lines, like a cube, will land solidly in the mind. Thus the Greek dramatic poets, by breaking up their plays with choruses, created subdivisions marked out into cubic lengths. And in this way the actors make the authors' words memorable [5. Pref. 3, 4].

Renaissance commentators have interpreted this puzzling passage differently (see below, 1.9, 1.10; and in the Rome, 1486 edition of Vitruvius 216 became 250). But one thing is clear: Vitruvius is linking memorability, number, writing, and by implication, architecture under "cubices rationes." And cubices rationes involve special cubic numbers and distributions.

Unfortunately, so far as I can judge, Vitruvius did not compose his own treatise according to cubic principles. But he does employ something like them when he describes Greek temples. These descriptions are attempts to translate the buildings as much as possible into words and numbers. (Very occasionally Vitruvius refers to diagrams but these have not come down to us.) He calls the temples themselves "signifiers" (*quod significat*) and the descriptions of them "signifieds" (*quod significatur*, 1.1.3). This notion of a description that is a kind of explanatory model or miniature, and also the "meaning" of the thing described, is common in classical thought (Vitruvius 34n–35n). Unlike the signifier, the signified is portable, transmittible, and storable. It is more permanent than the signifier since it can be written, multiplied, committed to memory, and spread among men. It is also a method of measuring and controlling the signifier or building proper, for it clarifies or confirms the latter's numerical and geometrical values and proportions. As Vitruvius asserts several times, "geometry indeed reigns over [protects, guarantees] architecture with all sorts of defenses and resources" (1.1.4). The signified is one of these. It is through number—through description, through the signified—that architecture establishes its status as a science (1.1.16).

Vitruvius does not develop his concept of signifieds and signifiers in his descriptions of buildings. But these descriptions are nonetheless signifieds in his sense of the word: they are buildings that have been transformed into words and numbers so that they can be accommodated to a book or sheet. A typical Vitruvian temple-signified has four parts:

1. Plan. A pseudodipteral or exostyle temple, for instance, *must be* eight columns wide by fifteen long (Fig. 0.2). Its cella (A) *must be* four columns wide and centered. The walkway (B) around the cella, inside the peripteral colonnade, *must* measure two intercolumniations plus the upper diameter of a column (3.2.6). If in addition the spacing of the columns is to be eustyle, these intercolumniations are to be 2½ diameters (or d) except at the central intercolumniation, front and back, which is to be three (3.3.6).

Indeed, under Vitruvius' system, a Greek temple plan is a rectangular plane plotted out into a grid by more or less regularly placed column bases, separated by regular "counts" or distributions of intercolumniations or diameters. That is, the transformational technique by which Vitruvius changes the mental building into a diagram presupposes a hypostyle temple with some of its columns removed (shown in white) and others converted into walls (Fig. 0.2).

2. Scale. Such rules might seem applicable at any scale. But this possibility is inhibited by Vitruvius' second system, which prevents the temple from being too small. This system provides that the steps on the stereobate, which must always comprise an odd number, must have 9–10 inch risers and 18–24 inch treads. The risers in turn comprise a given fraction of the stylobate to which they lead up. And the stereobate itself must be 1½ diameters high (3.4.4). Though this limits the possible smallness of the temple, its possible largeness is not so limited. But presumably a truly huge temple, say one approached by 59 steps, and consequently with a stereobate about 44 feet high and columns of 29-foot diameter, would still achieve human scale through its human-sized steps.

3. Upright planes. Vitruvius' third design system consists of the rules for the orders. These are so familiar that we need not go into them. Let us assume that our temple will follow the rules for Ionic (3.5). By saying this we construct the column type which is repeated to make up the temple's two pairs of facades, one pair for the short and one for the long side (Fig. 0.3).

0.2 Vitruvius' hypostyle Greek-temple matrix (imaginary columns in white)

linear diagrams called "idéae." The front elevation is divided into 24½ parts on a horizontal axis (3.3.7). He calls these parts "modules"; he uses the word in its literal sense, meaning "small modus" or measure (cf. the Renaissance term *piccolo braccio*). As Ferri points out (Vitruvius 54n–57n) the related word "model" also expresses this notion of the miniature. Idéae are hence explanatory models done in

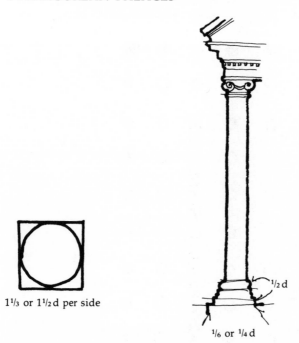

1¹/₃ or 1¹/₂ d per side

¹/₆ or ¹/₄ d

¹/₂ d

0.3 Vitruvius' Ionic formula (simplified): base (left) and column (right)

lines: diagrammed signifieds. In Vitruvius' scheme, columns are one module wide (hence 1 m[odule] = 1 d[iameter]). Bases are ¹/₂ m high and project either ¹/₄ or ¹/₆ d from the shaft, and so on. With these prescriptions Vitruvius sets up, at least *in posse*, modular coordinates that begin to form a planar grid across the front of the temple (Fig. 0.4).

These systems are not always mutually consistent. But that is not important. What matters is the attempt to *translate* a temple entirely into an algorithm, by which I mean a formula using words and numbers that entails other such formulas. The first three parts of Vitruvius' signified do this. The fourth part is a graphic record of the first three. Hence Vitruvius' Greek temple description, his "quod significatur," can be called an illustrated code.

This fourth system as noted also starts up a planar grid across the front end of the temple. Each square in the grid is 1 m². This being so, and the temple being a three-dimensional working out of the measures of the front facade, each square is also the face of a cubic tessera, 1 m³. Such tesserae, plotted down the flanks of the building as well as across the front, would create for it a complete enclosing armature (Fig. 0.5). In this way the temple is not so much cubic in its own shape as in the way it is diagrammed inside a cubic container which "protects and reigns over it." We can call this container the temple's actual cubica ratio. The idéai that form it are an invisible perfect body, pervading it just as Earth's sphere is pervaded by an

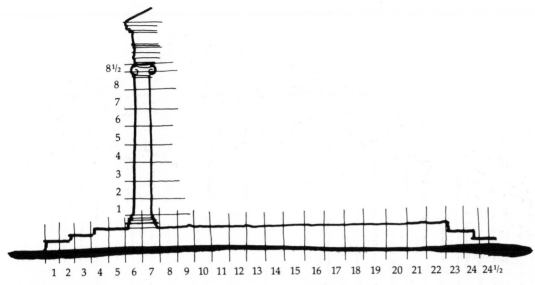

0.4 Vitruvian idéae

imagined cube. While Vitruvius does not ask us to perform this last operation—to extend the temple's incipient planar grid into a three-dimensional one—Renaissance architects will do so in discussing their own buildings.

0.3 Vitruvius' Cubic Hierarchies. Let us also note that Vitruvius has constructed his Greek-temple signified in the form of a hierarchy. He had first arranged points, that is column bases, into a grid. He then bounds these points with a linear structure—the stereobate and its steps. Then comes the order. This constructs the four planes of the facades, which automatically produce the final result, a solid.

I have said that the signified is a stored image. This storableness is not merely an advantage for future ages. It also does away, at least ideally, with all major design decisions at the site. In other words the patron has only to *utter* a signified: "I want a eustyle Ionic pseudodipteral octastyle temple with a module of two feet and a three-step stylobate." This statement, with its various subsidiary formulas, is the design. It is the temple completely translated into an algorithm. The constructed

Table 2. Vitruvius' Greek-temple signified

Number	Form	Signified
1	point	column base
2	line	bounding step
3	plane	order
4	solid	whole

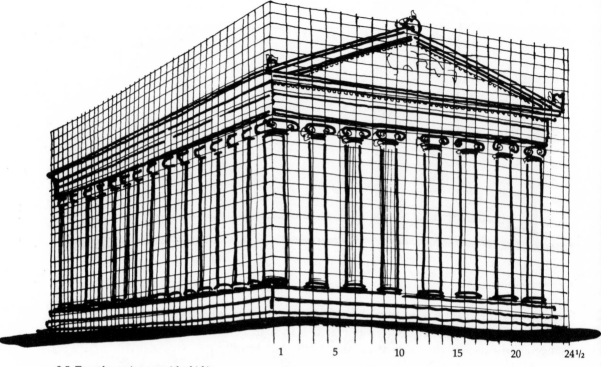

1   5   10   15   20   24¹/₂

0.5 Temple set into a grid of idéae

temple is the transmitted command. By contrast, a patron cannot say "I want a six-room saltbox house" and be sure of the same degree of reproducibility.

I should emphasize finally that Vitruvius' system does not work for just any building—only for Greek temples. There are no such detailed signifieds for Roman temples, basilicas, houses, or the like. But this is understandable, even necessary. To Vitruvius the Greek temple was a basic building. Other kinds of buildings were its dependents, its offspring. The Greek temple was the solid cubic father of mobile, derivative children. It was their origin and their destination. Hence the Greek temple signified, like the Greek temple signifier—the thing described, like the description—was properly nobler and more complete than other kinds of signifieds and signifiers.

Vitruvius contributes four components to the architecture we will study in the following pages: 1) he promotes Pythagorean cubic doctrines; 2) he claims that certain cubic principles are the best method of recording information; 3) he shows how a temple can be condensed into an illustrated code, that is, converted into transmittible information; and 4) his code can be thought of as a Pythagorean hierarchy. But as I have also suggested, Vitruvius doesn't integrate the four notions. He advocates cubic numbers and forms but doesn't consistently apply them in his designs. He believes in cubic descriptive principles but doesn't seem to follow them either in his treatise as a whole or in his individual signifieds; nor does he explain clearly what these principles are. And the hierarchy that stands behind the principles remains, for the moment, my own inference. In essence the Renaissance Pythagorean palace is an attempt to remedy these deficiencies.

0.4 Organization of this Book. The first four chapters trace the emergence of cubic principles in Renaissance architectural theory. The fifth chapter examines these principles as they appear in several material buildings. The period covered is c.1440–1615. I shall confine my investigations entirely to Italy, and more or less to the following writers: Alberti, Filarete, Ficino, Francesco di Giorgio, Leonardo, Cesariano, Serlio, Daniele Barbaro, Palladio, Lomazzo, and Scamozzi. I will present their ideas on the cubic analysis of architecture (Chapter 1), their definitions of the hidden coordinates or "linee occulte" that structure and are discernible in buildings (Chapter 2), and their notions about the human figure as the procreator of geometrical surfaces and as a hidden inhabitant of wall and column (Chapter 3). I shall then describe the three-dimensional "corpo transparente" or invisible cubic jacket that the initiate was supposed to be able to discern in material buildings or "raise" on two-dimensional plans. The fifth chapter, on material palaces, is intended only to illustrate the first four, and not as a systematic survey.

1. Point: Reducing a Building to Its Cubic Source

1.1 Alberti's Cubism. Challenged by Vitruvius' four unsolved problems, we are ready for the Renaissance. Alberti immediately raises the ante. He gives the cube a more paternal-divine role than ever. First of all, the cube's stability, he says, results from its unique unity. *All* good proportions spring from the First of Cubes. From its immediate products, 2, 2^2, and 2^3, and from 12 (which he erroneously says is the square of the cube's diagonal), the architect builds his sequences of ratios, distributions, and dimensions (831). Thus for Alberti an 8 x 12 rectangle would be "cubic" on the grounds that it is really $2^3 \times \sqrt{12^2}$ (pardon the latter expression!), the offspring of the cube of the duity, 2, and of the square of the cube's diagonal. Alberti also conflates (as Vitruvius had done by implication only) cubic and perfect numbers (821). For Alberti, one might say, the cube is the direct practical source of a building's numbers—of its "firmitas" and also of its "venustas," or as Alberti says, "the fulfillment of its parts."

Alberti tells us how we can discover the cubism, or lack of it, in a building through the systematic interchange of number and form (831). A given number is considered a line. That number's square is then seen as a geometrical square, and its cube as a geometrical cube. In other words a building is translated into dimensions, distributions, or proportions and the resulting numbers reduced to their square and cube roots. For the building to be truly cubic, the numbers must be "immediate offspring" of 1.

Meanwhile the building can also be seen, via these same numerical squares and

Table 3. Cubic reduction in Alberti

Number	Form	Reduced number: squares	Full number	Reduced number: cubes	Full number
1	point	1^2	1	1^3	1
2	line	2^2	4	2^3	8
3	plane	3^2	9	3^3	27
4	solid	4^2	16	4^3	64

cubes, as a complex of imagined volumes. Hence Alberti is actually making a set of equivalents or affinities.

1.2 Duity: Cubing the Uncubic. So far Alberti's system works only for numbers that really are the squares and cubes of "immediate offspring" of the First of Cubes—that is, for the numbers listed in Table 3. What about other numbers? For these Alberti develops what he calls the principle of duity. This is based on 2 (831), which is "mobile." Mobile numbers, for Alberti, are a variation of the Pythagorean pairs. They are applied to the distribution of openings and rooms. The arrangement and "count" of such features, says Alberti, must comprise equal entities on either side of a real or imagined central axis. That is, right must correspond with left, top with bottom, pair with pair (471).

Alberti does not explain this point further. But almost certainly what he has in mind is a characteristic practice in Pythagoreanism similar to the one mentioned in the Introduction (0.1), to wit: a "mobile" number can be reduced to cubic form by isolating a central, cubic factor or factors and flanking this with two equal cubic remainders. In his *De divina proportione* Fra Luca Pacioli defines "proportion" as the mean between two extremes, and says that all rational quantities should be divisible in this tripartite way (36).

To give an example of this sort of factoring, 9 can be written 4 1 4, or 3 3 3, or 2 2 1 2 2. And an even number, 8, can be seen as mobile when written 4 0 4 or 2 2 0 2 2. The only necessity is that there must be an axis, usually 1 or 0, and that the whole sequence must form a numerical palindrome. This arrangement is what Servius, for example, has in mind when he says that 3 has a beginning, middle and end (this is especially clear in the "classical" form iii; Servius, *In Virg.*, Ecl. 8.75). A proper building is pervaded by these Pythagorean dualities in all directions, and they must always be constructed, Alberti adds, along straight lines and at right angles (470).

If my diagnosis of what Alberti means by duity is correct, he has given us a complementary method, adapted for noncubic values, of interchanging numbers so as to reduce them as near as possible to 1.

In sum, in Alberti's system we are to analyze a building's volumes until we arrive at or near the First of Cubes, 1. And we are to analyze the distributions until we get binary structures also composed of cubic numbers. Finally, it must be obvious that *any* number can be "reduced" in one of these ways. All *numbers* taken by themselves are hence potentially cubic. But not all *dimensions, distributions,* and *proportions* are; far from it. Thus, for example, a 17-foot-long wall presumably noncubic in dimension, can move to a cubic state by being articulated (for example with pilasters) into zones of 4 3 3 3 4. These numbers, and their sums and products, are all direct offspring of the First of Cubes. On the other hand, if the 17-foot dimension, when subdivided, becomes 5 7 5, or even 3 11 3, it has not been cubically reduced.

Turning from theory to practice, we should not be surprised that most of Alberti's plans and elevations are based on true squares or on rectangles directly derived from true squares. Thus the area of a forum must be a double square, as are the areas of some churches and of windows (717, 551, 627). Alberti describes other rectangles in language which makes it clear that these forms are really only modified squares: he uses terms like sesquitertial ("a square-and-a-third") and sesquialter ("a square-and-a-half"). The 8 x 12 rectangle mentioned above would therefore be cubic both in dimensions and in shape (it is a sesquialter), a "perfect" example of formal and numerical cubic reduction.

1.3 A Cubic Analysis of the Etruscan Temple. For a fuller illustration, let us glance at Alberti's famous Etruscan Temple (555–57). I have made a sketch of its plan in Figure 1.1. (I follow Alberti's text as closely as possible; the result differs considerably from earlier reconstructions.)

The plan of the Etruscan Temple (Fig. 1.1 A) indicates an aggregation of square-based parallelepipeds—"partes," Alberti calls them—five wide by six deep. There is no designated height. Assuming that the "parts" of all four sides correspond to column placements as in Vitruvius' hypostyle (Fig. 0.2), we get a grid where all elements fall on the coordinates set up by these columns, and where the crucial intersections mostly fall on column placements. Only the back wall (right side of A), marked off in ten half-spaces controlling the placement of the cella partitions, is an exception. I have expressed the immured columns as pilasters.

Given this hypostyle structure or network of intercolumniations, we can easily apply Alberti's reductive method. We count the columns, both real and imaginary, to get a 6 x 7 structure with 42 columns in all. In this case the cubic-perfect number 6, across the front, is multiplied by the mobile number 7 down the flanks. The cubic number can in fact be broken down into 3 0 3, a value that is especially appropriate given the strong central axis of the whole. The mobile number 7 can be seen as the "duity" 2 3 2, that is, with the two freestanding portico columns forming the left-hand pair and the two outer pilasters on the right, the right-hand pair (Fig. 1.1 B). The whole assemblage of columns also breaks down into cubic units. The 42 columns are a sort of platoon divided into the two squads or ranks of 12 portico columns and 14 immured columns, and leaving a perfect square of 16 invisible freestanding columns in the center. Cubically reduced, these values come out to:

4^2 freestanding invisible columns

12   freestanding portico columns

10 + 4   immured columns

Other breakdowns, equally cubic, are of course possible.

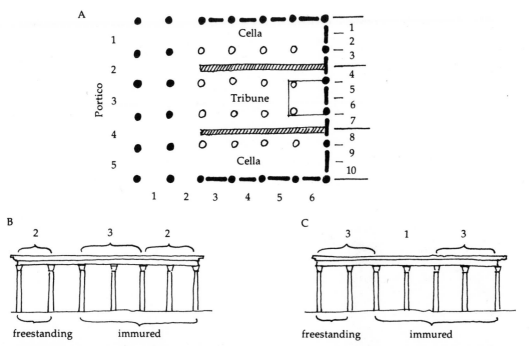

1.1 Alberti's Etruscan Temple as hypostyle

Alternately, one can analyze the volumes of the temple rather than its columns. Under this system the portico becomes a troop of ten bays or hollow tesserae, while another twenty make up the temple proper. The cellae consist of four sesquialter-plan bays and the tribune is composed of four bays based on double squares. Or looking again at the long side of the temple, we can make the arrangement seen in Figure 1.1 C. I have made these reductions on my own, though I followed Alberti's suggestions. But Alberti does specifically request us to divide the ten parts of the rear elevation into the duity 3 4 3. Also, he derives his whole formula from the cubic number 6 (the number of parts in the length).

Some readers may fear that I have now pushed things too far. The Etruscan Temple's hypostyle matrix in particular, and Alberti's duity principle in general, partly depend on inferences. For the present, therefore, I will let these notions stand as a personal reading of Alberti's thought. However, I will show in the following pages that regardless of what Alberti really meant, his successors explored the routes I have indicated here.

Alberti's achievement, then, was to revive three concepts: 1) the notion of cubic number and form, 2) the idea of the hypostyle matrix, and 3) the idea of the primacy of the square. The result, when analyzed in the Etruscan Temple, firmly links Alberti's cubic theory to Vitruvius' conception of the Greek temple.

1.4 Design Hierarchies. Writing in the 1460s, not long after Alberti, Filarete puts some of these same notions in a mysterious, almost sacral light. Sometimes his language even has the flavor of the occult. Ideal forms "lie within" his words—not, he implies, to be discerned there by every fool who comes along (13v, 107v). This is part of his wider conception of architecture, which involves unseen drawings and books written in difficult languages. Filarete's real treatise is not in fact the volume we hold but a certain Golden Book, written in Greek, whose cover is inscribed with the words "Memoria, Ingegno, Intelletto" and whose contents are not directly divulged. The Golden Book is consulted only by privileged characters in the tale, though it is illustrated—closed—for our benefit (Fig. 1.2).

1.2 Golden Book, from Filarete (Courtesy Yale University Press)

The Golden Book contains the "true" detailed diagrams for buildings to be erected; they are more summarily sketched in the margins of Filarete's treatise. There is also a third architectural book in Filarete's tale. When the Duke plays designer, laying out a fort without compasses and ruler, he does so by dictating numbers, that is, proportions and dimensions, to his architect. The architect becomes his amanuensis, his acolyte. He, the professional, transforms the numbers of the nobleman into lines (37v–44r).

In all, then, there are three books in Filarete's story, and they operate at three different levels. There is the Golden Book—secret, abstract, universal, and containing the prototypes for the localized sublunary structures at the seaport that Filarete and his patron are planning. There is the book compiled by the Duke's draftsman-architect, which translates spoken numbers into inscribed lines. And there is the treatise, where everything is explained, simplified, and applied to material cases. In other words there is an upper source, and then successive lower stages in which information from that upper source is simplified and divulgated.

A similar sensibility pervades Filarete's conception of design and construction. Here is another hierarchy of roles. He begins again with the notion of difficulty—of insights and truths not available to all. Thus, while Alberti had said it was hard for him to find words for his architectural thoughts (441), Filarete, admitting that verbal architecture is difficult, adds that graphic architecture is almost equally so. "One cannot," he says, "put these things into words, and even with drawings it is difficult to express them" (99r). Even the Duke himself says that "it is impossible to make these building matters understandable if one doesn't see them drawn out, and even in a drawing it is difficult to take in. And no one can understand [building] if he can't interpret [drawings], so that it takes more effort to interpret a drawing than to make one. This may seem unreasonable [but it is so] since many people will draw for exercise without really knowing what they are doing" (40r).

Drawings are more difficult to understand than the buildings they portray. Interpreting a drawing is more difficult than making one. And describing a building purely in words (or let us say in an algorithm) is the most difficult thing of all. This hierarchy descends from the verbal level to that of line verbally interpreted, to line manually drawn, to the material building. Or in concrete terms, on 53v, when the Duke's son is learning architecture, the boy himself is supposed to acquire the skill needed to make drawings, but wooden models, which are cruder and more comprehensible things, are to be made for him by craftsmen.

Summarizing Filarete's notions one can establish four streams of descent: 1) from Golden Book to material building, 2) from number to material building, 3) from noble patron to the many plebeian laborers, and 4) in the latter instance, from 1 to 100,000.

Table 4. Filarete's design and construction hierarchy

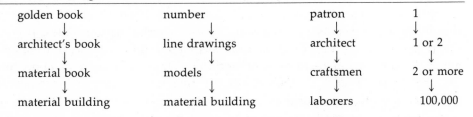

golden book	number	patron	1
↓	↓	↓	↓
architect's book	line drawings	architect	1 or 2
↓	↓	↓	↓
material book	models	craftsmen	2 or more
↓	↓	↓	↓
material building	material building	laborers	100,000

Note that as we move down through these levels the amount of judgment needed decreases, to be replaced by skill and finally by simple strength. There is also graduation from small to large throughout. Hence Filarete's descents are cousins to the Pythagorean hierarchy in Table 1 and to Alberti's hierarchy just discussed.

1.5   Ficino and Neoplatonism. Marsilio Ficino's architectural thought relates to that of the Neoplatonic Filarete, to that of the rational Alberti, and to that of Vitruvius the Pythagorean. As a mathematician Ficino was the Buckminster Fuller of the Renaissance. Ficino indeed possessed by far the most powerful intellect of any of the writers we are discussing, and so set his fantastic stamp on a great deal of later architectural writing.

Ficino takes up the second of Vitruvius' notions, after that of cubic reduction, the notion of signifiers and signifieds. One problem with my numerical translation of the Etruscan Temple was that, while I was applying Alberti's principles to his specific plan, the application itself was mine, not his. And it was that application that constituted the building's signified or numerical/verbal meaning. Alberti avoids the whole business of quod significat and quod significatur. However, Ficino (who praises Alberti as a "Platonic mathematician" and author of a "most beautiful book on architecture"; 2¹.1464r) makes up for this. Indeed Ficino's commentaries on Plato's *Timaeus* might well be called a Neoplatonic essay on the theme of signifiers and signifieds in cosmic architecture. As a result of his concern for elaborate verbal and numerical explanations of mental buildings, architecture was a nobler, more universal thing for Ficino the philosopher than it ever was for Alberti the architect.

For Ficino a building is a model both of the human intellect and of the cosmos. Designing and erecting a building helps us understand the way we think and act. These activities also help us understand the way God thought and acted when he created the universe and mankind. This is true for an Alberti-like reason: because architecture is at once so mathematical and so material. Indeed, after mathematics itself, architecture is the highest of the sciences (2¹.1267). By imposing mathematical form on matter, whose natural state is formlessness, man imitates God and struggles against what might be called the entropy of material creation. In Ficino's terms one might even define civilization itself as man's making an architecture out of a chaos. The very numbers that measure the sizes, distances, and compositions of the spheres, says Ficino, "come partly from history and partly from architecture" (2¹.1486). And "a soul surely cannot judge how to express absolute proportions, either in the air with music or in a body by its [material] nature, unless it possesses the causes of these proportions, and unless that harmony subsists in itself over and above the harmony made in these other things. Our soul consists of all proportions, like the *anima mundi*. . . . Our minds, in their natural strength, are not only to judge mathematical proportions but to contrive and create them" (2¹.1417[1453]). Any change in the mathematical ordering of material reality, or of an individual soul, reflects and is reflected by a similar change in the numerology of the cosmos (2¹.1458).

Hence the creation by man of mathematical harmonies has cosmic effects. Man-created harmonies are the signifieds of cosmic ones. Or to put it differently the ar-

chitectural mathematician, God, constructs signifiers and then explains them in signifieds. God's signifieds contain all knowledge. They are not simple prose passages
or algorithms as in Vitruvius. They take the form of a principal Neoplatonic artifact,
the affinity table or scala. This is a Pythagorean grid, or even a "temple," in which
objects and qualities are distributed into hierarchies culminating in Idea, in the
mental image in God's mind that has fathered them all.

All of this differentiates Ficino from Alberti. Ficino's ideas take off from Alberti's
in another way too. In saying that architecture is the most transformational ("Mer-
curialis") of arts, Ficino seems to have in mind something like Alberti's interchanging of numerical and formal squares and cubes ($2^1.1267$). But he adds a new ingre-
dient. He posits a specific building and a specific observer of that building. Cubical
reduction takes place in perspective from a viewpoint in space. And it takes place
in two different modes: thus, says Ficino, when we see a facade elevationally we
are led to calculation. When we see it retreating in perspective we are led to speculation and contemplation. Hence "Platonic mathematics" in architecture should
lead to surmise as well as to computation. And a proper building should be deeper
than wide (like my version of Alberti's Etruscan Temple). Similarly, says Ficino, the
various rectangles that are the square's offspring demonstrate not only their distribution in that square's family tree or scala, but depending on their position,
they give rise to certain sequences of emotions and thoughts (ibid.). Thus Ficino is
even more concerned than Alberti with cubic volumes; for he endows them with
philosophical functions. More importantly, he conceives of architecture not as a
corpus of general principles, as Alberti does, but as a corpus of specific buildings,
as a body of signifiers observed by individual, calculating, speculating minds. The
process involves emotion as well as intellect and imagination. A single speculating
individual mind can produce a complex signified, a scala of relationships extend-
ible to the remotest areas.

1.6   Cubism and Spherism. Like Alberti, Ficino claims that the most beautiful
form-source for architecture is the cube. And like the Pythagoreans he identifies the
cube, in its solidity and stability, with Earth. But for Ficino, Earth is not *only* a
cube; it is a cube pervaded by a sphere.

As a cube, Earth is One, unity, a monad or irreducible compositional unit. In its
unity it represents "the single work by the one God," just as a building is a single
work by one architect. All God's created species and varieties lead back to this
single image, "whence whoever would know the ideas of things [Ficino like Vitruvius uses the word "idea" to mean "visual concept"] must find them in the mind
of the Architect of the World" ($2^1.1444$). For the one God is like the one world, the
number 1, and the one form from which all things proceed. The one God makes
many material objects just as the human architect in his domination of matter can

produce many buildings stamped from a single mold. "The cube [of Earth] has six sides and is called a cube or die, and the cube stands for Earth because it has solidity and firmness." Here Ficino is playing the Pythagorean; he may even be echoing Vitruvius. But he then develops this notion neoplatonically: "as a solid [Earth] stands for action, as point stands for essence, line for being, and plane for virtue" (2^1.1447).

Table 5. Ficino's scala of Earth-as-cube

Number	Form	Philosophical state
1	point	essence
2	line	being
3	plane	virtue
4	solid	action

Philosophical states are added to number and form; but the scala also contains, says Ficino, "the species, figures, quantities, magnitudes, and proportions of all things" (2^1.1446). Just as a Vitruvian algorithm, when it says "Ionic Order," automatically activates an elaborate subformula, so Ficino, when his scala says "action" or "essence," automatically entails a spectrum of ancillary numbers and shapes. Indeed everything on and in Earth can be integrated into scalae and thence traced back to a cubic source. The quod significatur of Earth-as-cube is immense. It is part of an even larger grid that contains the animal and sensible worlds, the four quarters of the universe, and the four armies of its inhabitants; and the gods of the world, angels, daemons, and individual souls. Within the larger table, which also includes metals, jewels, colors and the like, cube-Earth is the equivalent of the solid, the number four, the world of sense, and the army of individual souls (2^1.1445–47, also 1415–25). Cube-Earth can be projected outward, invisibly, so as to fill the cosmos and rearrange the cosmic hierarchies of number and form, of beings and qualities. Ficino's scala for Earth-cube proper, and the larger scalae within which it is set, go beyond the possibilities of two- and even three-dimensional presentation. They constitute an infinitely multiple frame of reference for the philosopher-viewer of this great temple, as he speculates on its endless perspectives and calculates its numberless elevations.

So much for Earth-as-cube. Earth's simultaneous spherical nature involves it more in heavenly and invisible matters. Earth-sphere is the most indissoluble and capacious of forms. Where Earth-cube had been the principle of action, springing from a motionless base, and had been solid and material, Earth-sphere is the principle of motion and of space (2^1.1444). And space—volume, interval—in Ficino's scheme of things is as important as line, plane, and solid. Space is what *allows* mobility. A spherical/spatial signifier is the work of an "invisible" architect as opposed to a visible one: for such a signifier is based on the 2-principle, that is on what I have called duity; on those mobile numbers that move and disappear under the pressure of cubic analysis, but which for this very reason contain an energy not possible for immobile, cubic forms and numbers.

Hence Ficino makes a crucial distinction between space and form. Out of this will come the Renaissance conception of two mutually pervading architectures in a single building, one invisible, the architecture of space, and other visible, the architecture of solids. (I have already suggested these two architectures in my analysis of Alberti's Etruscan Temple, which can be seen simultaneously as a hypostyle of 42 columns and as a cluster of 30 spatial tesserae.) Yet according to Ficino space and form are equally susceptible to numerical analysis. Space is indeed what he calls "invisible geometry" ($2^1.1461$). And from this notion he not only lays the groundwork for invisible architecture but elaborates his vision into all sorts of antitheses between temples and antitemples inhabited by visible and invisible populations, and even between visible architects and invisible ones, the latter being the offspring of Earth-sphere rather than Earth-cube, heavenly or hellish unseen colleagues of the human builders.

1.7   The Copulation Explosion. Taken together, mobile and cubic numbers are more active and democratic in Ficino than in Alberti. Cubic and mobile numbers pair up, either with their own kind or with members of the opposite camp, on sexual principles. In Ficino, that is, numbers copulate and procreate children, families, tribes, armies, and populations. The duity principle (Ficino calls it "duitas," $2^1.1417$–18) reveals a given number's sex. Even numbers are female because when halved there is 0 at their center. Odd numbers are male because under the same circumstances the cubic (and phallic) 1 remains on axis ($2^1.1421$), as what Martianus Capella calls the "sole procreator" (7.731).

It is possible for two numbers of the same sex to copulate, and even for a number to copulate with himself or herself. Indeed, the "nobler" a number is the more it tends to be autogenous. Thus 27, the cube of 3, is his own father and mother and his own grandfather and grandmother on both sides. Yet at the same time, when a number copulates, especially if it is "electissimus," that is cubic, it unites large families or moieties of beings and states. Let us say that 3 copulates with 4. The female, 4, is then "occupied" by the male, 3. And the offspring 12, manifests lines of relationship with various noble groups of twelve, including, Ficino tells us, the twelve Antediluvian Kingdoms, the twelve orders of the gods, the twelve faces of Earth, the twelve parts of the zodiac, and the twelve parts of the elements. Twelve is also the "universal number of the forms of the World, the governor of human and civil forms for the multiplication and transformation of all things" (2¹.1415, 1418, 1420–21). A "sterile" number, for example an irrational one, does not have these relationships, or at least not as many of them.

Every number is also a geometric form. A form does and is everything that a number does and is. In this sense Ficino's numbers are like what the Pythagoreans called "figured numbers." But because Ficino gives his version of figured numbers such a powerful role in the design of the cosmos, I am calling them "number-forms." This word will describe not only the identity of number and geometrical form but that of action and being. Hence when 3 occupies 4 and she produces 12, at the same instant a 3-unit line joins a 4-unit line to make a 12-unit rectangle. And that rectangle is as related to the twelve-orders just listed as is the number 12 herself. Similarly (I will here assume), a palace that has four groups of three windows, let us say, proclaims the procreation of a new twelve-something, another child of the cubic power and the solid state, a child who equally carries in her blood the number of the twelve-orders. For Alberti, 12 had been one of the elect simply because it was the number of the cube's diagonal. But with Ficino it was a more extensive, more royal and angelic kinship structure.

These notions are developed from Plato's ideas about the nuptial number. Ficino's most important essay on the subject is, indeed, in his commentary of 1463 on Plato's *Republic* (2¹.1414–25), the dialogue in which the nuptial number is discussed. But Ficino's picture of the numberforms' behavior lacks the sense of respectability that Plato's discussion has. Plato's notion was that the ideal society's leaders ought to copulate at moments best suited to a specific rhythm of fertility and gestation, and in accordance with a corresponding cosmic rhythm established by the muses. Ficino draws from this the conclusion that the arts ought to determine these cycles and incite people to obey them. And he greatly increases the amount of sexual activity by extending Plato's vision of state-controlled copulation by human couples into the realm of numberforms. For Ficino not only do social leaders copulate in accordance with these cycles, so do an endless host of numbers and shapes, numbers and shapes that pervade every cranny of existence, defining the proportions of humors in the body, its mensurational symmetries, its chemistry, movement, and appearance. Everything is structured for good or ill around this dense, endless mass of mathematical coition.

The unions between Ficino's numberforms are promiscuous, brief, multiple, and polysexual. They are orchestrated so as to temper all oddities and excesses in the ultimate progeny: "Many brides, with as many husbands, are made to copulate in public ceremonies. Strong passions are mixed with softer ones, and the rich mate with the poor, so that the whole city is made even-numbered after being odd-numbered, as wine is mixed with water to make a temperate drink" (2¹.1424). The unions not only take place between odd and even, however, with all that entails, but can be happy or unhappy, plane or solid, consonant or dissonant, harmonic, geometrical, or arithmetical. They take place between couples or trios, or even among larger groups. The best sort of union, says Ficino, is one that reveals unsuspected similarities between the partners: this is generally the harmonic series (which of course requires a minimum of three partners).

Let us look back for a moment at Alberti's Etruscan Temple (Fig. 1.1) and give it a Ficinian reading. The plan can now be seen as a numbered scala, whose numbers tell us about the relationship of the visible temple (the columns and walls) to its invisible counterpart (the bays). As an invisible temple it measures 5 x 6. That is, along the front the ignoble male 5—the object of the viewer's calculation—mates with the perfect and cubic female 6 along the side—the object of the viewer's speculation. The offspring of this union is 30, a number that is feminine or tempered in its evenness, and doubly cubic—as 5 x 6, and as 3 x 10. As a visible temple on the other hand we have 6-calculation mated with 7-speculation: 42, another equable and tempered number with only a single cubic parent. So the visible temple, quite appropriately, is slightly less noble than the invisible one. Furthermore the original five-bay front can be seen as the duality 2 1 2, in other words as two females flanking a male "sole procreator," while the six-bay flank consists of 3 0 3, two males on either side of a female. These numbers can be thought of as the parents of 5 x 6 and the grandparents of 30. In terms of the visible temple we could have, as grandparents, 3 0 3 and 3 1 3. Thus 42, in its own way, is the ultimate offspring of the First of Cubes.

One can go further still on the basis of our Ficinian warrant. The 16 invisible interior columns were born from the union of front-as-1- 4-1 columns and flank-as-2- 4-1 columns—the latter an unbalanced duity. In other words the two axial 4-values in the two groups mated with each other. The 12 portico columns are the children of 6-calculation and 2-speculation. In each case each number, whether male or female, parent or offspring, calculative or speculative, can be joined in the observer's mind to its group in the cosmic scala, as the twelve columns of the portico join the twelve orders of the gods and so on. In this way the Etruscan Temple leads the knowing mind from sublunary materiality on to the cosmic temple which it epitomizes. It accomplishes this by recomposing itself into a polyvalent structure of numberforms, or to use Ficino's phrase, a "mathematical image" (2¹.1446).

Ficino's commentaries are philosophical and mystical signifieds describing or hoping to describe God's cosmos. One way of doing this is through the image of earth-as-sphere-and-cube, a geometrical construct which God the architect has made as a partly visible, partly invisible temple. An earthly temple is a miniature, a model/module, of this unseen or partly seen one. The earthly architect who makes an earthly temple exercises a godlike role. He is a kind of beneficent demiurge who imposes divine form on sublunary matter. Man the philosopher, contemplating this earthly temple, expands it, through its perspective and its elevation, into a child of calculation and surmise, and thence back to its original celestial proportions. This process occurs via the cubical number analysis of its visible and invisible parts, which are discerned and imagined into the armies, families, and individual couplings of numberform hosts.

1.8 Families of Solids and Voids. While not directly influenced by Ficino, Francesco di Giorgio's treatises on architecture provide a notion of how certain Ficinian ideas apply to practical design. Ficino's commentaries suggest that an architectural treatise could consist almost entirely of signifieds—of descriptions of specific buildings—rather than of general propositions as was the case with Alberti. In addition, Ficino's notions lead to the suggestion that building layouts—facades and plans—can be interpreted as scalae, as hierarchical grids of shapes and functions. Francesco's treatises, as we shall see, embody both these ideas.

For instance Francesco groups building types and rooms into genealogies. These are not dissimilar to the number genealogies I adduced for the Etruscan Temple. Thus when Francesco illustrates Vitruvian temple plans in his earlier treatise (Fig. 1.3), he abandons Vitruvius' system for establishing depth and width. Instead he substitutes a kinship structure, showing the descent of rectangles, proportions, and plans from the square (345, 345n). As the square's seed descends, procreating new rectangles, it changes its relation to its cube-source, 1, in terms of number, geometrical state, and proportion. The next-to-last column, with its irrationals, tells us at each point what that change in relationship consists of. The sequence ends in a new "rational," the double square. Francesco then uses exactly the same series for a family of rooms at the bottom of the page, with the addition of a $2\frac{1}{3}$-square sala. (For simplicity's sake I will disregard the octagonal and circular rooms, and the oval temple.)

Table 6. The genealogy of rectangles

Number	Form	Temple plan	Square-relation	Proportion
1	point	square	1	1:1
2	line	sesquitertial	$1\frac{1}{3}$	4:3
3	plane	sesquialter	$1\frac{1}{2}$	3:2
4	solid	double square	2	2:1

By arranging these shapes before us, and describing in the text their bloodlines to the square, Francesco is describing two cubic families, one of interiors and the other of exteriors, one of solids and the other of voids, one visible and the other invisible. By displaying their descent from a numberform Adam, they affirm the Adam's existence and procreative role. More remote progeny also carry Adam's

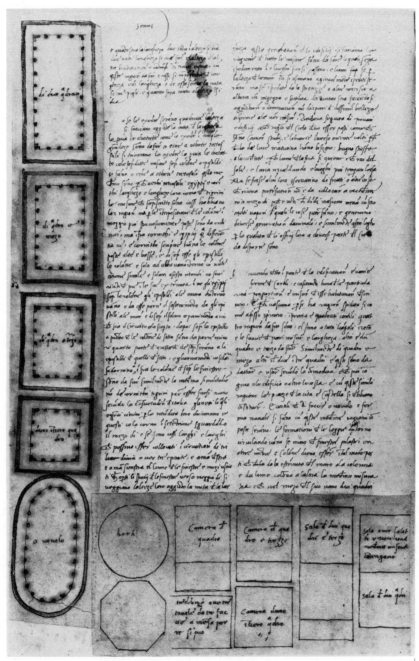

1.3 Temple and room genealogies, from Francesco di Giorgio (Courtesy The Beinecke Rare Book and Manuscript Library, Yale University)

seed. Vestibules and loggias with proportions as high as 8:1 by this very extremity stress the more cubic proportions of the rooms they lead up to. A proper sala should be close to the cube itself (345; the sala in Fig. 1.3, second from the right, is an exception). Attendant rooms *ought* to be the humbler, more distant kin of the cube. Hence within any building there is a hierarchy or population of rooms that we might call paterfamilias, adults, and servants; or ruler, nobles, and bourgeoisie. And since all these rooms are also numberforms, they also have the sexual and generative characteristics I have been describing.

All this is a variation of Ficino's notions about numberform procreation. In the earlier treatise Francesco also plays with Alberti's scheme for squaring and cubing numbers so as to "reduce" or telescope the building's numerical population. Francesco tells us that numbers are proportional when the first is to the second as the third is to the fourth. Numbers are in *continual* proportion, on the other hand, when the first is to the second as the second is to the third as the third is to the fourth. If four numbers are proportional, he adds, the proportion between the first and the second is called the "first portion," that between the first and third the second portion, and that between the first and fourth the third portion. "And," he concludes, "the second portion [is the] square of the first, and the third portion is the cube of the first" (119–20).

Now we have a new version of the sequence 1 2 3 4, point/line/plane/solid. In its new form the sequence 1:2::2:3::3:4 "procreates" a trio of ratios paired by two equal-signs or "equalities," as Francesco calls them. In other words the ratios themselves are the "portions" and the "equalities" are the "pro-portions." Let us assume that the first portion, 1:2, generates a second, which Francesco says is its square, $1^2:2^2$, that is, 1:4. This is the "first portion." The second portion would be $1^3:2^3$ or 1:8. The third is then $1^4:2^4$ or 1:16. The two "pro-portions" reside in the fact that $1^2:2^2$ is as *like* 1:2 as $1^3:2^3$ is *like* 1:2 (since 8 = 2x4). And this, from the viewpoint of cubic theory, is a lot neater, though more complicated, than calling, say, an 8:1 vestibule an octuple square. It explains the bloodlines of a shape that is in fact geometrically far from the square by mating two numerical values. The calculations are harder but the kinship structure is simpler. Above all Francesco's scheme enriches the Pythagorean sequence. At this point the integral values of such squares and cubes (1, 4, 8, 16; 1, 8, 27, 64; 1, 16, 81, 256) become parts of the cubic

Table 7. Portion and proportion in Francesco di Giorgio

Number	Form	First portion	Second portion	Third portion
1	point	1^2	1^3	1^4
2	line	2^2	2^3	2^4
3	plane	3^2	3^3	3^4
4	solid	4^2	4^3	4^4

family too. With the addition of these we get a table identical to Table 3, which showed Alberti's reductions of cubic numbers. Therefore Francesco's system of portions and proportions grafts the Ficinian kinship system we have been examining onto the more purely Pythagorean notion of the cube as source of number and form.

In sum, one of Francesco's contributions to cubic theory is to knit new connections, to arrange (in Ficino's sense) new and unlikely but ultimately harmonious copulations between members of a given numberform group. Francesco also applies this idea to sequences of volumes and solids, thus managing to suggest both diachronic lineages and synchronic families or societies.

1.9 The Sectioned Cube. Vitruvius' third seminal notion, after those of cubic reduction and signifier-signified, was that of cubices rationes. For Renaissance developments of this concept we turn naturally to the commentators on Vitruvius' text. The first important contribution is Cesare Cesariano's in 1521. He translates the passage on cubic principles to say that the Greek mathematicians wrote treatises *about* these principles (5.72r) rather than saying, more correctly, that they cast

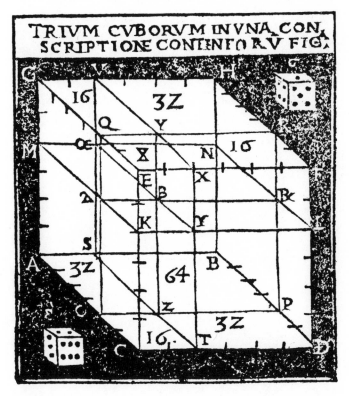

1.4 Sectioned cube, from Cesariano

their treatises in cubic form. Thus at one stroke Cesariano suggests the one-time ex-istence of a classical literature of cubic theory. For him the passage in Vitruvius is no longer a puzzling numerological dead end but a possible key to a lost treasure of geometrical and architectural theory. Hence he devotes a good deal of space to cubices rationes.

He connects them with a geometrical problem called the "sectioned cube." This involves subdividing a cube so as to produce two smaller cubes inside it (Fig. 1.4). The larger outer cube is composed of 216 tesserae, themselves cubic in form, like the dice used in gambling (which Cesariano also illustrates, Fig. 1.4, lower left). The two different-sized squares mapped out on the outer cube's surfaces are the bases of the two smaller cubes inside the large one. In other words by removing the certain parallelepipeds—in this case the one marked by CAST and EGVX and the one by COPD and EQRF—one of these inner cubes, namely ZSBP and $\beta \alpha$N₿ (A in Fig. 1.5) is isolated. The second cube (B in Figure 1.5) can be revealed in the same way. Cube B is formed of 8 tesserae and the larger cube, A, of 64. Thus we get a total of three *geometrical* cubes that are made up of the following *numerical* cubes: 2^3, 4^3, and 6^3. In the present case we have the cube of the duity, that of the first "solid" number, and that of the first perfect number. Meanwhile the numbers 2, 4, and 6 are in themselves a cubic hierarchy or family, of course, as they also are when cubed. Thus Cesariano's arrangement is not too different from that established by Francesco di Giorgio. Thus too, Cesare's 216 tesserae, and the whole numerical-

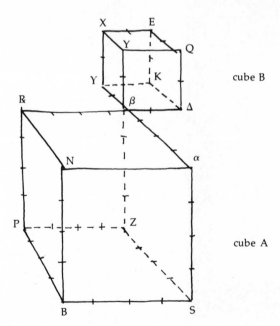

cube B

cube A

1.5 Explanatory diagram of Cesar-iano's sectioned cube (rotated 180°)

geometrical context it symbolizes, "land in the mind with motionless solidity," as Vitruvius would say. And they are also, says Cesariano (but without further explanation) the equivalent of 216 lines of text.

But the main point is that for Cesariano 216 is the climax of three progressions: two of them very distinct, a numerical one and a geometrical one, and the other, a verbal one which is fainter. And as the cube of 6, 216, the climax of the whole triple process, is *the* cubic power of *the* cubic number, "cubo expressissimo," as Cesariano puts it.

Cesariano's sectioned cube has another interesting aspect. The two inner cubes are packed into the outer envelope by means of a stuffing or interface of parallelepipeds. These are made of cubic tesserae but are obviously less perfect in form than the three cubes. Hence we not only have a sequence from cube to cube, 2^3 4^3 6^3, but another sequence, a stratigraphical one, that goes from outer envelope through these "leftover" spaces to the two inner goals. Exactly this same sequence, from outer cubic envelope, to interface (vestibules, porticoes, etc.), to inner cubes or

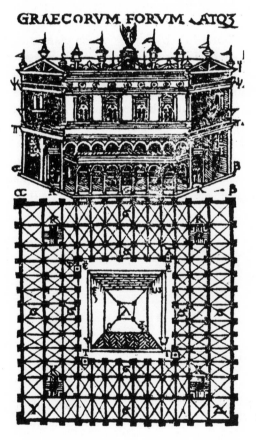

GRAECORVM FORVM ATQ3

1.6 Greek forum, from Cesariano

salas, shows up in Renaissance palace architecture. Even the Etruscan Temple can be seen this way. In plan it is a near-square. It is approached via the portico, which consists of two rows of quintuple squares. Within is the invisible, perfect group of sixteen columns, four by four: from near-square outer jacket, to interface, to inner square.

Cesariano himself prints practical designs that can be studied in terms of his version of cubices rationes. There is for instance the plan and section of a Greek forum (5.72v; Fig. 1.6). It is square in plan. We can easily read the hive of cross-vaulted compartments as hollow tesserae like those in Figure 1.4. In the center of the forum is an open plaza, obviously an invisible continuation of the surrounding visible tesserae. The forum as a whole is thirteen bays square, that is, with 169 bays per floor (including both the visible and invisible bays). But the bays are of three different sizes. Around, and in, the courtyard are small square ones, marked a on Figure 1.7 A (which represents one-quarter of the whole). Branching off from these a bays, to fill the center section of each side, are sesquialter-plan bays based on a (a plus $^1/2a$), which I will call b. In the corners of the forum are groups of four large square bays derived from the longer side of the sesquialters. I will call these c (b plus $^1/2b$). All this constitutes a cubic distribution of each quarter of the plan. But I am still not counting the axial bays, which I will declare to be *hors concours*, and will designate as 1's, or "sole procreators" in line with the duity principle. The building, then, consists in its main-floor plan of four square groupings, each corresponding to the distributions in Table 8 and separated by cross-axial divisions. Each grouping is reducible to a state that is very close to the First of Cubes.

Furthermore, in these progressions we have something directly akin to the sectioned cube setup. There is an exterior square, and there are two interior squares of different sizes (Fig. 1.7 B). Serving as interface between the two are parallelepipeds. The basic plan of each quarter of the forum is in fact that of the sectioned cube itself (Fig. 1.7 C).

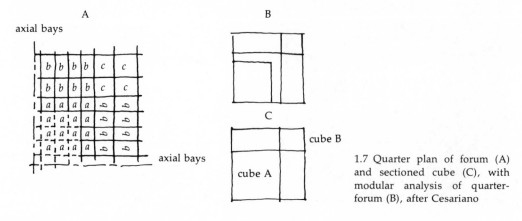

1.7 Quarter plan of forum (A) and sectioned cube (C), with modular analysis of quarter-forum (B), after Cesariano

Table 8. Cubic module distribution in Cesariano's Greek forum

Square	Bays	Distribution	Reduces to
1	a (invisible)	9 ⎱ 16	4^2
1	a (visible)	7 ⎰	4^2
1½	b	16	4^2
1	c	4	2^2

Finally, returning again to the duity principle, we get readings along the facade of the Greek forum of 2 3 1 4 2. And in this case, of course, 2 doubly equals ½ x 4, that is, it does so both numerically and geometrically. Cesariano applies similar ideas to house plans, where the atrium serves as the courtyard and the vaulted compartments become rooms, appropriately enough called "cubicula" (Fig. 1.8, upper right). But the true monad-tesserae in Cesariano's system are not even these: they are the very bricks of the fabric, which he also illustrates in various cubic forms and even in patterns similar to that of the sectioned cube (Fig. 1.9).

Cesariano linked the sectioned cube with cubices rationes and then designed

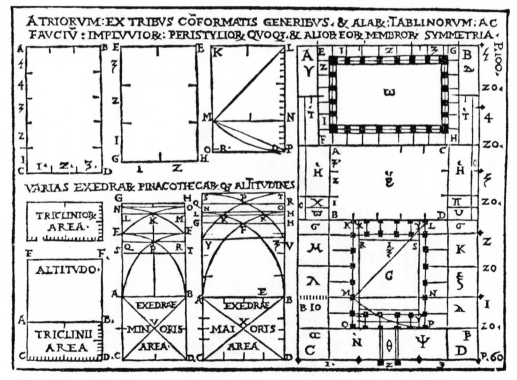

1.8 Methods of establishing room volumes, from Cesariano

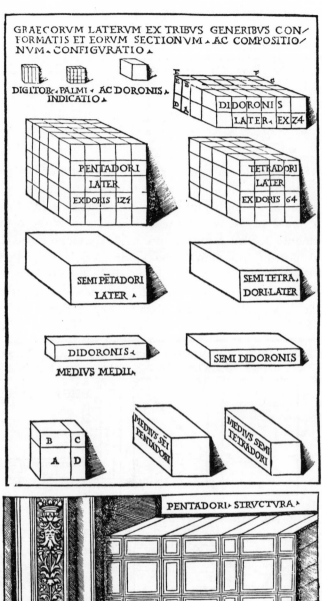

1.9 Cubic masonry, from Cesariano

buildings on cognate principles. This represents a great leap forward from Vitruvius. In Vitruvius cubices rationes had merely been a way of vaguely suggesting common properties between solid geometry and verbal and numerical description. Cubices rationes had also been akin to, but not the same as, Vitruvius' notion of signifieds. The integration of Vitruvius' three ideas began when Ficino supplied planar and solid grid-shaped signifieds—his scalae—which housed a host of verbal, numerical, and geometric components. Cesariano completes the integration by providing a graphic signifier that is a cubic solid, in the manner of Ficino, but which can be drawn out on paper—that is, which is applicable to a visible building by a visible architect.

1.10 Horizontal and Vertical Affinities. Our next authority is a better translator of Vitruvius, if a less inventive commentator. He is Daniele Barbaro, whose edition appeared first in Italian in 1556 and then in a corrected Latin version (which I am using) in 1567. Barbaro spends more time than any earlier writer on the problem of Vitruvius' cube:

The cube, as unity, produces a natural series of odd numbers. If you add the first two of these you get the first cube. The next three make the second cube and the four after that, the third. For instance $3+5$, the first two odd numbers, make 8, the first cube [2^3]. Then $7+9+11=27$—the second cube [3^3]. Next, $13+15+17+19=64$ which is the third cube [4^3]. In a similar way a point in motion creates a line, and a moving line makes a plane. A moving plane in turn makes a solid. Is not this like the numerical series just mentioned? A unity, 'continued,' creates a linear number which, continued again, makes a [planar number, which continued still further makes a] solid number [157; see Table 9].

Table 9. Horizontal and vertical affinities in Barbaro

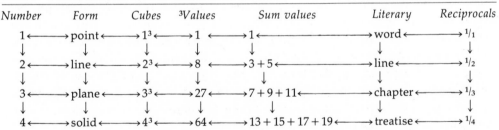

Number	Form	Cubes	³Values	Sum values	Literary	Reciprocals
1	point	1^3	1	1	word	$1/1$
2	line	2^3	8	$3+5$	line	$1/2$
3	plane	3^3	27	$7+9+11$	chapter	$1/3$
4	solid	4^3	64	$13+15+17+19$	treatise	$1/4$

I will discuss the two right-hand columns in a moment. The column marked "³Values" shows that by *adding* consecutive integers we can arrive at what Ficino would call the procreated offspring which also occur from cubing. Barbaro then directly links these two types of progression, one in Ficino's terms copulative or parental and the other a progression by issue or birth, to the Pythagorean sequence. He emphasizes the continuity of these sequences. The force that moves them onward, he adds later, is desire. Thus a 2 "wishes" to cube itself so as to match $3+5$. Point "desires" to become line and also to match 2^3 and $3+5$. I have indicated the directions of these affinities by arrows in Table 9. To understand the scala in Barbaro's fashion we must be able to see in a number like 8 both the additive components (Lomazzo will later on call this phenomenon "friendship"), such as $3+5$, as well as the parental components like 2^3.

Barbaro is at variance with Cesariano on the subject of cubices rationes. He pays no attention to the idea that treatises *about* such principles were involved, but sticks to Vitruvius' actual statement, that is, that the treatises were written *in accordance* with cubic principles. But he does deal with the sectioned cube. He describes the three cubes in a way that accords fairly well with Cesariano's diagram, and adds that Vitruvius had meant that the numerical equivalent of such an arrangement ought to govern the number of verses or lines in a treatise *and also* that such an arrangement ought to govern the sequences and proportions of the chapters or books. Both distributions, of lines and of "planes" or chapters, would come from calculations based on 3, 4, and 5. Thus 27 is the first usable cube (2^3 he dismisses as too small). Then 4 is cubed to get 64. The sum of these two cubes in turn is 91. The cube of 5 is 125 which added to 91 makes 216. Thus Barbaro again makes use of his additive-versus-cubing principle. Cesariano's cubices rationes sequence 8 64 216, is replaced by 27 64 216, that is, Barbaro is replacing 2^3 4^3 6^3 with 3^3 4^3 6^3. But both are equally good routes back to 1, and both are comparable to the route 4^2 4^2 2^2 used by Cesariano for his Greek forum.

Barbaro's new sequence is also more useful than Cesariano's for the composition of treatises. An ideal treatise might for example have 27 books consisting of 64 chapters of 216 lines each (though this would not obey Vitruvius' rule that there ought to be no more than three 216-line units in any treatise). More important, Barbaro makes it clear that in his system of cubices rationes the words are points, the written lines are like drawn ones, the chapters are planes, and the whole treatise is a solid. Such a treatise, if it were devoted to architecture, would therefore establish a new affinity between signifier and signified. Both the building-as-object and the building-as-description, the temple on the one hand and its numerical and verbal translations on the other, would be identically descended in different families from an original cube-source (Table 9, next-to-last column).

1.11   The Ratio of Silence to Space. Barbaro has another new wrinkle: he is skeptical as to Vitruvius' description of the dramatic poets and the alleged "cubic" lengths of their productions. He knows of no such plays, and says that cubices rationes were not a matter of particularly memorable line-counts but rather of the length or distribution of the pauses in the acted productions, especially the sung parts. Thus Barbaro implies that cubices rationes cover silences as well as sounds.

And these silences he likens in turn to geometrical spaces (158), that is, what Ficino called "invisible forms" or "invisible geometry." In line with this Barbaro comments on the genealogical proportions—the sesquialter and the like. Here again he links number and shape, along with pitch and interval, to silence (80–81). This equation of space and silence and of solid and sound has a Ficinian ring. So does Barbaro's concept of proportion.

Proportion, says Barbaro, penetrates all of life: "Such is the power of proportion, and such its necessity, such indeed its usefulness in business and politics even, that one cannot eliminate it from any of the senses—ears, eyes, even the mind itself—or from any pleasure or delight, unless you are doing this on purpose, for a game, or so that you can illustrate some harmony, some calculation, some comparison. Even then it will sneak back into the senses" (80). For Barbaro proportion is nothing less than all measured perception of difference. He extends the earlier lists of allowable numerical ratios, setting them out (for the first time in an architectural treatise, I believe) in graphic scalae (81–87). He goes as high as 39:10. But in these scalae he is always careful to give the verbal version of each ratio. And the verbal version he gives, whatever it is—say, "quadripartiens quintas" (that is, 5+4:5 or 9:5)—firmly anchors the proportion to its parent square. Furthermore, just as Francesco had introduced ratios of ratios (in the sense of $1:2::1^2:2^2$) Barbaro, more directly, makes double, sextuple, and octuple versions of simple ratios—for example, "duple undecupartiens duodecimas," 34:12. Finally, again following Ficino's lead, Barbaro praises harmonic ratios and says that not only are 1 2 3 4 basic components of number theory but that so are their reciprocals (Table 9, last column).

Barbaro, then, injects Cesare's cubic principles with a dose of Ficinian mysticism. He links the sectioned cube more firmly with the Pythagorean hierarchy and adds new values to the latter, including literary ones. He establishes within the scala both horizontal and vertical, or erotic and friendly, relationships. Earlier number genealogies are compounded. Finally, in his concept of space as silence, Barbaro equates the unseen with the unheard and hence with Ficino's notions of invisible architecture and geometry.

1.12   Extended Void Hierarchies. The Cesariano-Barbaro phase has turned out to be complicated. It is a relief to turn to Sebastiano Serlio, who operates on a simpler level. But Serlio is nonetheless a Pythagorean and a Neoplatonist. Indeed, for him the square and cube take on a more clearly divine role than they ever did for Cesariano and Barbaro. Serlio is also the first of our group to illustrate graphically the genealogy of canonical (i.e. allowable) rectangles derived from the square (Fig. 1.10). Though he allows far fewer proportions than Barbaro—no such ratios as 34:12 are given—like Barbaro he rules out irrational ("sterile") ratios. "One cannot find any proportion with the perfect square in this progression," he says (1.15r). And

Le proportioni quadrangolari sono molte : ma io quiui ne pongo sette principali, delle quali l'Architetto a diuerse cose se ne potrà seruire,& accommodarsene in più accidenti, & quelle che non farà fier vn luogo, potrà seruire ad vn altro, come saprà vsarle .

Questa primiera forma è d'vn quadro perfetto di quattro lati vguali, & quattro angoli retti.

Questa seconda figura è vna sesquiquarta , cioè vn quadro , & vn quarto .

Questa terza figura è vna sesquitertia , cioè vn quadro , & vn terzo.

Questa quarta figura si dice proportione diagonea,laquale si fà così; fia tirata nel quadro perfetto vna linea a schiancio da angolo ad angolo , & quella linea darà la longhezza di questa proportione , laquale è irrationabile , nè si troua proportione alcuna dal quadro perfetto a questo crescimento .

Questa quinta figura farà sesquialtera, cioè d'vn quadro & mezo .

Questa sesta figura farà di proportione superbipartiens ter- tias, cioè partito il quadro perfetto in tre parti vguali,& à quel lo aggiunteuene due .

Questa settima, & vltima proportione farà doppia , cioè di due quadri, & sopra questa forma nelle cose buone antiche non s'è trouata forma che ecceda alla doppia, eccetto anditi , loggie, qualche porte, & finestre , lequali ban passato di alquanto : ma di vestiboli, sale, camere,& altre cose babitabili non si compor- ta fra gl'intendenti, perche non è commoda.

1.10 Genealogy of canonical rectangles, from Serlio

not only must shapes *derive* from the square, they must, in a more philosophical way, return to it. "Among the quadrangular forms I find the rectangle the most perfect. And the more the rectangle moves away from the perfect square the more it loses of its perfection, even though it is bounded by a line of the same length" (Fig. 1.11). With a Neoplatonic flourish he then likens this geometrical departure from and return to the square, to the individual soul's departure from and return to the mind of God (1.9v).

Related to this is Serlio's notion of cubic or dual hierarchy. Throughout a design, he says, openings ought as nearly as possible to be equal. Thus the ideal plan would have a cubic number of equal volumes arranged in a square, and with completely uniform fenestration (7.168, 232). But of course this is not always possible, and anyway *total* uniformity would rule out the degrees of distribution and dimension that are necessary in order to exalt higher as opposed to lower spaces—a sala as opposed to a loggia. Serlio makes lists of room types and gives allowable proportions for them, as follows (7.148; see Fig. 1.12). The lesser shapes are always the more contingent and have a greater number of possible proportions. Long thin shapes (as with Francesco di Giorgio) must be limited to "anditi, loggie, qualche porte, e finestre." Long shapes are expressly forbidden to salas and cameras, and also (unlike Francesco) to vestibules, be it noted, because of their offensiveness and incommodiousness to "those who know" (1.15r).

But all these rooms, whatever their place in the family hierarchies, are square-derived. Serlio is even more of a square enthusiast than his predecessors. He derives round columns from square piers, the reverse of the usual procedure. In fact he lays it down as a general proposition that "round things come from square" (2.34v). Even the curves of arches and circles are developed in perspective out of squares and rectangles.

So great is this primacy of the square for Serlio that its invisible presence can be sensed even in the remotest contexts. The principle here is the familiar one of "discordia concors" (7.122). An ultimate harmoniousness, hence squareness, is achieved via preliminary discords or nonsquarenesses. Partly this is related to duity. If there are inequalities or nonconformities on the left, there must be exactly similar ones on the right. The same goes for upper and lower. But if the principle of discordia concors includes duity, it also transcends duity. If a site is irregular it must be regularized, this time not with a matching site but through internal squaring up. The perimeter of the building becomes as much as possible an assemblage of rectangles. And further movements back to the square are made with the interior plan: "A form of different, unequal sides will have lines of different lengths joined together, and even when it has seven sides, with the angles all obtuse, it can very well be seen as a second figure, with fewer sides, so disposed that it will have right, acute, and obtuse angles; and similar figures can be found by the architect at

DI M. SEBASTIAN SERLIO

Tra le forme quadrangolari io trouo la più perfetta il quadrato, & quanto più la forma qua-
drangolare si discosta dal quadro perfetto, tanto più perde della sua perfettione, quantunque sia
circondata dalla medesima linea, che era il quadrato : essempi gratia farà vn quadrato a'angoli
retti circondato da quattro linee, & ogni linea sarà dieci ; talmente che la linea che'l circonda
sarà xxxx. farà vn'altro quadrilungo circondato dalla medesima linea, la longhezza della quale sarà xv. & la larghezza sarà v. & nondimeno il quadro perfetto moltiplicato in se farà cen
to, & il quadrilongo farà settantacinque, perche moltiplicati li lati del quadro perfetto diremo dieci volte dieci, cento: & moltiplicati li lati del quadrilongo, diremo cinque volte quinde-
ci, settantacinque, come quì sotto è dimostrato.

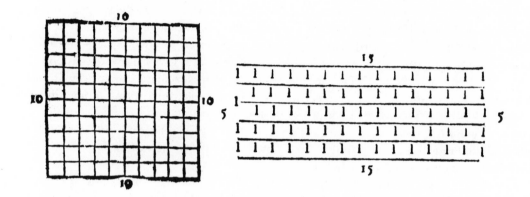

Et più farà il sopradetto quadro perfetto del valore di cento, & farà vna forma quadrango-
lare più longa della prima, cioè longa xviij. & larga ij. che saran due volte diciotto, trentasei;
& due volte due, quattro. che son quaranta, & nondimeno moltiplicati li suoi lati diremo, due
volte diciotto, trentasei ; & quini si vede che forza hanno li corpi più perfetti delli men perfetti, & così fa l'huomo, che quanto più s'auicina con l'intelletto a Dio, che è la istessa perfettione,
contiene in se più di bontà , & quanto più si allontana da esso Dio, dilettandosi di cose terrene ,
perde più di quella primiera bontà a lui primieramente donata . Lo essempio di questa dimostra-
tione si vede quì sotto figurato, & questa propositione sarà di gran giouamento all' Architetto,
nel conoscere all'improuiso che differentia sia da vna forma all'altra circa il ualore, & non pure all'Architetto, ma alli mercanti che molte cose comprano così ad occhio , & a molte altre
cose, ch'io lascio all'industrioso ad inuestigarle.

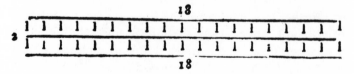

1.11 Tessera analysis of rectangles, from Serlio

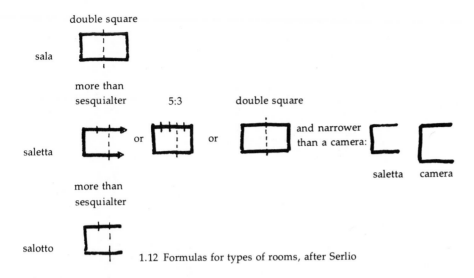

1.12 Formulas for types of rooms, after Serlio

different sites. From these figures I will give the rule at the end of this book [of the treatise] for reducing them to the form of a perfect square"—that is, subdividing them so that their area is reckoned in terms of squares (1.3v). This kind of reduction in Serlio is a purely geometrical equivalent of Alberti's geometrical-numerical interchange of cubes and squares.

Hence it is both as a practical and as a philosophical matter that Serlio asks the architect to "reduce" a shapeless area to cubic forms. The architect first perceives possible but hidden perfections in the imperfect—concord in discord (1.4v); and then he imposes square-derived rooms, arranged in hierarchies, on the irregular masses. He thus transforms a material chaos by colonizing it with a family of canonical volumes (Fig. 1.13).

Serlio is able to discern these invisible geometries in situations that at first look rather unpromising. For example, the Pantheon is "cubic" because its length is the same as its height, which shows that it "proceeds from a single source." This is brought out also by the lighting, which comes from the single eye in the dome (3.50r). Over and over again he praises ancient buildings for being "di forma quadrata perfetta per ogni verso" (e.g. 3.63v). What he often means is that the buildings are simply *inscribed* in squares. All sorts of shapes—Greek crosses, circles, ovals, and the like—can thus be "forme quadrate." Just as an irregular lot can be measured and related to the ideal by internal invisible cubic forms, so through external ones a building is perceived within or procreates a mental envelope.

1.13   The Hypostyle Adam. There are two diagrams in Serlio that make a perfect bridge between these theoretical notions and the more detailed forms of palace ge-

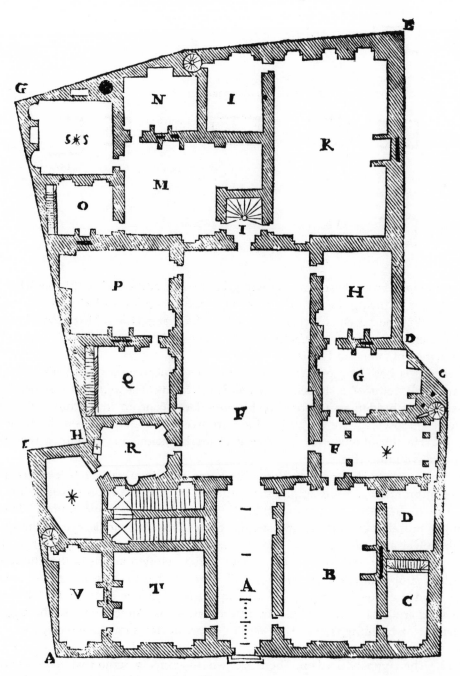

1.13 Redeeming an irregular building, from Serlio

ometry that I will discuss in the following chapters. These diagrams appear in Book III (along with diagrams of the Pantheon and Poggioreale. We will study the latter further on). One diagram is a plan of the water storage vaults in the Baths of Diocletian (3.96r). This appears as a honeycomb of 4 x 7 bays (Fig. 1.14). Each bay is cross-vaulted and is twelve Roman feet square, with four-foot piers. The other diagram (Fig. 1.15) is the plan of the main floor of a 100-column hypostyle structure that Serlio derives from a description of "an Athenian Council Chamber," almost certainly the famous Bouleuterion (3.96v). The Bouleuterion plan is even more cubic than that of the water storage vaults; it has ten columns per side. Each tessera is square, as is the whole. The scale is colossal, Serlio tells us, and two men together could not embrace one of the columns.

The Bouleuterion is Serlio's only Greek building. This uniqueness makes it significant in a further way: it is an architectural Adam. It is produced by Serlio as the creation of "the first inventors of good architecture." And Serlio's follower in architectural matters, Giovanni Paolo Lomazzo, promotes this 100-column hypostyle even higher. He makes it the ancestor, and basic building, of *all* good architecture. "Whence," adds Lomazzo, "the moderns, opening their eyes, have themselves adapted such a plan or quadratic form, as Poggioreale in Naples proves" (*Trat.* 96).

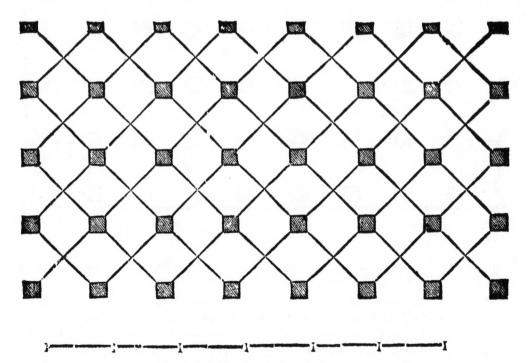

1.14 Plan of water storage vaults, Baths of Diocletian, from Serlio

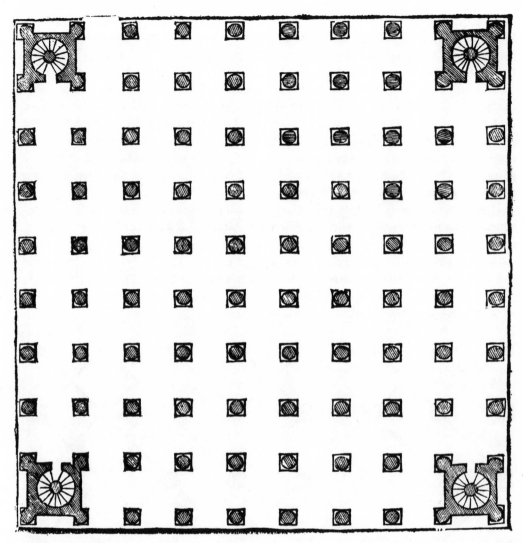

1.15 Plan of council hall, Athens, from Serlio

Thus in 1584 Poggioreale is actually designated a sort of New Architectural Adam, a cube-procreator of a renewed family of "good architecture."

Serlio thus appears on our stage as a simplifier and divulgator. But he believes firmly in cubic reduction and the source-role of the square. He extends the duity principle, which is now subsumed in the notion of discordia concors. He carries on Francesco's notion of shape parameters for different types of rooms and makes a more precise list of their names; once again, a development, in a table of affinities, between name, shape, and number. And with Serlio, as perhaps no earlier writer, a building is also seen as an object inscribed within an imagined plane or envelope, something like the sectioned cube. Finally, Serlio prints the plans of two hypostyle ur-temples as cubic ancestors of good architecture.

1.14   Cloning the Cubic Adam. Our last contributor to the story of cubic reduction is Vincenzo Scamozzi. His book appeared in 1615 but his ideas belong to the Cinquecento. Scamozzi reiterates Ficino's grandiose definition of architecture and elaborates its central notion that the architect "reduces" matter to form (1.12). For Scamozzi, indeed, the commissioning, design, and construction of buildings is part of this philosophical process (8.275). The patron is the "prime or motive cause" of a building. The "formal cause" is the architect. The craftsmen and workers are his "instruments." The building's "secondary cause" is its material, its "final cause" its function.

Within this philosophical framework Scamozzi creates a world of Pythagorean order, or I should say, orders. Each column module is divided into 60 parts or minutes, "this being the product of two perfect numbers, 6 and 10. Therefore it [the module] is *perfectissimo,* and is comprised of 10 complete subdivisions, on the analogy of 2, 3, 4, 5, and 6, among lower numbers, which [subdivisions] create $1/30$, $1/20$, $1/15$, $1/12$, and $1/10$ [of the order respectively] and hence 10, 12, 15, 20, and 30. The [former sequence has reciprocals of] $1/6$, $1/5$, $1/4$, $1/3$, and $1/2$. And all these values are to be understood as portions of the module, but beyond these one can form others, for example $1/7$, $1/8$, and $1/9$ and so on." In other words Scamozzi creates new values out of his basic 10 and 6 by measuring the order in modules, marking off those measurements as fractions, and then utilizing the fractions and their reciprocals. He does the same with dimension units. And his real "cubic source" is not 1 but 10. Ten is such a source because it is the goal of so many different ascents; not only is it the sum of $1 + 2 + 3 + 4$ but also of the duities $2 + 8$, $3 + 7$, $4 + 6$, and $5 + 5$ (2.4).

Scamozzi, following Barbaro, also shows how cubices rationes affect signifiers and signifieds through letters and words as well as through number and form. Even the letters of the alphabet, which form the words of his descriptions and the codes of his diagrams, are a species of numerological geometry (1.30). A, for example, is a surface, and an upright 60-degree angle, that is, its shape is "the product of two cubic numbers, 6 and 10." Thus are planes, numbers, and letters harmonized by these hidden affinities.

Scamozzi continues Serlio's discussion of the square. The square, he says, stands at the center of all architecture; it is the most commodious and compact shape for buildings, it generates subdivisions in the most convenient way, and it creates corresponding exterior facades on the fronts and sides of buildings. "Therefore we have used square forms, and near-squares, many times in churches, monasteries and public buildings, as also in private houses in the city, the suburbs, and the country. In this we have followed the ancient Greeks and Romans, as we have discovered from many authors and from the ruins of the ancients' buildings" (1.41). Scamozzi finds not only literary but archaeological evidence in favor of his cubic source. Like Serlio and Francesco di Giorgio he limits the longer rectangles to anterooms and the like. Indeed he emphasizes the parallel between the transient shape and the transient functions or "final causes" of these secondary rooms. They are rooms for waiting, for circulation, for storage. The irregular, conditional interface between exterior and interior, between Nature and Art, should affirm the fact that it is a transition from one thing to the other.

Finally, Scamozzi redefines and illustrates the hypostyle matrix as a tool in practical design. He mentions the Bouleuterion but applies the hypostyle concept to the reconstruction of a classical Roman villa. He "clones" or reconstitutes this vanished ancient palace by positing an invisible structure which can be more or less automatically filled out, given the room names in the classical account (he cites a letter to Gallus by the younger Pliny, 1.260–66). This is possible because of Scamozzi's exceedingly detailed rules for the shapes, sizes, and distributions of rooms, rules approaching in rigor the level of Vitruvius' temple algorithms.

In making such layouts Scamozzi first imagines the hypostyle. He subtracts columns and adds walls so as to transform the hypostyle into a practical building (Figs. 1.16, 1.17). Or as he describes it:

I divide [the plan] into equal spaces of convenient width as if they were intercolumniations, and from center to center of column or pilaster, making the entrances, and the stanzas and salottos, all of three spaces, but with the middle one rather larger to give majesty to the act of entering [cf. here Vitruvius, Fig. 0.2, and Cesariano, Fig. 1.6]. The widths of the rooms are two spaces and the lengths of the lesser rooms also two spaces. The major rooms are three and four spaces wide. The stairs and camerinos are one space wide. The walls are understood to be between one space and another, as if they were columns or pilasters. In the same way all the openings of the facade correspond to the dispositions of the inside walls, and those of the right to those of the left. This arrangement means that all parts of the building have correspondence and proportions among themselves. Such correspondence and proportion can never exist when the compartmenting is done in palmi, piedi, or braccia [i.e. with dimensions rather than modules] [1.48].

When we analyze Scamozzi's passage visually (Fig. 1.17), applying it to the main block of the villa, we see the full logic of his description. In the lower left-hand corner I have put the imagined hypostyle with its invisible and visible columns, some of the latter connected by walls. Next, in the upper left-hand corner we see the tesserae laid out as in Cesariano's Greek forum: 6 x 7 or 42 in all. In the upper right-hand corner I show the clusters of tesserae coming together to make the modules for the actual rooms 2A, 3A, 4A, and 6A. This then leads to the finished plan (lower right).

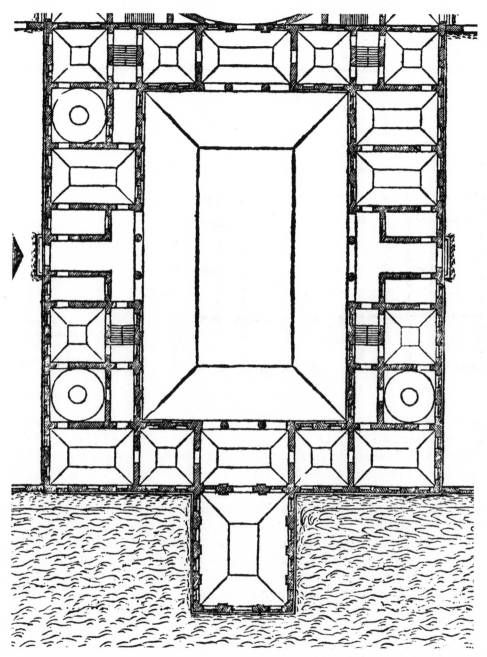

1.16 Plan of classical villa, main block, from Scamozzi

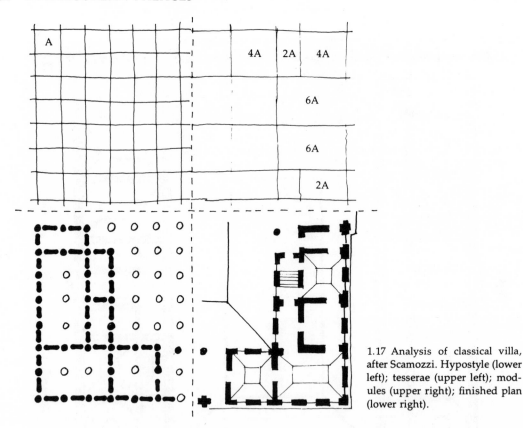

1.17 Analysis of classical villa, after Scamozzi. Hypostyle (lower left); tesserae (upper left); modules (upper right); finished plan (lower right).

As to distribution of the tesserae, there are in all 7 1 7 bays on the sides and 6 1 6 across back and front. Of the total, 195, 77 are invisible and in the courtyard. These invisible bays are divided into the male duities of 3 1 3 and the mixed duities of 4 3 4. Looking at the facades, on the short side we get 2 2 2 1 2 2 2, that is, a trio of mobile female 2's on either side of the male cubic axis-bay, 1.

Each double and each single tessera belongs to a room. And the interior volumes are exactly reflected in the exterior fenestration. On the long sides of the villa we get 3 2 2 1 2 2 3, with a similar correspondence between tesserae and windows.

Hence Scamozzi's villa is practically perfect in its shapes and distributions. It has been derived from the diffuse and complicated traditions of the earlier authors discussed in this chapter. The scheme fulfills almost all the ideals and requirements of cubic reduction. It can be traced back to Vitruvius' temple formulas; it is based on a regular grid or scala; it is built up from an imagined hypostyle temple; it is easily convertible into a numerical, geometrical, and verbal signified; it has a flexible scale; it has cubic distributions and proportions; and it is partly visible and partly invisible. The only thing wrong with it is that it appears 150 years after the material palaces that it explains or "signifies" had begun to be constructed. In other words, a number of problems had to be solved before such a clear distillate as this could appear. The next three chapters will deal with these problems.

2. Line: Lineamenta and Linee Occulte

2.1 Lines and Lineamenta. The Introduction and first chapter presented the cube as the source of form and number—that is, as the equivalent, among solids, of the point. In this chapter I shall concentrate on line, or lines: specifically, the lines Serlio called linee occulte. Linee occulte are the unmarked or partly marked axes, edges, and coordinates of cubic architecture. They are graphic metaphors for invisible affinities. And, obeying Neoplatonism's pattern of metempsychosis—of descent from and return to God—linee occulte have two basic roles. They help architecture to descend from Idea to materiality, and they help it to rise back. Physically, linee occulte are two different things. They are the "unseen" stylus or pencil lines with which the architect makes a geometrical grid on which to cast his plans and elevations. And after the building is erected, they are the imagined geometric scaffolding that the critic applies to the structure he sees. This imagery of lines clarifies the building's proportions and distributions and squares up the material edifice by imposing on it a more exigent, imaginary architecture.

The earliest mention of something like linee occulte that I have found is in Manetti's life of Brunelleschi. Manetti describes the architect and Donatello in Rome measuring the ruins: "And where they could, they estimated elevations, either [getting the heights] from the intervals between column bases, or from the foundations, jogs, or the vaults of [buried] buildings. And they set up strips of parchment which they transferred to a squared paper marked with Arabic numbers and letters which only Filippo understood" (52). I take this to mean that the two men constructed a full-scale grid across the site to be measured, using ribbons of parchment, and that they then reproduced the building's outlines on what we would call graph paper. Elevations were extrapolated, I presume, via formulas for the orders and the like—from intercolumniations, column diameters, and wall thicknesses. The use of such a temporary grid for measurement, transfer, and change of scale; the fact that the squares or rectangles of this grid were projected vertically as well as horizontally, thus becoming cubic tesserae like Vitruvius' idéae; and the difficulty or secrecy of Brunelleschi's algorithms or code—these notions all reappear in the later history of linee occulte.

64

The phrase itself, however, belongs to the sixteenth century. Earlier, there had been confusion about what to call these lines; there were various terms for the grid coordinates and for the visible ink lines of architectural drawings. And often writers seem to be talking about lines in the sense of "lineaments" or outlines, or as when we say today that a building has "good lines." The word "lineamenta" itself could mean most of these things. It could also mean something like idéae, as noted, and even Idea itself (e.g. Scamozzi 1.52). This confusion may stem from the fact that in classical Latin the singular "lineamentum" means a stroke made with a writing instrument while the plural "lineamenta" means designs, drawings, or portrayals. In modern translations, as Susi Lang has shown, the word has been rendered as design, drawing, form, outline, plan, sketch, and even definitions. Or in the Italian form of "liniatura" it can veer towards "overall ornamental scheme" (Colonna 36, 38). Thus like cube and cubic, and square and squared, lineamenta has overlapping senses. But it rarely contains the notion of thickness or plasticity. It retains at least a flavor of Idea and can as well mean something like "coded geometric drawing." The word appropriately emphasizes the diagrammatic, linear character of Early Renaissance facades and plans. More philosophically, lineamenta are preliminary graphic descents from that higher architecture that is only possible in the realm of words and numbers. They are demonstrations of truths but not the truths themselves. They are less noble than algorithms but more noble than perspectives, models, or material buildings.

To emphasize this philosophical aspect of architecture, Alberti often remarks that he wants to promote it as a liberal art, a speculative science, a literature. I believe that the lack of diagrams in *De re aedificatoria* comes from Alberti's desire to translate "edificatory matters" as far as possible into words and numbers.

Yet Alberti was well aware that drawings do have to be made in the practical process of design. His solution was to conflate the notion of the drawn plan with something more like "architectural surface geometry." "The whole business of building," he says, "consists of structure and lineamenta, and the whole power and purpose of lineamenta is that an absolute, straight manner be used for the adjustment and joining of lines [*lineae*] and corners into which the facade of the building is inserted and framed" (19). Lineamenta thus assign distribution and number throughout the building. They are at first entirely mental; it is proper, says Alberti, to lay out entire designs in the mind and soul without reference to materials. And "the lineamentum [here, unclassically, the drawn design] is to be a sure and constant record, conceived in the mind, expressed in lines and angles, and realized by resourcefulness and learned talent" (21). Hence lineamenta, though comparable to idéae, have greater primacy. They transcend and pre-exist the material building, which is checked against them. A single set of lineamenta can reappear intact in many different buildings. In themselves, therefore, lineamenta are monadic or cubic; applied, they produce multiples. They are the intermediary between the unique universality of Idea and the repeated local imagery of the material world.

2.2   Filarete's Two Grids. Alberti's language suggests that lineamenta are disembodied linear diagrams. Filarete produced a more practical and more complicated version of the same thing based on the grid. For Filarete the grid establishes number and translates it into drawings and three-dimensional models. Then the grid is established at the site to determine the actual building at full scale. The last stage, with the full-scale grid marked out on the site, is described and illustrated when Filarete talks about laying out a piazza "in paralli tutta lienata" (Fig. 2.1, 101r). This sounds more or less like Manetti's account of Brunelleschi and Donatello in Rome. After choosing the site, says Filarete, "I first had the cords stretched according to the gridded drawing [*disegno lineato*], . . . the square compartments having been marked out across the area of the site . . . according to the squared-off plan" (101r). No doubt the procedure was commonplace, but this is the first illustrated description I know of. Filarete's full-scale grid, if not precisely magical, is at least evanescent. It appears first in the design process, then temporarily at the site, and finally disappears.

2.1 Grid of linee occulte marked out on site, from Filarete (Courtesy Yale University Press)

But at this point Filarete's use of the grid takes off in two different directions. In the above case, and elsewhere, he uses it as a simple transfer device. As such it is purely a method of dimensioning and locating, like the grids used to transfer figure drawings. There is no necessary relationship between the coordinates of the grid and the forms of the drawing. Such grids as these are like the coordinates of a map. The geometric web of latitude and longitude is simply imposed on the pre-existing land masses and boundaries. On the other hand, when new territory is being explored, often the grid that measures also determines permanent man-made

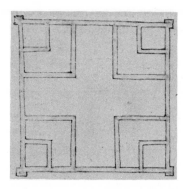

2.2 Plan of Sforzinda Cathedral, from Filarete (Courtesy Yale University Press)

shapes. An example is the western United States. Here states, counties, and townships often have rectilinear boundaries following coordinates of latitude and longitude. Allowing for a few intractable mountain ranges and rivers, these settlements and regions are "rational" and geometric in form. Such coordinates, which simultaneously measure *and* bound, are what I call linee occulte. They are different from the grids that simply measure, for they remain as determinants—partially visible, partially implied—of the civilization they portray, in the form of street patterns, vegetation patterns, and the like.

The grid that locates, measures, and then forms Filarete's plan of Sforzinda Cathedral consists of these linee occulte. The cathedral is laid out in 25-braccio (hereafter abbreviated br) squares, 36 of which demarcate the whole (Fig. 2.2, 49v). Two of the squares form baptistries and two others sacristies. These compartments are visible statements of the invisible or partly visible tesserae or modules of the remainder. Similarly the hospital on folio 79r (Fig. 2.3) seems to be formed, and not merely measured, by 4-br tesserae grouped into larger modules. Filarete says that first a rectangle 400 br long by 160 deep is measured on the site of the hospital (Fig.

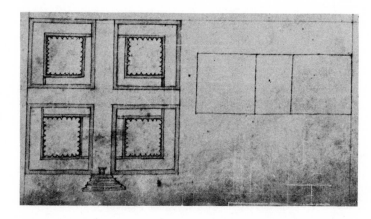

2.3 Plan of hospital, from Filarete (Courtesy Yale University Press)

2.4 A). He then divides the long side dually as follows: 160 80 160. Thus there are two 160-br squares flanking a vertical double square derived from one-half the side of the squares. This layout is then subdivided into 4-br "quadretti" which will be the tesserae forming the smaller compartments of the hospital. Margins of 80 br are marked out around the squares and the whole configuration is then repeated below to make the outer perimeter of the hospital a square 400 br per side, with a Greek cross 80 br wide imposed on it (Fig. 2.4 B). Thus do the linee occulte first measure, then locate, and finally become, walls and canals (Fig. 2.4 C).

Linee occulte grew out of the notion of an invisible or partly invisible graphic architectural design of strongly geometric origin. These "hidden lines" could be erased guidelines on the draftsman's sheet, or the temporary grid used to lay out

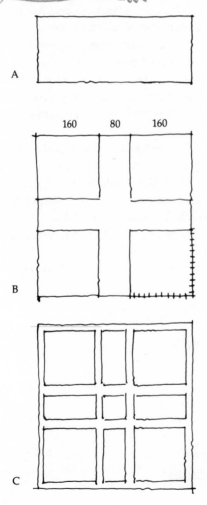

2.4 Analysis of Filarete's hospital layout

foundations *in situ*. Alberti had a somewhat similar notion of geometric drawing which he called lineamenta, and which was the earliest physical manifestation of number during the design process. Filarete makes Alberti's conception more concrete. He exploits a grid plan based on subdivided squares, that is, produced via number-genealogy. Filarete's related family of squares and subsquares locates and forms all the main parts of the building.

2.3   Gameboard Plans. Francesco di Giorgio takes a further step in the elaboration of linee occulte. The earlier version of his book had featured thick-walled plans in the manner of Filarete (Fig. 2.5). But when in the 1480s Francesco rewrote his treatise on the basis of a more reliable Vitruvius text, he substituted new plans.

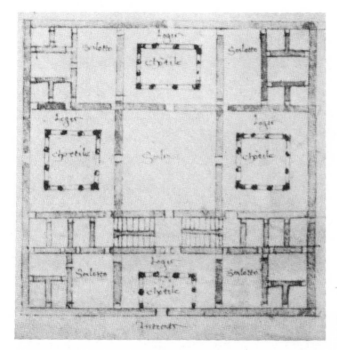

2.5 Palace plan, from Francesco di Giorgio (Courtesy Edizioni Il Polifilo)

These are more schematic than the earlier ones, with single-line walls and emphatic grid matrixes formed of continuous coordinates that are partly inked in and partly erased or omitted (Fig. 2.6). Indeed, some diagrams still retain the scored lines with which they were made. Sometimes, too, the illustrator used the horizontal guidelines that had been prepared for the scribe who wrote out the text. On one occasion, in the Spencer manuscript (New York Public Library), the linee occulte of a Greek-cross church are in pencil and the walls in ink (Fig. 2.7).

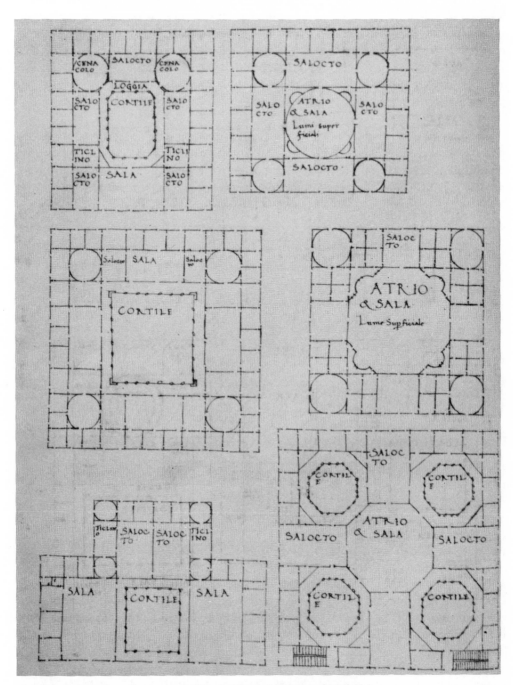

2.6 Palace plans, from Francesco di Giorgio (Courtesy Edizioni Il Polifilo)

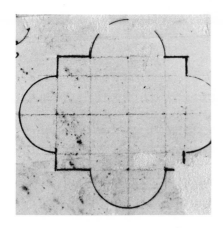

2.7 Church plan with linee occulte in pencil, from Francesco di Giorgio, "Trattato di architettura" (ms copy, courtesy Spencer Collection, The New York Public Library, Astor, Lenox and Tilden Foundations)

Francesco's linee occulte assign and govern spaces in a newly rigorous way. As had not normally been the case with Filarete, his tesserae tend to be of uniform size. We can lay out the left-hand center palace in Figure 2.6 on a grid that is uniform (like Filarete's) and regular in spatial components (unlike Filarete's). It is a construction of 121 squares, 11 per side, which in turn forms a hypostyle temple of 144 columns (Fig. 2.8). Within this scheme there is cubic distribution; the four facades, each of 12 columns, make a square perimeter of 44 columns. The courtyard is composed of 16 invisible columns in a 4 x 4 block; the corner blocks are 4 x 4 and the areas between them 4 x 4, and so forth.

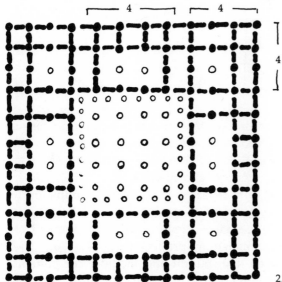

2.8 Square palace in Figure 2.6 as hypostyle

But there is more. Analyzing the tesserae rather than the columns (Fig. 2.9), we find that the rooms are distributed with cubic regularity. The courtyard (whose *visible* columns, the small circles, are unfortunately out of register) is composed of 25 tesserae, 5 x 5—all noncubic values. But the rooms themselves consist of two "cenacoli" or dining rooms (4 tesserae), two "salotti" (4 tesserae), four salas (6 tesserae), sixteen rooms of 2 tesserae each, including the stairwells, and twenty-four rooms of 1 tessera each. Hence all are cubic in shape and distribution. Furthermore, the whole is cubic in its layering: there is an outer chain of 1- and 2-tesserae monads and "duads," so to call them, then inner sequences of 2-, 4-, and 6-tessera rooms—that is, rooms that are both larger and with a higher count of invisible coordinates—and finally the central 25-tessera courtyard, which is made up entirely of invisible bays.

A	2A	A	A	A	A	A	2A	A
2A	4A	2A		6A		2A	4A	2A
A	2A						2A	A
A								A
A	6A			25A			6A	A
A								A
A	2A						2A	A
2A	4A	2A		6A		2A	4A	2A
A	2A	A	A	A	A	A	2A	A

2.9 Tesserae in Figure 2.8

The names of the rooms also adhere to this scheme, and at this point, in consistently identifying the functions of his rooms, Francesco marks another advance from Filarete. Francesco's plan is in fact so regular that we can convert it into a scala that shows function as well as modules, tesserae, and distribution.

Once a cluster of tesserae is systematically repeated it becomes a module on its own (last column), a practice we will see over and over again later on. The larger a volume, the fewer its appearances, and the smaller a volume the more frequently it occurs. There are very similar inverse matching progressions, 1–24 and 25–1 (marked by arrows on Table 10) between distribution and modular components. Francesco's plan is indeed more of a numberform scala than an actual building.

Table 10. Function, distribution, and module composition in Francesco di Giorgio's square palace

Function	Distribution	Tesserae	Module components
Courtyard	1 ⎤	25 ↑	25A ↑
Sala	4	6	6A
Cenacolo/Salotto	4	4	4A
Duads (including stairs)	16	2	2A
Monads	24 ↓	1	A

Many other plans in the second version of the treatise are similar—what might be called graphic versions of Albertian lineamenta, or even of Ficino's social scalae.

Such plans appear in notebooks of other architects. Codex Ashburnham App. 1828, for example, in the Biblioteca Laurenziana, Florence, contains a square palace plan (Fig. 2.10) very close to the one just discussed. It could be a copy, though if so the copyist has transformed two 6A salas into smaller rooms. But here again we get a constancy of function, that is, a constant ratio is maintained between the shapes, sizes, and distributions of the larger rooms. There are similar things in the Sangallo sketchbooks. In the Uffizi album of Antonio Sangallo the Elder (the so-called Geymüller Sketchbook) is a plan of the Basilica of Maxentius laid out with a pencil grid but with inked walls. The pencil grid presumably helped the draftsman assign the ruined remnants to their original places. So the technique of measuring ancient buildings with grids was still alive at a time when architects were designing new buildings in which these same grids were used as linee occulte. The latter act as family ties—unseen "lineages" between ancient monuments and modern palaces.

2.4 Duity, Symmetry, Self-Measurement. Francesco exploits linee occulte with a new thoroughness. He also states the theoretical position derived from this practice, and from its cubic background, more completely than his predecessors. First of all he makes a clearer, stronger case for three-dimensional vertical and horizontal alignment of all walls and openings. He is more rigorous in applying Albertian duity than Alberti himself: "Openings must be over openings," he says, "volumes over volumes, solids over solids, supports over supports, columns over columns" (412). And in the earlier version of the treatise he had written:

It seems to me that one of the most excellent arrangements that a building can have is the concordance and conference [conferenzia] of each thing, as one tribune to another, windows to windows, chapels to chapels, columns to columns, one member to another, void over void. Thus all parts have consecutive [or linked-up] correspondence. And above all the framings of cornices, friezes, architraves, and bases, inside and out, are erected so that at no point are there interruptions. Also one must take care that the wings, fronts, and facades of the churches, their surrounds and members, are not broken into by any interval, and that the parts of windows, either right or left, are not cut into [48].

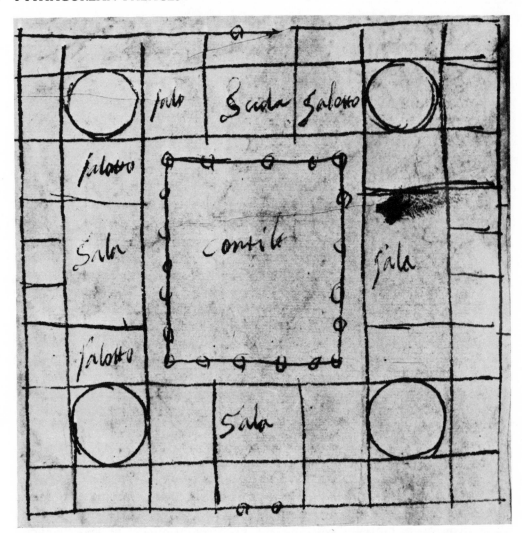

2.10 Palace plan, from Codex Ashburnham App. 1828 (Courtesy Biblioteca Medicea Laurenziana, Florence)

This is a more circumstantial case for chains of binary sequences than anything we have read so far. Any building with such pairs of components is using them as coexisting modules. A left-hand tribune creates a right-hand one and by implication front and back ones. The visible tribunes "state" that the building is so many visible and invisible tribunes in extent. The same goes for other binary sequences—such as sextets of windows. In a similar way single or odd-numbered elements must be disposed into equalities flanking their central axis (89). Concordance and conference, as Francesco defines them, demand that a building be self-measuring not merely in terms of some single feature or module, but with many different sets of intraposed module-features. The cathedral is so many tribunes in extent, but also so many window-squads, pilaster-files, dome-groups. The building is *symmetrical* in the literal sense of the word. It admits of different, coexisting measurements via modules composed of its decorative and spatial components. The presence of these coexisting families, these pairs, trios, and septets of mobile and stable, male and female, odd and even values, and their visibleness and invisibleness, their continual copulation and reproduction, create the building.

2.5 The Republican Town Hall. I can illustrate some of the practical results of this theory by taking advantage of another novelty besides Francesco's use of the grid and his insistence on duity. This novelty is his detailed assignment of functions to different rooms.

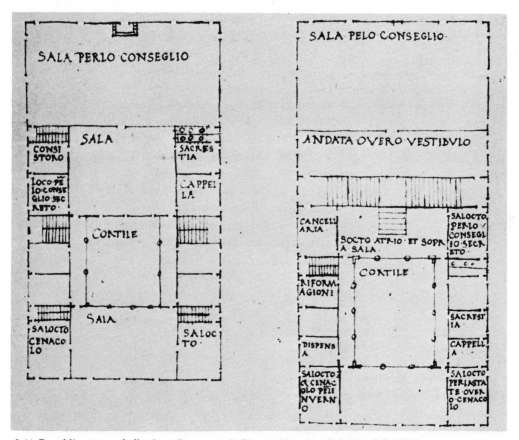

2.11 Republican town halls, from Francesco di Giorgio (Courtesy Edizioni Il Polifilo)

For examples of this, we can look at two plans of town halls for a republic (Fig. 2.11). In perimeter the plan on the left is a "superbipartiens tertias" (5:3) rectangle, the other a double square. The two are similarly though not identically subdivided in ways one might find advocated by Filarete, with lateral cubicula or tesserae, and axial, dominant salas. Francesco says:

The houses of republics . . . must be fronted by the city's main common square. . . . The palace should be freestanding and unencumbered all around. There should be only one doorway, though there may be false doors so as not to destroy the orderliness of the design. Through the entrance one arrives at an atrium and then goes into a courtyard around which are the entrances to all or most of the offices that a well-governed republic is expected to have. . . . [He is describing the right-hand plan; cf. Fig. 2.14 B.] The first and principal staircase ought to rise from the [second] atrium. From this one enters a room [the vestibule, marked "Andata overo Vestibulo" in Fig. 2.11] from which one enters the council hall and all the other apartments around. At the end of [the vestibule] is the consistory or audience chamber [i.e. directly over the second atrium and flanking the room marked "private room" in Fig. 2.14 B] connected with the chancellery [Fig. 2.11] and similarly [on the other side] with the bathrooms or necessaries that serve the council hall and these others. . . . Near the chancellery there is to be a chapel with its sacristy, and another, private place. Near this is a room for dining like a staff dining room. And nearby is the room for the butler and the pantry, with a stair leading to the upstairs kitchen [350–51].

It is not always clear which of the two plans in Figure 2.11 Francesco is talking about; but no matter. His description is more detailed than any earlier comparable one I know of. It is our fullest attempt so far to translate a building's functions into words, to make, that is, a functional *and* formal, as opposed to a merely formal, signified.

One can express this new degree of informativeness in several ways:

1. Relationship of Hypostyle to Tesserae. If we draw out the right-hand plan on a grid (Fig. 2.12), we produce a 6 x 15 hypostyle temple with horizontal sesqualter bays and 90 columns in all. If we then subdivide these totals into visibles versus invisibles we get:

    visible columns
        42 of them in 7 squads of 6
        24 others
    invisible columns
        16 of them in 4 squads of 4
        8 others

—in other words excellent cubic reduction.

Looking at the same temple as a set of modules (Fig. 2.13), we find the tesserae arranged in 7 rows of 4, with 14 A's and 14 B's. All the coordinates between these tesserae are walls or partitions except for α and β, which are main axes, and 1, which is a sight line. But while the tessera and hypostyle breakdowns adequately

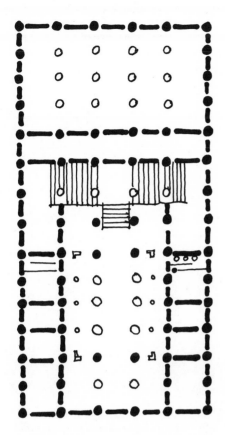

2.12 Republican town hall as hypostyle

explain most of the plan, they do not fit the cross-hatched strip through the center, which includes the main staircase (just beneath β). This strip will therefore have to be declared noncubic territory.

2. Relationship of Tesserae to Modules. But we need not leave things in this semi-cubic state, that is, with seven unindividuated rows from top to bottom. The tesserae come in two sizes: A is a square each of whose sides is two times the width of one of the hypostyle bays in Figure 2.12. B is a rectangle whose base equals one bay's length and whose altitude equals twice a bay's width. These B's are distributed into two files running down the sides of the building, with seven modules in each file. But these files are broken by the nonmodular strip into groups of three above and four below. In the center is a double file of seven A's, also divided by the strip into groups of three and four. Thus while neither 7 nor 14 is a cubic value, 3 + 4 certainly is, as is 6 + 8—the sums of the upper and lower files of A's.

This kind of duity is not as neat as that discussed in the last chapter. But it does yield cubic results corresponding to the stated axes of the building.

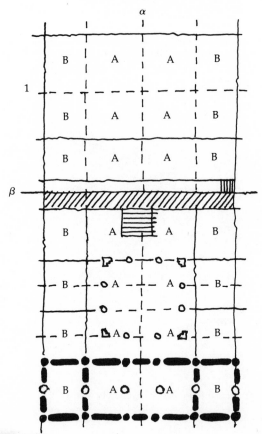

2.13 Modules in republican town hall. Tesserae (A,B) differ from intercolumniations as shown in lower row.

3. Relationship of Modules to Distribution. If we now align the room-modules with the room-functions and distributions, we get other interesting relationships. First, there is a cluster of four A's in the center of the council hall which matches the four A's occupying the courtyard. These two appearances of the same cluster make it a supermodule, 4A. For the rest, the whole plan is readable as a scala-hierarchy. In other words there is a *unique* distribution of modular components for the council hall, the courtyard, and the vestibule. This is Group I. Then there is a slightly larger group of rooms, including the chancellery, the private room ("Salotto Segreto"), and the two dining rooms, all defined by module B. Finally there is the largest group, including the pantry ("Dispensa"), the chapel, the sacristy, the legislative committee room ("Riformagioni"), the toilet, and two nameless rooms, where all the spaces consist of subdivisions of B. The first group of rooms may be called "noble": the rooms are large and unique. The second group is "bourgeois": all four rooms are the same—respectable, symmetrically distributed (in the modern sense of the term), but formed entirely from the secondary or derivative module. Finally there are "plebeian" rooms which include such things as pantries, latrines, stairs, undesignated space—and the chapel, a true piece of italianità, this. These all are less than B in extent. The nonmodular staircase in the center can also be grouped with these servant spaces.

Further, the noble rooms have a hierarchy within themselves. If we assume that A, the square, is nobler than its rectangular offspring B, then the noblest space is the supermodular courtyard, which is all A and which is made entirely of invisible architecture. The council hall also contains 4A but has flanking pairs of B's and is in large part visible. The vestibule is down a peg from this: 2A plus a B on each end. There is no noble A blood at all in the rest of the building except what was inherited through B.

Table 11. Function, distribution, and module composition in Francesco di Giorgio's republican town hall

	Room	Distribution	Module or Supermodule
Group I (noble)	Council hall	1	4A plus 4B
	Courtyard	1	4A
	Vestibule	1	2A plus 2B
Group II (bourgeois)	Chancellery type	4	B
	Chancellery	1	B
	Private room	1	B
	Dining room I	1	B
	Dining room II	1	B
Group III (plebeian)	Pantry type	8	less than B
	Pantry	1	less then B
	Chapel	1	less than B
	Sacristy	1	less than B
	No name I	1	less than B
	Legislative committee room	1	less than B
	Latrine	1	less then B
	Private stair	1	less than B
	No name II	1	less than B

In terms of size, finally, there is a graded downward sequence from the series of three unique noble rooms, to the four bourgeois ones, to the eight plebeian. This matches a corresponding upward movement in modular size, as noted in Table 11.

Compared with the more formalistic analyses in the last chapter, Francesco's designs, while still firmly cubic, yield information about the social organizations he had in mind. One might say that he has used not only geometric but functional linee occulte to establish social hierarchies.

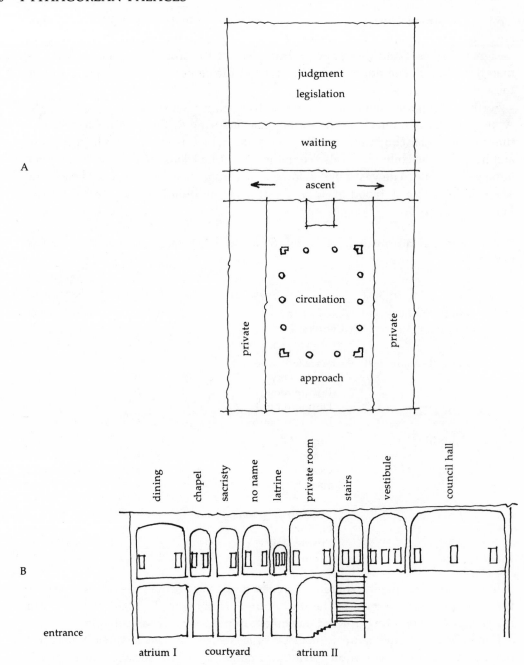

2.14 Functional analysis (A) and section (B) of republican town hall

Francesco's development of linee occulte greatly enriches cubic theory. His game-board palace plans are graphic equivalents of Alberti's lineamenta. The republican town hall is a three-dimensional social or governmental scala (Fig. 2.14). In Neoplatonic terms, the building consists of parallel streams of descent and ascent leading from a cubic source-space at the head of the plan, the council hall, down through grades of activities ranging from worship and deliberation to climbing and walking, to what Scamozzi would call the palace's "rump"—that is, pantries and dining rooms (Scamozzi 1.241).

2.6   Linee Occulte and Perspective. We come now to Serlio, as far as I know the actual coiner of the term linee occulte (2.25r). I hasten to explain that by this expression Serlio meant both more and less than what I have indicated in the preceding pages. For him, linee occulte are the guidelines drawn to construct a perspective view (Fig. 2.15). They are what we sometimes now call "vanishing lines." But by this term we usually mean only lines that *lead to* a vanishing point. Serlio's term emphasizes the fact that these lines (like Francesco's pencil lines, or even Brunelleschi's parchment strips and Filarete's cords) were eventually removed. They *vanished*

figure b

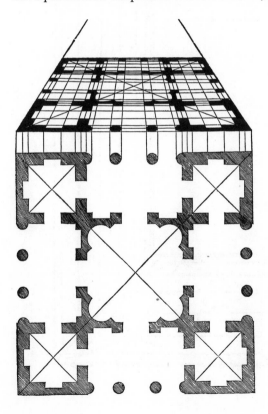

2.15 Perspective plan, from Serlio

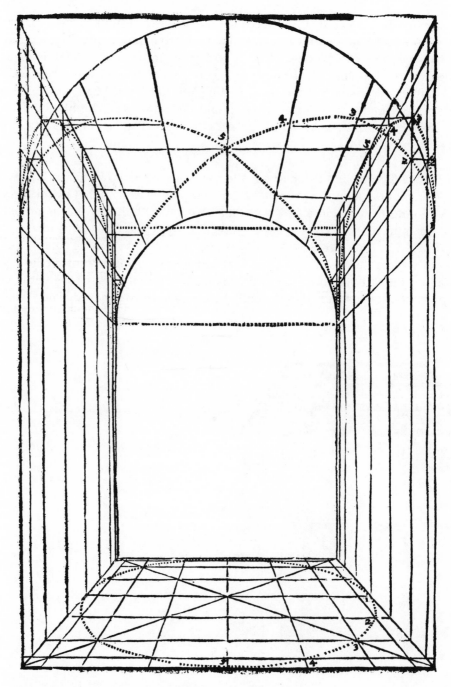

2.16 Vault in perspective, from Serlio

after they had structured the desired figure (2.21r). And this brings Serlio's definition of linee occulte closer to the definitions given earlier. Serlio's linee occulte are loosely comparable, even, to Alberti's lineamenta. But Serlio goes further (for example, in Book VII). He includes scales of feet (*piedi*) and inches (*once*) in his layouts so as to imply a continuous dimensioning grid that pervades the building's plan and elevation, and even the space around it. The idea suggests more than the invisible envelope he describes for the Pantheon; it suggests the continuous, infinite geometrical grid, orthostatic in elevation but oblique in perspective, of Ficino's cosmos.

In other words, Serlio's notion of vanished perspective guidelines leading to infinity links up cubic theory with perspective. In elevation and plan, and in perspective projection, the vanished guidelines are uniform three-dimensional grids. The "true" orthostatic grid creates the building's plan and elevation and prepares it for transfer from drawing to material structure. The obliquely seen scenographic grid of a plan in perspective—which is an *imagined* or *contemplated* orthostatic grid—is used to construct views, as in Figure 2.16. Thus Serlio composes architectural planes and locates openings in a double sense, both in terms of real space and in terms of the representation of real space. He shows how, once the air is filled with this transparent armature of linee occulte, all kinds of forms—polygons, circles, anything you like—can be inscribed within it (Fig. 2.17). And in this practical graphic way he reinforces the link Ficino had made between speculation and perspective.

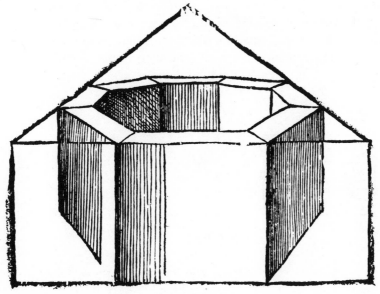

2.17 Octagonal ring in perspective, from Serlio

The notion of a fully three-dimensional, transparent armature is encountered elsewhere in Serlio's pages. I have already mentioned the Pantheon's cubic envelope, and we shall see in Chapter 4 how Serlio goes about drawing out such an armature as a full-fledged transparent solid. He also emphasizes the likeness of such all-purpose, see-through architecture, or geometry, to the study of human anatomy, with its hidden frameworks and its practice of peeling away outer layers: "As those draftsmen who have seen the anatomies of men and of animals are worth more, and understand art better, than do those who pass it all by superficially, abiding only by outward appearances, so those perspectivists who want to understand well, and memorize the hidden lines, will know art better than those who content themselves with drawing the visible parts" (2.25). One must be able to draw the lines of invisible architecture mentally, just as one draws the lines of visible architecture physically. One must always think metonymically, that is, and be able to calculate and imagine the whole of which the built building is only a part. One does this via linee occulte and the invisible tesserae of a mental armature.

2.7 Linee Occulte and the Occult. Philosophically, linee occulte are secret connections that, when perceived, show unsuspected relationships between separated things. They explain correspondences and actions-at-a-distance. They are the "influences" through which forces such as gravity, love, and friendship—all important in Renaissance architecture—exert themselves. Hence they are the architectural equivalent of the lines that Giordano Bruno was to draw, in *Articuli adversus mathematicos* and elsewhere, to show the invisible, multiple-imaged structures of the cosmos and its worlds (Fig. 2.18). Bruno's diagrams are simultaneously the objects of calculation and of contemplation. They recede in perspective and at the same time present themselves as elevations. The longer one examines them the more

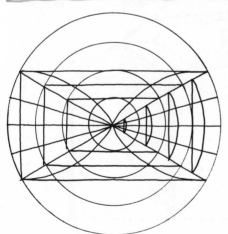

2.18 Diagram redrawn from Giordano Bruno, *Articuli adversus mathematicos*, in F. Fiorentino et al., eds., *Opera latine conscripta* (Naples: Morano, 1879)

relationships and forms one sees. They can be mentally measured or calculated, and so become the procreators of numbers. I assume that Ficino had this same activity in mind, this same continuous fabrication of form and number, when he tells us to calculate and speculate in the presence of a building.

Lomazzo, the most hermetic of our theorists, even equates the process of drawing itself with linee occulte in this sense. In the *Trattato* (483), writing after he himself had gone blind, he stresses the notion that a blind man sees more acutely in his mind than does a man with sight. He likens himself in this way to Homer, Democritus, and Plato. "Vista interna" sharpens the image of Idea; and a sighted artist, with sharp vista interna, "more easily draws objects on a ground that is not extreme or contrasty, as very white paper would be, and with an instrument that is not very sharp, as a pen dipped in ink would be, but instead with softest pen dipped in watercolor . . . so that, there being little difference between the color of the design and the paper, without the confusion of a [too-physical] object, that which is in the mind quietly affirms itself." Lomazzo cites Leonardo as a practitioner of this system. Similarly, in *Idea* (106) he advocates that the artist draw with the thinnest possible lines, and with frequent guidelines. With faintest outline, and embedded in a network of geometrical diagrams, Lomazzo envisages the form emerging from the surface of the paper like a ghost materializing.

Even more than Lomazzo, Scamozzi attributes hermetic virtues to line drawings. Plans, elevations, and sections, he says, are the true ways to "know" a building; and not only do we thus know a given building but we ultimately know all its supernatural counterparts—the worlds of which it is a model—in the cosmos. Drawing miniaturizes the celestial and terrestrial worlds and brings them into comparative scale. It readies them for contemplation. Drawing or "disegno" in Scamozzi is almost a form of conjuring. By making architectural diagrams one summons invisible presences and invokes hidden affinities. It is not a human but a divine activity (1.47). When, like Serlio, Scamozzi shows how irregular lots can be articulated into squares and rectangles (Fig. 2.19), he has made these ideal forms imposed on matter, the measures of the redemption of chaos (1.128). The leftover, irregular spaces equally measure the architect's *struggle*, which has of course been only partially successful, to impose divine disegno on this chaos. One notes in this plan the 6-x-6-column square central court, which is the noblest space, and its flanking rooms which descend from the 5:6 "entrata," flanked by square anterooms, to the more irregularly formed, trapezoidal chambers on the perimeter. The regular spaces are located and shaped by the linee occulte of the grid; the outer, rougher and more natural spaces defy the grid. Thus the plan of the palace becomes a model of the perfect and divine inner worlds of squares and cubes, and it equally "models" the material world of rough nature, illustrating a redemptive procedure: the gradual and hierarchical imposition of cubic form through the action of linee occulte.

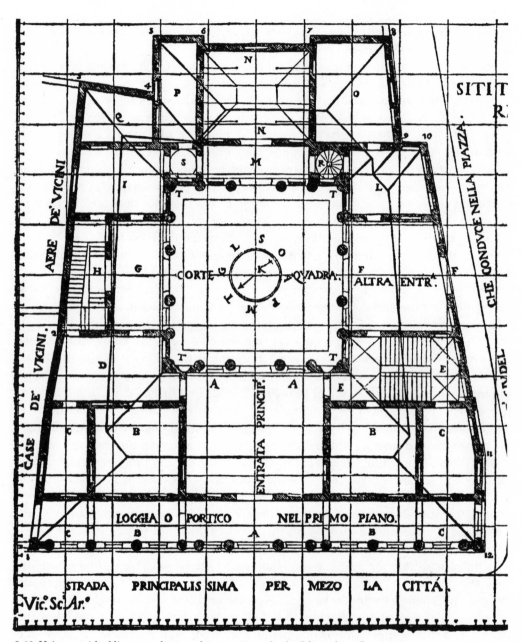

2.19 Using a grid of linee occulte to redeem an irregular building, from Scamozzi

Serlio, then, connected linee occulte with perspective and hence with infinity. He endowed these powerful lines with a projective, three-dimensional character. They became for him a continuous unseen network within which the plans and facades of buildings, and the spaces between, occur. For him a building is only a visible, finite part of an infinite invisible jungle gym. In post-Serlian theory linee occulte become even more fully the magic forces the name implies. They link the different hermetic worlds with lines of influence, and form scalae that may be defined in the literal sense as heavenly ladders.

LINEE OCCULTE

LINE OCCULT

3. Plane: Man the Beautiful

3.1 The Human Figure and Its Geometric Offspring. Our theorists believed that geometrical surfaces were procreated by the human figure. Such physiques were invisibly sensed within geometrical and architectural perimeters, and they generated number sequences affecting the planes that they produced. Because they possessed physiques, palaces could also contain working organs like those of an animal or person. Meanwhile the columnar orders could be seen as social orders.

These notions grew out of Vitruvius, and out of Ficino's social and sexual ideas. But Lomazzo expressed the basic relationship behind them with the most concision: "The cube is formed from the square, and the square in turn is formed from the man of perfect proportions" (*Idea* 194–95).

Where did this concept come from? Vitruvius had described Dinocrates' offer to rebuild Mount Athos in the form of a male statue holding a city (2.Pref.1). In the story Dinocrates attracts Alexander's attention by oiling his handsome body, curling his hair, and dressing in fur so as to appear like Hercules the city-founder. Dinocrates thus tries to "seduce" the emperor into decreeing that the city shall be built. In another famous passage Vitruvius sets forth in detail the proportions of the ideal male physique. We need not concern ourselves with the actual values involved, except to note that, as we saw in the Introduction, Vitruvius claimed that 1, 2, 3, 4, and 5 feet respectively measured $1/6$, $1/3$, $1/2$, $2/3$, and $5/6$ of the ideal body (3.1.6). To this we can add two corollaries: 1) Vitruvius does not mean an abstract foot but the actual foot of the man in question, so that each body carries with it its own foot-module (3.1.7); and 2) these numbers exist in sequences leading up to a final stable value transcending in importance the sequence proper. Vitruvius calls this ulterior stable value the "summa figuratio" (3.1.4). Thus 6, the height of a man, is a Pythagorean goal, a stable state at the end of a mobile or relatively mobile set of preliminary steps, like 4 in 1 2 3 4, or 216 in 8 64 216.

Just before this passage Vitruvius had described his famous man-in-square-and-circle (3.1.3). He had said that if a man—and we must note here that he means *any* man, not necessarily an ideal one—lies down on the ground and spreads his arms

88

out so that they are even with his shoulders, a perfect square can be fitted around his head and outstretched limbs. And, says Vitruvius, the same can be done with a circle. In both cases, furthermore, the center will be the man's umbilicus. Vitruvius thus makes a proto-Neoplatonic affinity between the human body and two ideal surfaces. We can add that the body creates the figures by gesturing, by spreading its arms; that the center of the two planes is located at that point in a man's body which marks his birth; and even that the square, circle, and man "pervade" each other very much as Earth-cube is pervaded in Ficino by Earth-sphere. Finally, Vitruvius describes the famous encounter between the architect Dinocrates and the patron Alexander as in part sexual; and he remarks on a human-shaped city plan that resulted from this relationship.

3.2 Courtship and Column Physique. Filarete is even more of an anthropomorphist than Vitruvius. He imagines the processes of patronage, design, and construction as forms of courtship, copulation, pregnancy, and childrearing. After alluding to the Dinocrates story he describes the "love affair" between the architect and the patron, a relationship which energizes the whole enterprise of planning and building (2.11r). This is no casual metaphor. Filarete pursues it throughout his book.

Transforming the metaphor slightly, Filarete also draws parallels between father, mother, and child on the one hand and architect, patron, and building on the other. The Idea of the building in the architect's mind is like a fetus in the womb. The line drawing of a building's floor plan is its birth (ibid.). Filarete then speaks of the building as growing through infancy into manhood as it passes through the stages of plans, model, and completed structure. We could thus add a fifth column to Table 4 reading downward through Fetus, Infant, Youth, Man.

There is another way in which Filarete anthropomorphizes. He equates different types of human physique with different rectangles, and these with the orders. Thus the lowest, most primitive order, Doric, the order of the muscular man, is sesquialter. Ionic, a matron, is diagonal, that is, more or less 5:3. And Corinthian, the order of the maiden, is a double square (8.60r). This is a simple but early and eventually important link between the human physique, geometry, and the three orders. For future reference I have expressed it in tabular form.

Table 12. Hierarchies and affinities of the orders in Filarete

Order	Numberform	Physique
Corinthian	double square (2:1)	maiden
Ionic	diagonal (5:3)	matron
Doric	sesquialter (3:2)	muscular man

3.3 Amorous Beings, Visible and Invisible. With Ficino an even richer stream of anthropomorphism enters architectural theory. I noted above in section 1.9 how he explained the multiplication of numberforms sexually, and I outlined the implications of that explanation as they affected cubic architecture. But there is another, more human side to it. This side Ficino investigates not only in the Plato commentaries but also in his translation of the *Pimander* (1463), one of the supposedly ancient Egyptian books attributed to Hermes Trismegistus.

The *Pimander* presents images of man and his body very different from those of traditional Christianity or of the Old Testament. Nor is man a mere ape of nature in the medieval sense. With Hermes, instead of being made of dust, man is "comparable to the celestial gods" (2².1849). He is so beautiful that after his advent on earth Nature falls in love with him and puts herself at his disposal. Indeed God himself is in love with him (2².1837, 1854, 1959–61). And even man, on seeing his own reflection, falls into a narcissistic passion, "and loved that [image] and desired to copulate with it. . . . And he embraced Nature and she, also smitten by love, folded herself into him and they copulated." As a result, says the translation, man alone of all creatures is both mortal and immortal (2².1837). Hence man-as-body is involved in erotic relationships with God, Nature, and himself—all of which are in some hidden way look-alikes: those who know can discern images of man's physique in all of them.

These notions help account for the power of Renaissance art in its time. They foster a basically erotic attitude towards external visible reality and its depictions. If for Vitruvius a man's body begets a square and a circle, for the Renaissance hermetist a square or circle begets a man. The man is a "figura occulta," metonymically seen or sensed within an ideal frame. This hidden man is the object not only of internal vision but of passion. He is a love-object, an adored "constructed god" to use Ficino's term. He is the Lord of Nature and central being of the universe. He is everywhere, eternally mobile, mixing with daemons and angels, with the elements and with the directions, a creature of all dimensions, mortal and immortal (2².1859–60).

As God's inescapable and multiple self-portrait, idol, and lover, man becomes an imitator of God in another way. He fashions images or idols of himself from material substances. "Thus," says Ficino's translation, "from human art to the conceiving of divine art [God] lifts us up" (2².1857). It is by reaching down to us through the beauty, the proportions, and the forms of these man-made idols that God raises us to his bosom. The human physique, strained through the proper numberforms, possesses a redeeming erotic power that Ficino calls "seminal virtue" (2¹.1424–25). Through their seminal virtue the idols speak and do miracles. And the highest form of this self-worshiping self-portrayal is human procreation under proper magical conditions—that is, in obedience to nuptial numbers. Sculpture, painting, and architecture are lesser forms of it. And all procreations are repetitions of the initial act of creation by God. In Ficino's or Hermes' view, in sum, man not only loves himself, Nature, the World, and God, he makes love *to* them; and families and tribes of identical offspring result. Hence do there come to be families and societies of humans, and equally, families and societies of works of art.

The idols made by artists, and of course the geometric frames or numberforms they procreate or are procreated by—their niches, their altars, their temples real or mental—can through their seminal virtue abridge Nature's laws. They can get her to "put herself at man's disposal," to sacrifice her regular rules. In this sense nature-defying machines, like miraculous works of art, are magical. Especially so are "works of lifting art." Instruments that make use of hitherto unknown natural laws, like some of Leonardo's inventions or the construction machinery praised by Scamozzi, break the apparent or "old" taboos. Man has his will of Nature. It is for this reason, I believe, that Neoplatonism tended to give human attributes, and often forms, to automata and other prodigious machines. These were "constructed gods" par excellence.

But there were not only human, artistic, and technological constructed gods, and beautiful idols, hidden or visible. There were also invisible but equally beautiful hosts of spirits. And these spirits inhabited cities of invisible temples, cities reflected or exemplified in part by visible earthly architecture. We noted in the first chapter that Ficino equated the cube itself with the army of individual souls, the point with the gods of the world, the line with the army of angels, and the plane with the army of daemons ($2^1.1415$). But these are only a few of space's inhabitants. There are all sorts of other armies, gods, beings—governors, decans, various kinds of angels, and so forth. It is no wonder that the sixteenth century saw the creation of so many dome frescoes filled with thick choirs of beings—invisible beings made visible through the "magia naturalis" of art, and contained within spherical perspective views of the cosmos. Such beings, mobile and feminine, circled over the stationary, earthly, manly cube of the church's crossing, countering its silence with their song (Fig. 3.1).

Indeed, states and qualities as well as angels and daemons were given ideal physiques by Ficino. These became the animal spirits with which Plato, "like an architect"—that is, as the disposer of incorporeal beings throughout the temple of the cosmos—made the intellectual world apparent to us ($2^1.1519$). Thus is the cosmos a vast building filled with or even composed of images of man.

Finally, God's original act of creation was in a sense also one of artistic procreation. Ficino writes: "The ancient theologians say that animal beings once lay beneath Earth. The primal matter of the World was at first female. Later, Jupiter, the craftsman god of the world, formed the lesser gods—that is, living beings, from the elements and stars" ($2^1.1298$). I interpret this to mean that the basic act of creation

3.1 *Choirs of Angels* (1565–1571), by Giovanni Paolo Lomazzo, Foppa Chapel, San Marco, Milan (Courtesy Soprintendenza alle Gallerie, Milan)

was a sexual/sculptural one. Jupiter the male scooped living female matter out of Earth and shaped it into human forms according to astral *linee occulte*. Jupiter was not only a father and a sculptor but a midwife. The passage also conforms to what I have just quoted from Hermes: Jupiter created the armies of visible and invisible beings by fathering them on the worlds who were their mothers.

This attitude, and certain corollaries drawn from it, was re-expressed a generation later by Cornelius Agrippa:

Man is the most finished and beautiful work and image of God, and a smaller version of the world. Therefore in his more perfect form and sweeter harmony, and in his more sublime dignity he has all the numbers, measures, weights, motions and elements, etc. All component things stand within and are sustained in him, all things are in him as in the supreme artificer, and he has a supreme destiny beyond the common range of other creatures. As a result all ancient peoples first counted their fingers and then established [abstract] numbers from them. And all the articulations of the human body itself, and all numbers, measures, proportions and harmonies that they found were measured against it. Whence, from this commensuration, temples, shrines, houses, theatres and beyond them boats and machines and all sorts of technical devices and craft objects, and buildings in all their parts and members e.g. columns, friezes, bases, antae, stylobates and so on and so forth, were born and brought forth from the human body. . . . And there is no member of the human body that does not respond to some point or sign, some star, some being, some divine name within the archetype of it all, God [2.27.160].

3.4 From Male to Female. Francesco di Giorgio gives similar notions new visual embodiments and applies them more aptly to practical architectural design. Thus he is the earliest Renaissance theorist, so far as I know, to visualize graphically Vitruvius' anthropomorphic imagery. He has several versions of Dinocrates' city and illustrates the statue-mountain (Vitruvius does not say what the colossus looked like) by making it a portrait *of* Dinocrates, a narcissistic idol wearing its seductive gear (Fig. 3.2). Where Vitruvius, anticipating Filarete, had made Alexander the patron-father and Dinocrates the architect-mother of the "son," Mount Athos, Francesco adds that that son is also an image of the mother. (On the other hand, he omits the incident of the seduction itself from his text, though he does develop, more than Vitruvius, equivalences between parts of the city and parts of the human body, for example likening walls, gates, and streets to skin and arteries, [361–62].

Francesco also refers to the city square as the "umbilicus" of the city and almost draws it as such (Fig. 3.3): "The reason for this similitude can be this: because as human nature at its beginning takes through its umbilicus every nutriment and growth [*perfezione*], so through this public place come [the city's nutriments]" (363).

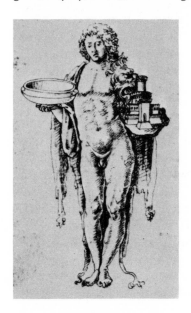

3.2 Dinocrates as Mount Athos, from Francesco di Giorgio (Courtesy Edizioni Il Polifilo)

3.3 Umbilical towns, from Francesco di Giorgio (Courtesy Edizioni Il Polifilo)

There is even more body imagery in Francesco. When he shows how the Ionic column is like a matron he removes (again, in the illustration but not in the text) her chiton (Fig. 3.4). And he makes a number of other interesting changes in the story. He does not say that the Ionic column is specifically a matron, only that it is based on a woman's form. And he adds that this type of column came in after the male Doric because, though woman is an imperfect animal, "she is more attractive than the male in appearance, especially in youth." In this spirit he likens the Ionic capital to an ornamented coiffure. This is an early instance of a growing preference among our theorists for female proportions, numbers, and figure occulte (375).

Like his columns, Francesco's church plans and facades can immure hidden human figures. In the text he mentions, in medieval fashion, the model of the crucified Christ. But in the illustrations the figures appear as naked, curly-headed Dinocrates-types (see Figs. 3.5, 3.6). The textual Christ is transformed in the illustration into something closer to Vitruvius' square-and-circle procreator.

With Francesco, then, we have several important new ideas: the troops or squads

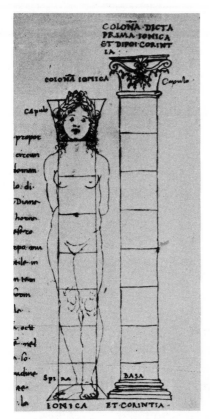

3.4 Ionic and Corinthian columns, from Francesco di Giorgio
(Courtesy Edizioni Il Polifilo)

of columns in a hypostyle are groups of male and female beings. There are also colossal hidden physiques in plan and facade, and even larger fragments of colossi—their stomachs or umbilicuses—in city layouts. There are three different worlds of scale, in other words, unified by their use of the human physique. And there is also Francesco's affirmation that the trio, Doric, Ionic, Corinthian, is not simply a group, as with Vitruvius and Francesco's other predecessors. For Francesco the three orders form a progressive sequence, a hierarchy, with one order leading on to the next so that Corinthian is a "perfection," as Francesco calls it, or even a summa figuratio (expressed by the arrows in Table 13 below).

Table 13. Hierarchies and affinities of the orders in Francesco di Giorgio

Order	Height (in diameters)	Physique
Corinthian ←————————→	9 ←	————————→ perfected woman
↑	↑	↑
Ionic ←————————→	8 ←	————————→ woman
↑	↑	↑
Doric ←————————→	7 ←	————————→ man

3.5 Cubic Columns, Plans, and Facades. What about the cubic content of all this? Nothing could be easier to express graphically than Francesco's columns and their proportions. (Francesco's diagrams express the diameters as squares, more-over, so that the squares composing the columns are cubic numberforms—for example in Figure 3.4.) In the sequence of heights we progress from the noncubic 7 up through 2^3 to 9, which is doubly cubic, as the first true number self-multiplied, and as the square of the first true number—a sequence that becomes a progression from man to woman to perfected woman.

As for the cubic values of the two man-procreated churches, they require more explanation. In the plan (Fig. 3.5), considering volumes only, the transepts each consist of two vertical superbipartiens tertias rectangles on either side of a crossing square on which a circular dome is mounted. The nave consists of four horizontally set 5:3 rectangles. The basic tessera of the plan is $1/15$ of a module, the 15 tesserae in each module-rectangle being in a 5 x 3 format with 120 in all, plus 25 forming the crossing square. The narrow end of each module terminates in a segmental apse built on a circle whose radii equal two tesserae in length. The main chancel area is one tessera by 5, and the apse behind it has a radius of 3 tesserae, the center being marked just at the man's chin. The main apse is indicated by the man's head, the transepts by his arms, the crossing dome by his chest, the nave by his lower body.

The facade (Fig. 3.6), which is for a different church, is based on modules of horizontal double squares arranged in rows of 6 9 9 6, with the male figure $9^1/2$ modules high. The slope of the aisle roofs is given by the man's outstretched arms, the main door height by his knees. Two horizontally set half-modules comprise the frieze of the main cornice. Counting the pediment areas as full modules, there is a grand total across the front of 30 modules plus 6 half-modules.

3.5 Church plan with recumbent colossus, from Francesco di Giorgio (Courtesy Edizioni Il Polifilo)

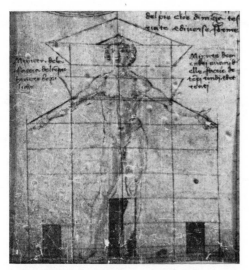 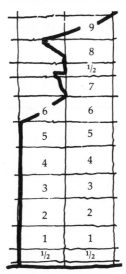

3.6 Church facade with standing colossus (modular analysis on right), from Francesco di Giorgio (Courtesy Edizioni Il Polifilo)

By introducing the human figure into this numberform world we have reinforced the sexual and social meanings of both the figure and the numberform. Dinocrates and Alexander, Vitruvius' man-in-square-and-circle, Ficino's polymorphous-perverse Man the Beautiful, Filarete's architect and patron, and Francesco's columnar maidens and planimetric Dinocrateses—all to one degree or another project seminal virtue. They are real or potential parents. In a sense cubic geometry is only a device that builds bowers for these "occult" lovers, though the development becomes more practical as we move from Vitruvius into the Renaissance. Filarete explains not merely the orders, but the whole process of design, anthropomorphically. Thereupon in Ficino's sexual/social cosmos the worlds of buildings, like the worlds of numberforms, become kinship structures. In Vitruvius' work Dinocrates had presented himself as a love-object, while for Francesco di Giorgio it was Dinocrates' city—his self-portrait and offspring—which played that part. Also for Francesco the orders *progress* from Doric to Ionic to Corinthian, so that Corinthian represents the maiden's triumph. She is the daughter, the heiress-child of Doric and Ionic. And she prevails over them through her superior Neoplatonic beauty and greater seminal virtue.

3.6 Gesture and Passion. At this point Leonardo briefly appears. He was not himself much of an anthropomorphist but he contributed to the anthropomorphism of others. I am thinking particularly of the famous Venice Academy drawing of 1485–1490 (Fig. 3.7). It is based on Vitruvius' ideas but with important differences.

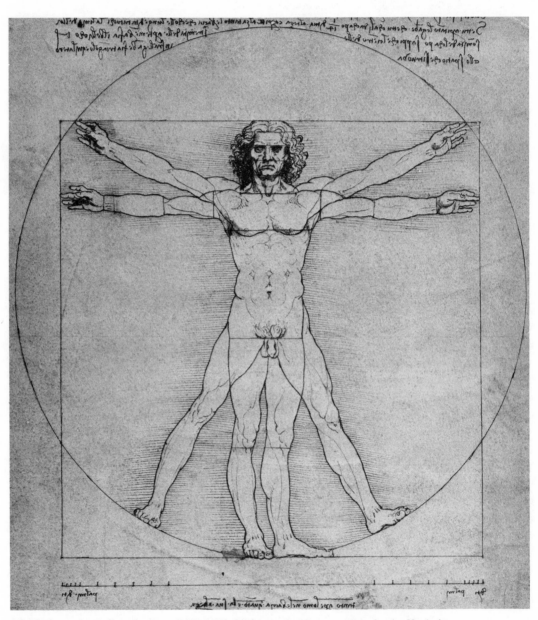

3.7 Ideal man in circle and square (1485–1490), by Leonardo (Courtesy Accademia, Venice)

By inserting Vitruvius' modular measure of the *ideal* male figure (Vitr. 2.1.3) into the square-and-circle procreated by Vitruvius' everyman (3.1.3), Leonardo has conflated two ideas that were distinct in the original. He has also shown his man standing up rather than lying down. Thus the man is generating vertical surfaces like Francesco's man in Fig. 3.5, rather than horizontal ones as in Vitruvius. Then too Leonardo has apparently studied Vitruvius' instructions about arm and leg positions. He says that the circle is created *when the height of the body is lowered by* 1/14. This is achieved by spreading the legs and at the same time raising the arms slightly above the horizontal. In this pose, Leonardo writes, annotating the drawing, the legs make an equilateral triangle. Thus does a third ideal geometric form spring directly from the man's loins. Meanwhile the center of the circle is the umbilicus, as Vitruvius specifies.

For the square, a different pose is necessary and a different center point results. Now the legs are together, the arms horizontal. The center is the base of the penis. Hence the square is not *within* the circle but overlaps it, having its base on the circle's lower perimeter. With two different centers and an irregular relationship between the two perimeters, the only connection between the two surfaces becomes the man himself. Leonardo seems to be stressing that this is a single individual making two gestures—otherwise he would have probably made two different drawings. So in this sense Man the Beautiful procreates both square and circle.

Leonardo has modified Vitruvius in another way. As noted, Vitruvius had supplied information about the measurements of the ideal man. These measurements are all modular, that is, drawn from the parts of the body: "pedes" (feet) and "palmi" (palms). Leonardo takes these measurements and applies them directly to his drawing. It is these marked-off feet, palms, and cubits (forearms)—and not the circle and the square—that tell us we are looking at the ideal man of Vitruvius (3.1.1). There are also scales of palms and inches at the bottom. The square is (again as the result of experiment?) just less than 24 palms per side, and the circle has a radius of 14 palms. Leonardo also gives relationships within the body (not quoted by Richter). One palm = 4 inches (*onci*, "thumbs"), 4 palms = 1 foot, 6 palms = 1 cubit, 4 cubits = 1 pace, and 24 palms = the man's height, which is also, of course, 4 cubits, or 6 feet, or 96 "thumbs." Hence the man (though Leonardo does not remark on this) has cubic summae figurationes in thumbs, palms, feet, and forearms. He is anthropometrically "symmetrical." (Below the figure, on the other hand, Leonardo has written a list of bodily locations expressed as fractions of the total height. In the main these are neither cubic nor symmetrical.)

Leonardo, therefore, for the first time makes explicit what Francesco and others had only implied: that it is the *ideal* man who procreates the ideal surfaces, and that this fact can be expressed "symmetrically," that is, in compatible measurements using different modules and arriving at cubic totals. This confirms our assumption that in Renaissance Pythagoreanism the word "symmetry" refers to quantity as well as, or perhaps more than, to distribution. The man generates his two surfaces, finally, via two gestures and from two different bodily center points. And because he moves in this way, for Leonardo it is the man who procreates the forms, not the other way round.

But paradoxically we can add here on our own that the circle *does* procreate the man, in the sense that he is "attached" to it by his umbilicus, while in turn the man procreates the square with his penis. One can even say that the square is the man's mate. In terms of Ficinian kinship the man is the son of the circle-mother and at the same time the square's lover-father.

While Leonardo locates the center of the square at the man's own erotic center, he says nothing about an emotional relationship, filial or otherwise, between the man and the two planes. For this sort of thing we must turn to Francesco Colonna. His book, the *Hypnerotomachia Poliphili* (whose title I translate as "The Dreaming, Loving Struggle of the Lover of All Things"), was published in 1499. In it, architecture is described in what might be called the poetry of numberforms. The story concerns an amorous quest in which Poliphilus, the hero, searches for his human inamorata. During the search he travels through a garden filled with buildings that arouse his passionate admiration, a feeling he expresses by describing the buildings' measurements and geometric shapes. Thus on seeing a monumental pyramid topped by a cube and then an obelisk, he says in wonder:

The face of the square of the base, beneath the start of the slope of this admirable pyramid, . . . was six stadii [over 3000 feet] in longitudinal extent. Multiplied by 4, as its circumference, the said equilateral base occupied an area of 24 stadii. Then, in altitude from each corner, using the profile or outline as measure, the perfect pyramidal shape constituted or measured out a dimension equal to that of the summit line of the plinth, i.e., all four lines running up to the top and meeting at the center [290ff].

There were, he adds, 1000 + 400 + 10 steps leading up to the top of the pyramid. (Note the cubic breakdown.) At the top, reached by the last ten steps, "was placed a stupendous cube, solid and firm, and whose monstrous bulk made one wonder how it had been raised to this place." This cube formed the base of an obelisk which, as Poliphilus exclaims, "contained so many marvels that I remained in an insensate stupor" (293).

Thus does the Ficinian calculator and speculator reduce material architecture to numberforms. The effort climaxes in a transport of emotion. The causes of the transport lie in the symmetrical sums of the measurements, all cubical, in the ideality of the geometric forms, and in Poliphilus' wonder at the magical or marvelous ways in which these great objects were hoisted into place.

However, Poliphilus' passion is greater still when he encounters a building that reminds him of his beloved. It is a triumphal arch or "miraculous portal" (Fig. 3.8).

3.8 Triumphal gate, from Colonna

Before this excellent gate, . . . visible to the eye, was a tetragonal piazza, 30 paces in diameter, with handsome paving of marble squares set one foot apart, of tesserae in various interlacings and connections and colors. . . . And at the far end of the piazza, on the left and on the right, towards the mountains, were, on the same level, two orders of columns with an excellent araeostyle interval between, according to the rules exhibited by the relations of columns. . . . And between one column and the next was a distance of 15 paces [308].

The lengthy account ends:

Through all which things, I being eager, and my flaming intellect afire with the joy of understanding the perspicacious architect through thorny scrutiny, thus did I subtly analyze [the portal's] dimensions, circumscribing lineaments and material substance [315].

(Note the sequence of the last observation, from number, to line and plane, to solid.) Poliphilus ends by acquiring a portrait of this gate, which he describes as its "figure transported into the small."

The effort of the hero's thorny scrutiny is to my mind the "machia" of the book's title, while the "eros" is his love of a once and future architecture, seen in the dream or "hypnos." And Poliphilus himself is a typical polymorphous-perverse son of Neoplatonism, for whom all things are reducible to anthropomorphic number-forms that radiate seminal virtue.

3.7 Symmetry and Suffering. Cesare Cesariano brought Leonardo's innovations into conformity with Vitruvius' and at the same time added a dose of Neoplatonic eroticism. Cesariano returns to Vitruvius by illustrating modular symmetry and the circle-in-square as two different things (Figs. 3.9, 3.10). His first illustration is entitled "The Measurement of the Human Figure, and All Symmetries Corrected and Proportioned to Correspond with a Geometrical Program." The man stands with his feet together and his "symmetries"—inches, palms, feet, and forearms—mapped and measured on a uniform 30 x 30 grid of three-finger squares. The grid is also marked off into larger tesserae of nine squares each. There are ten of these each way. Meanwhile, corresponding to key points in the man's body, the grid is subdivided at intervals, the heels at 0, the knees at 8, the penis base at 15, the umbilicus at 18, the heart and arms at 24, the chin at 26, the mouth and nose at 27, the eyes at 28, the forehead at 29. Only one of these numbers, 15, is thoroughly noncubic, a great improvement over Leonardo. Meanwhile, radiating from the top of the central vertical axis AB are lines going downward to the man's extended arms. G and Θ are the termini of the "bracchial, manual, and pectoral lines," says Cesariano (48r–52v). We can interpret them as special "influences" between the microworlds of hands and head. The corner axes HG and LK, meet at O, the base of the penis and center of the entire construction. The subsidiary diagonals MA, AN, NB, and BM create a square, MANB, set diagonally within HLGK, intersecting the main diagonals at SQRP, which thus becomes a third square set inside MANB—much like a horoscope or Nativity, as it was called, hence another suggestion of goemetric birth and kinship.

This method is far more informative geometrically than either Vitruvius' or Leonardo's diagrams. "By which," says Cesariano, "not only can we distinguish any [size?] exemplary figure that we wish; we can estimate [*assumere*] all the areas and surfaces, of whatever integral [*elementale*] quantity we wish, either on land or water" (49v). And he adds: "It is convenient that skillful architects know this system, for it computes not only simple surfaces but cubic volumes, so as to arrive at the depths of excavations."

Thus is the ideal physique turned into a universal cubic measure. One fly in the ointment is that the module-squares given below the figure, which have four-digit tesserae, do not correspond to the squares of the grid proper, which have three-digit tesserae. Also, from the viewpoint of summae figurationes, Cesariano's man is

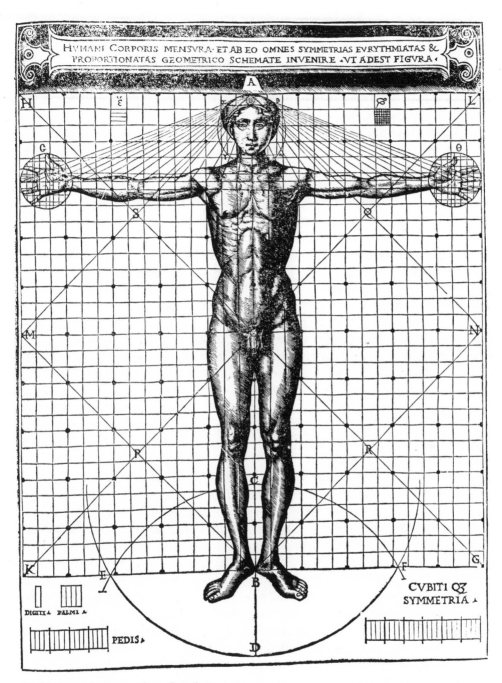

3.9 Ideal man in square, from Cesariano

less perfect than Leonardo's, for he is 24 palms or 4 cubits high, but only 5^3/$_4$ feet. But everything else agrees; indeed Cesariano's scheme involves a perimetric square and several interior squares as well. The body procreates all sorts of inner surfaces, like a sectioned cube or like a colossus within a church plan or facade.

On the other hand Cesariano's man-in-square-and-circle (Fig. 3.10) is uncomfortably spreadeagled. This gives him a single bodily center, the umbilicus, within a set of concentric geometric figures. Like the penis, the arms and legs of this man are extended to their utmost. The man's erection may be intended to suggest the procreation, as opposed to the static measurement, of geometric form. He is actually in the process of fathering the square and circle. But he is also their lover, one guesses, for it is his embrace that actually forms them. His arms and legs establish the corners of the inner square, and hence also the perimeter of the circle which in turn generates the outer square.

In this way Cesariano is more loyal than Leonardo to Vitruvius' directions. But he makes it equally clear how impossible to follow those directions really are. The outer square in Figure 3.10 is again a 30 x 30 grid. The man's feet are at the level of the fifth square up, his knees in the tenth, his umbilicus at 15, his heart in the twentieth, the top of his head in the 24th, the top of his hands at 26. Neat, but not fully cubic.

Most of this I have extrapolated from Cesariano's illustrations. Almost nothing is said in the text to support these readings. On the other hand, in the commentary Cesariano does push the concept of modular symmetry further along. Symmetry, he says, involves not merely the arm, foot, palm, and finger, but even the knuckles and the spaces between them, even the veins, nerves, skin muscles. "All the flesh," even hairs and pores, are modules. And they all must be numerically compatible when the body is used as the hidden structure of a building, or of any form "built or to be built by architectonic science."

This gives us another hint of Cesariano's attitude toward the plane-creating ideal man. In Leonardo's drawing the geometric frames generated by the figure project no sense of discomfort. With Cesariano's man there clearly is such a sense. Geometrically he may be having an orgasm but anatomically he is on the rack. And Cesariano develops this idea. He illustrates Vitruvius' tale of the Persian Portico (7r) whereby different echelons of captives, or statues of those captives, were transformed by their conquerors, the Spartans, into a loggia (Fig. 3.11). The figures act as columns supporting friezes of battlefield trophies. The arrangement of these "orders" follows a social hierarchy. Philosophers and kings make up the main floor and soldiers the second. In an alternative version (Fig. 3.11, right) there are three upper floors with, first, kneeling soldiers, then busts of philosophers or kings, then on top, kneeling homunculi.

Here, as in his prescription for knuckle and vein modules, Cesariano's implicit

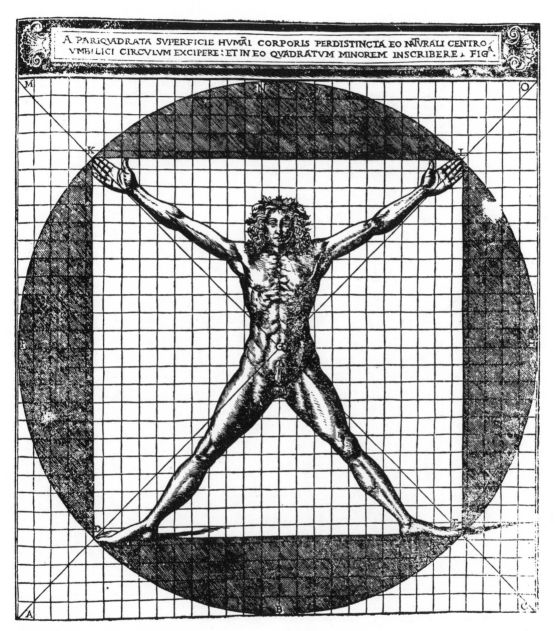

3.10 Ideal man as procreator of form, from Cesariano

3.11 Persian Portico, from Cesariano

attitude towards the immured human components of architecture is sadistic. The victors' gratification is increased by the sight of these architectonic sufferers who in turn are the legendary prototypes for all sorts of structural supports. Such a contrast of sensations would strengthen that sense of well-being which Serlio had claimed one feels on entering the Pantheon. This would of course be due in part to his soul's and body's harmonious rapport with the vast cubic temple; but also, at least for someone like Cesariano, the imagined, straining figures invisibly housed in the temple's walls would deepen the pleasure.

3.8   Columns as Characters. We have watched the orders being transformed into sentient beings. Already, for Francesco di Giorgio, they had been something like that, and Cesariano's caryatids have even more of a sense of life. Now Serlio applies Vitruvius' notion, whereby a temple order's physique is supposed to match that of the god or goddess worshiped, to Christian churches, private houses, and ultimately to their builders' or inhabitants' personalities. For instance, he says, a Doric house suits a strong, short, warlike man. If this man also possesses a certain elegance in his character the order ought to be correspondingly attenuated (4.139r). Ionic is more suited to scholars (4.158v), while of course Corinthian is best suited to churches dedicated to virgin saints (4.169r).

Serlio in fact advocates the use of what might be called architectural metonymy. The full order is not necessary to express these ideas. A part will do for the whole. Details, or only the entablature, or sometimes only a clearly Doric or Ionic molding, will serve. (At this point we recall Filarete's Doric, Ionic, and Corinthian rectangles.) In this same vein Serlio differentiates between "hard" and "soft" details. Their hardness and softness can be expressive. A hard Doric pilaster might support a soft Corinthian entablature (making some point, perhaps, about the builder's build?). And not only are physical type, sex, personality, and profession thus expressible, but so are nationality and climate. In these ways Serlio takes over the social structure Filarete had used as a model for the design and building process only, and applies it to the building itself as a permanent commentary on (and hence as a signified of) its origins and functions.

To extend these expressive possibilities still further Serlio suggests the use of *objets trouvés* or trophies, or imitations of these. Broken tympana and ancient capitals can be added to a building. Even the bizarre and ugly have their place. Here we get more sadism, or at least expressive vandalism: the bizarre and ugly can be achieved by "breaking and spoiling" a beautiful detail. Such a partly destroyed metonym sends messages of the "Roma quanta fuit, ipsa ruina docet" type. Serlio even refers to a bestial order. He wants a complete range of beings among columns; he wishes to mix order-fragments so as to express an architectural individual, the offspring of several bloodlines. Thus of the arch in Figure 3.12 he says:

3.12 Rustic portal, from Serlio

This portal has something of the Doric, the Corinthian, the Rustic, and also (to tell the truth) of the Bestial. The columns are Doric, their capitals are a mixture of Doric and Corinthian. The archivolt [*pilastrata*] around the portal is Corinthian in its carvings, and so are the architrave, frieze and cornice. The whole portal is surrounded by the rustic, as you see. As to the Bestial order, one cannot deny that since there are several stones done in the natural state, and which have the form of beasts, that there exists [such a thing as] *opera bestiale* [6.17r].

In the plate, the rustic and bestial components are extruded through the more civilized ones into a genetic mosaic. The resulting personality is a compound of feminine and gross, bestial and refined—not a bad mixture for a Renaissance lord. Alternatively, you can look at the portal as a battle between a maiden and her beast-tormentor. The beast-faces in the spandrels glower at the elegant archivolt. The rustic stones seem to embrace or bind the flutes of the maiden's chiton, though her Corinthian hairdo is undisturbed. The violent breakages in the entablature and tympanum, the upper triumphing ruinous pedestals with their missing statues— these confirm the story of rape and pillage, as in a battle between Lapiths and Centaurs.

Serlio's ideas clearly extend the expressive ranges of the orders and their costumes. They add to the information we can elicit from the imagined figures of beings that stand within the volumes, surfaces, and ornaments of a building. They give these figures souls and personalities. They plunge them into activities. Serlio's world of the orders is the reverse of the world described in Vitruvius 3.1. Vitruvius presents a visible man circumscribed by invisible geometric and architectural forms. Serlio presents visible architectural forms that house, cage, or perhaps pour forth mental men, women, animals, and monsters.

3.9 Family Facades and Theater Spheres. The figure occulte in a plan and facade link the two latter things together. In some cases we might imagine the same colossus, first lying down like Vitruvius' man to procreate the plan, and then standing up like Leonardo's or better still Cesare's to procreate the facade. But there are other connections, in Pythagorean anthropomorphism, between plans and facades. As we have seen, this architecture is generally plan-oriented. Even the facades in Serlio's book are highly "planimetric" (Fig. 3.13). Not only do the lines that determine wall axes and rooms also determine facade axes and openings, but on the facade proper, the windows, doors, and panels can be read as planar vestibules, cameras, and salas. Stringcourses, pilasters, and quoins "portray" walls and partitions. And their implied regularities are the result of partly hidden, partly visible tesserae and linee occulte, just as in plans.

These linee occulte guide the stratification of the columns. They first pervade the mass of rustic or bestial matter we sense in a rusticated basement, as in Figure 3.13, and then establish the noble individuals of the piano nobile, in this case six

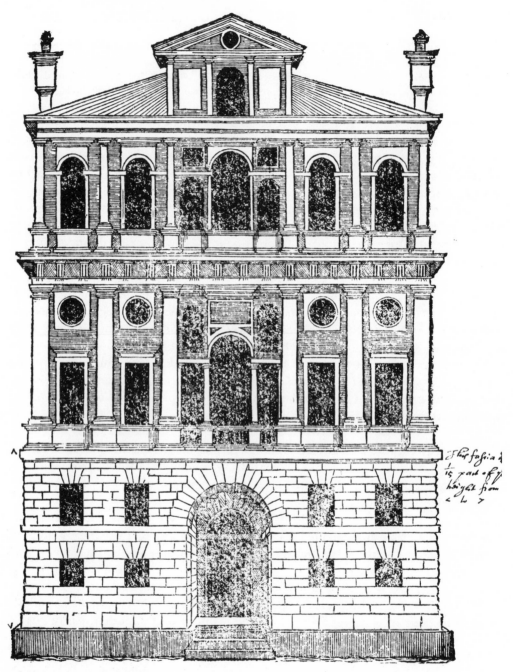

3.13 Palace facade, from Serlio

"statues" of Doric men, on pedestals, supporting a Doric entablature. The linee occulte thus set up the vertical filiations between one level and the next. Above is the lighter, frailer Doric of the bedroom story, supporting an Ionic or Corinthian entablature. In the center of both upper stories are smaller pilasters of the same order, almost like the family's children protectively centered among the adults.

Serlio extends these family notions to larger groups. In Book II, 43v and following, he illustrates a theater (Figs. 3.14, 3.15). This consists of a series of concentric semicircles which are stepped so as to form seating and are inscribed within a rectangular auditorium. Serlio divides this quarter-sphere into ranks and orders—much as Ficino and others describe concentric ranks of celestial beings. The hierarchy runs from the center outward. In the center are the "most noble" spectators. (G). At the perimeter are the "little people." Within these limits, families are arranged in ranks according to status (H, I). And outside the circular formation entirely are the nonnoble "plebi" (K). At the same time the quarter-sphere of this particular world becomes the fictive half-sphere, in another part of the theater, of the stage. Here, says Serlio, "in a small space created by the art of perspective are proud palaces and most ample temples" (2.44r). He evokes a society of buildings to match the society of spectators. Both societies occupy geometric and bodily hierarchies. In the same way, his famous scenes at the end of Book III—the Rustic Scene for satyr plays and the Comic and Tragic Scenes—are also based on social divisions not unlike those of a state: peasant, bourgeois, noble. And they are equivalents of a palace society, with its rustic basement, its "tragic scene" piano nobile, and its "comic scene" upper floors with their bedrooms, balconies, and belvederes. Even in his chimney designs Serlio continues with his social hierarchies, rising (Fig. 3.16) from Doric to Ionic to Corinthian to what he calls Bastard, from massive to moderate to small, from manly to matronly to maidenly to mixed (7.71r). Thus is the chimney a social model of the palace it ornaments.

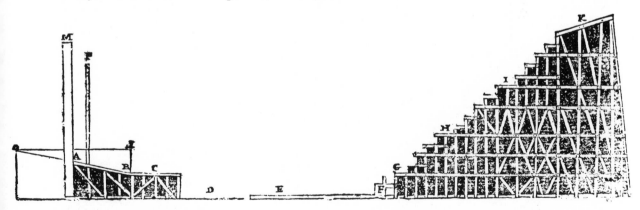

3.14 Section of theater, from Serlio

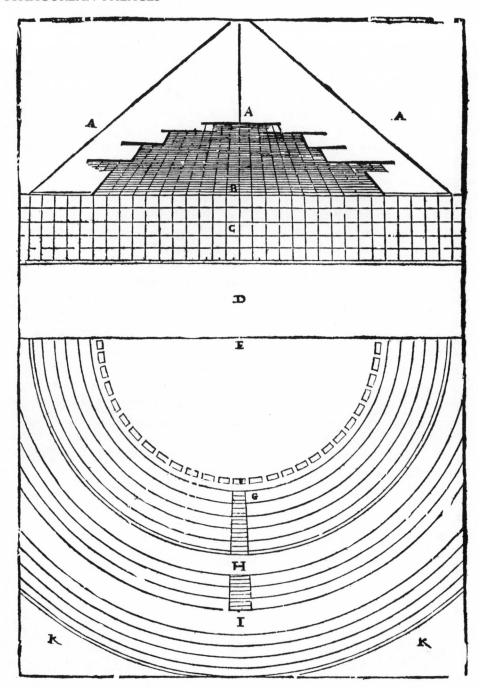

3.15 Plan of theater, from Serlio

3.16 Chimney design, from Serlio

3.10 Rooms as Organs. Palladio was a less fantastic thinker than Serlio. But he was imbued with cognate ideas. However, he applied his anthropomorphy to volumes and distributions rather than to ornament. Thus in Book II of the *Quattro libri*, on the subject of distribution, he says that the principal rooms must be large and magnificent, while the "small ugly spaces" must be located so as to serve the main rooms adequately:

For just as in the human body there are some parts that are noble and beautiful and others that are rather ignoble and ugly, but of which we have the greatest need and indeed would not be able to live without; so also in buildings there ought to be some parts that are respectable and honored, and others less elegant, but without which the former could not be free and would lose part of their dignity and beauty. But just as the Blessed Lord has arranged our organs so that the most beautiful are in the most exposed and visible places, and the less attractive in hidden places, so too we, in building, will locate the main parts, which are to be looked at, in visible places, and the less beautiful as far from sight as possible. And in these latter parts we will put all the ugly things of the house, everything that might cause shame and uglify the most beautiful parts [2.2].

Thus wood storage, cooking, and other such activities should take place underground or in the palace's "private parts." A palace is in fact metaphorically a clothed body, like one of Francesco's columns. The purpose of the clothes is to show off beautiful organs and hide ugly ones. And these organs are distributed in the palace after the manner in which God made man in his image. Francesco di Giorgio and Serlio had posited "ignoble" proportions for vestibules in order to highlight the nobility of the salas. Francesco had also differentiated between nobility and ignobility of function. Now Palladio applies that differentiation to a metaphor in which the whole palace becomes a sort of being.

Leonardo had suggested that when the ideal man procreates his square and circle he performs two different gestures. The man therefore procreates two brother-forms—though I have suggested the alternative process, whereby the circle makes the man and the man makes the square. In any event, Colonna provides an instance of the kind of erotic reaction to numberforms that is implied in Leonardo's centering the square on the penis. Cesariano, though attempting to reconcile Leonardo's active, ideal, gesturing man with Vitruvius' recumbent, not necessarily ideal, passive one, actually furthered some of the implications of Leonardo's drawing. In Cesariano the man generates a universal cubic measuring system. For him Man the Beautiful is not only the measure, but the measurer, of all things. He is, as Ficino described him, "the central being of the universe, who is everywhere, eternally mobile, mixing with elements and directions, of all dimensions" (2^2. 1859–60). Cesare's man-in-square-and-circle embraces and procreates. But in his agonized pose he is also an example of the captive personages who inhabit walls and columns. With Serlio the orders take on further social and human values. Used metonymically their fragments can become a code. They tell of incidents: a facade expresses a family group in its stratification and individual actors; a theater is a model of a society, a model in which, during performances, that society literally occupies its proper spheres. Finally, Palladio's notion of rooms as organs, and hence of the palace as a creature, forms an appropriate pendant (or tail) to the developments just described.

3.11 Elevations as Worlds. Lomazzo sees all of architecture as peopled by, or condensable into, metaphoric beings. He repeats most of what we have heard on the creaturely qualities of columns. Like Francesco di Giorgio he describes their ornaments as their "clothing." Tuscan and Doric are relatively unclad, and Ionic, Corinthian, and Composite are more decorous, or decorated (*Trat.* 78). Astragals, ovolos, cymatia, and other moldings are like necklaces and bracelets. The greater number of small ornaments in Corinthian and Composite architecture further suggests refined jewelry. Indeed, the Composite is a leafy fantasy version of Corinthian, as is Corinthian in turn of the more demure Ionic (*Trat.* 410ff.). So once again we have a generational relationship between the orders, in which the most recent is the most beautiful. Lomazzo at the same time claims to emphasize the orders' femininity, both by establishing a ratio of three female to two male and by dwelling on dress and ornament.

Lomazzo also sees the orders as populations. Accordingly he emphasizes the column types that are already most creaturely—herms, atlantes, and so on. The tale of the Persian Portico provides his point of departure, and not only the Persian slaves, he says, but hermaphroditic philosophers, satyrs, and combinations thereof can be used. Rustic supports ought to have satyr bodies growing out of tree trunks, or be peasant men whose legs are logs (*tronconi*). There can also be old, long-bearded men and gross women. These are for Tuscan and Doric. For the Ionic there are barbarian captives and of course matrons. Arches may be sustained by Persians in costume (*Trat.* 414–15). The basement Tuscans must be nude or seminude and have terrifying expressions and immense straining muscles. Near the top Corinthian maidens stand serenely with baskets of flowers on their heads. Above them, in turn, the Composite columns stand, the most fantastic and free of all. These are accompanied by sculptured nymphs in revealing costumes. So at the top, as at the bottom, there is again nudity; but in these upper regions it is the nudity of seminal virtue rather than bondage. Meanwhile the variety of physical types set forth by the orders, and the employment of creatures like the philosophers of mixed sex, complements the polymorphous perversity of numberform behavior. In fact, then, Lomazzo's world of the orders rises like a Neoplatonic scala through layers of social, functional, sexual, and physical change, and through changes of behavior and costume and even of mood. One is reminded of acrobats in a human pyramid.

These figures, for which orthodox columns are the received metaphors, coexist at different scales. The smaller figures are freer and more frolicsome, the larger soldier and more locked into the building's forces. Even in their pure state, as columns and without figure sculpture, their human, divine, or beast nature can be perceived since they possess the principal geometric forms taken from the human body, which is, Lomazzo tells us, the perfect example and model of all fabrics and works (*Idea* 137).

Lomazzo also discusses the narrative friezes and panels of "istorie" (historical or legendary works) that so often accompany the orders (*Trat.* 421). These too are controlled by expressive limitations derived from columns. Corinthian istorie depict songs, pleasures, miracles, marvels, and lasciviousness. Composite friezes deal with hunts, nymphs' games, and gardens. Ionic ones show councils, sacrifices, triumphs, judgments, and "honored, grave, religious deeds." In the Doric we have wars, discords, battles, rapes, conflicts, and melancholy and funeral tales, and for the Tuscan the more elemental accounts of agriculture, the times of day, and the events of the calendar (*Trat.* 421). Elsewhere Lomazzo adds that, in rooms, these choices are shaped by the room's location and purpose. For example, Mercury governs "bizarrie" and scenes of horror. A room situated in Mercury's region in a palace should therefore be decorated with such scenes, which means in turn that it should be Doric or perhaps Doric and Corinthian (*Trat.* 350).

Lomazzo claims, in short, that an order's affinities with numberforms, personality types, and events place it in a social world or scala. This scala can be stated in an abbreviated tabular form. Each type of column has a number, a geometrical shape or field, a proportion (both of the latter being derived from the pedestal), a being with a particular type of body and personality, and a realm of characteristic action. A facade or world comprised of these orders is a social structure that moves vertically through time, beginning with the Doric ancestor and culminating in the perfected, more sexually powerful Composite. In comparing this table with Tables 12 and 13, we note in Lomazzo a direct logical elaboration of Filarete, Francesco di Giorgio, and Serlio. There are now five orders rather than three. The sequence of heights is a Pythagorean hierarchy, limited to successive integrals and descending from the perfect 10 to the cubic 6. Rectangles and proportions, physiques and events, all follow along.

Table 14. The "social" orders of architecture in Lomazzo

Order	Height (in d)	Pedestal elevation	Pedestal proportion	Physique	Actions
Composite	10	double square	2:1	perfected maiden	hunts, gardens
Corinthian	9	sesquitertial	4:3	maiden	pleasure, marvels
Ionic	8	sesquialter	3:2	matron/scholar	councils, triumphs
Doric	7	diagonal	5:3	workman	battles, funerals
Tuscan	6	square	1:1	peasant/animal	calendar

But at this point Lomazzo adds something new. He says that the different physiques of Tuscan, Doric, Ionic, and Corinthian are derived from the characteristics of the peoples who originated them. And not only the particular proportion but the particular module used by the ancient race in question survives in the modern order (though with different values than Lomazzo had ordained in the discussion paraphrased in Table 14). The Dorians measured in feet and were six feet high. The Ionians measured in heads and a "ben quadrato" Ionian was seven heads high, and so on. The different gods and goddesses involved also fitted into this scheme with their characteristic modular symmetries (*Trat.* 77–79). Hence Lomazzo applies Serlio's population metaphor to a historical span. The superimposed ranks of columns express not only contemporary social/sexual/functional aspects of a society, they have historical, racial and religious dimensions as well.

3.12 Colossi Occulti. Lomazzo wrote in a period, the 1580s, when the colossal order, encompassing one and one-half, two, or three floors, had become common. Perhaps as a result he deals more than his predecessors with the question of large scale. The human-sized inch and palm can create colossi, he says, by being transformed into feet, heads, or arms. For example, the human body is 300 minutes long, 50 wide, and 30 deep. By a simple scale-up or quantum jump, Noah's Ark and the *Argo* were made human in proportions by being built with these same values in cubits. The minute, or ¹/₈ of a digit, becomes the forearm. Thus did these ships become recumbent floating giant men. Greek ships were even ornamented with heads and masks, and their sterns decked out with feet or tails, while there could also be "great arms" along the sides (*Trat.* 94ff.).

Lomazzo easily transfers this notion of the gigantic human form back to terrestrial architecture. Round temples, he says, take their roundness from the human body's roundness (ibid.). The circle that continues the profile of the Pantheon dome through the base of that building, and the similar circles inscribable in the elevations of Roman round temples, have their genesis in a supercolossal, "occult" physique, only a fragment of which is made visible as it pervades or forms a building. Other temples are derived from the square that a colossus procreates with his outspread arms (including the 100-column hypostyle of cubic theory). The sesquialter of any size is procreated by the distance from the base of the throat to the breastbone. "And from this point to the breast, with the greatest sagacity, the ancients drew another temple form, as one sees from the Temple of Peace [Basilica of Maxentius] in Rome." Arches of triumph, meanwhile, derive their plans from the body's trunk. More rarely a huge human foot provides proportions or key lineamenta, for example in the port of Ostia. Oval theaters derive their plans from the oval plan of the human head, or else from the contour of the hand, the lateral section of the body, or again, from the line from the base of the throat to the breastbone. These things also give numberforms to churches; and not only to rectangular ones but to those that are oval in plan, or oblong, pentagonal, hexagonal, octagonal, and cross-shaped. Lomazzo instances the ones in Serlio's fifth book—designs which, incidentally, he ascribes to Peruzzi. As a result of Lomazzo's vision we can imagine these superhuman forms standing over the visible temples of earth, temples which incarnate fragments of these giants' vast unseen bodies.

3.13 The Palace as Monster. Scamozzi, our last authority, also celebrates Man the Beautiful. Man is the procreator of squares, circles, and the like, and the hermetic model and source of architectural form. Thus while all architecture should be "square," it should also be an image of the human body. And symmetry means not only cubic distribution—integral value sequences achieving summae figurationes—but the *likeness* of the different parts of the body to each other, and the ability of one part to be intertranslated with another by modular measurement (1.38). Scamozzi illustrates Man the Beautiful as the procreator of square and circle (Fig. 3.17). The illustration is partly based on Cesariano's format: there is a basic grid, this one 21 x 21; the square's diagonal equals the circle's diameter; and the two planes are concentric on the man's umbilicus. But Scamozzi's man not only generates ideal concentric perimeters, he encompasses the three kinds of angles, obtuse, right, and acute. Further, by allowing the right half of the man's body to strike Cesariano's spread-eagled, mobile, surface-embracing pose (though with no implications of orgasm), while the left half strikes his standing, "cubic," proportion-generating pose, he further conflates the Vitruvian everyman with the ideal, and increases the geometric fecundity of both. From this more fecund central progenitor, then, are derived a whole surrounding family of squares, triangles, circles, sphere, and cubes—and of architecture as well: an obelisk, a column shaft, and two pediments.

Scamozzi's man is thus in his gestures the father of a good-sized family of geometric and architectural elements. But in Neoplatonic fashion this father is also a mother. He is a mother, particularly, in Filarete's sense, since he is an "architect" who produces a building out of his body. And Scamozzi then reflects on the procreation of the architect himself, or rather herself, in the same sense: architects, he says, who are in too much of a hurry to get jobs and who are careless in their designing are like "vile and abject animals" who have been too briefly in the womb and are full of imperfections. But those who refine and winnow their designs so as to make "a whole, perfect body . . . have come to imitate Nature who prudently commands that, for the creation of her jewels, for the raising of her noblest plants, and for the pregnancies of her more perfect animals . . . they must remain for long either in the earth's stomach or in their mothers', in order in the end to have finer qualities and more finish and perfection." Yet, though a mother, the architect is manly. He must brim with virile spirit and impose on his Idea "a certain heroic animosity" (1.47).

Scamozzi is fully anthropomorphic in his vision of the palace. He speaks of its "bones and nerves and orifices," and of construction scaffolds as "swaddling clothes" (1.20, 312). But this vision is even less ideal, and is more monstrous, than those of his predecessors. He advocates, as a form of "symmetry," the allocation of spaces as if they were organs, that is, in accordance with nature's distribution principles. Man, he says, has seven openings serving the four senses. These are located so as to conform to the relative nobility of their functions. Thus the eyes are the noblest for they are "eminent"—high up—and double. The ears are less eminent and indeed partly hidden. They bracket the forehead. The "foreheads" of buildings

3.17 Man the procreator, from Scamozzi

ought always to have their openings so disposed, that is, with the most important ones in the center and the others of lesser importance moved toward the sides (1.69). In other words duity is receiving a biological twist. Single "organs" (openings) must be in the center, and others arranged in flanking pairs. And ornament is also to be distributed in buildings as in the human body, assuming that the face and breast are the noblest organs and the stomach and rump the ignoblest (1.241). And not only is ornament (as in Lomazzo) like clothing; Scamozzi even has architectural sumptuary laws. Only the noblest buildings wear rich ornament.

In much of this Scamozzi is elaborating from Palladio's ideas. Thus he repeats Palladio's simile between the palace's central sala or courtyard and an animal's heart. But he adds that "all the veins of blood ought to lead to it" (1.304). Similarly, staircases are the palace's "veins and arteries." And Scamozzi does not stop here. He lays out certain rooms and sequences of rooms in terms of family functions, describing the needs of mothers, the young, the elderly, the head of the family, and its servants, even its animals. All these functions and statuses are affected by changes in light, temperature, and atmosphere throughout the day and throughout the seasons of the year. Rooms must respond to these changes. Therefore different suites are used at different times and seasons. Devices for controlling temperature, including blinds and air conditioning (*ventiducts*) bringing cold air from the mountains, are described (1.306ff.). And "kitchens are like the stomach of an animal's body. As, in the latter, food is warmed with its natural heat, so in the kitchen food is prepared and cooked by special fires." Scamozzi proceeds to write what must be one of the few Renaissance essays on kitchen architecture. The room should be large and long, lighted from the north, and contain a balcony from which the master or his butler can give orders and supervise important maneuvers without having to enter (1.311ff.).

Even the stones of a palace can be organs or separate creatures; they can speak and eat. He mentions "pietra Assia, in the River Gaga [Ganges] in Asso [?] and in Phrygia [which] is an eater of corpses" (2.181). He speaks also of an Ethiopian basalt that when touched by the sun's rays utters a near-human sound. Indeed the very word sarcophagus, Scamozzi points out, means "corpse-eater." Some sarcophagi were able to consume their contents (except for the teeth) in forty days (2.193).

Building stone for Scamozzi is like the race of humans itself; it is a society. "The nature of stones may be said to be like the nature of men, for some are noble, like the marbles and the mixed stones and so forth, and others are of middling nature, like the hard strong stones that take a polish, for example Istrian and certain others; and finally some others are rough like the *macigni* [blue-gray sandstone] and others similar, which for the most part make roughhewn structures without fineness. The heavy, dense stones are used because their material is lasting, and their heat so great that they [condense] humors." (2.194).

3.14   The Column as King. But if the interior, the openings, and even the very stones of a Scamozzi palace are thus geometrical metaphors of a creature's organs, or of societies of beings, it is nonetheless in terms of the ideal human body that everything is dimensioned and arranged. And the most patently human and ideal parts of a palace are its columns; these are the guardians of its "forehead and breast." Like Lomazzo, Scamozzi describes nude or seminude male Tuscan and Doric columns, while the female orders must be dressed with "honesty, modesty, and gravity, grace, and ingenuity, as are women themselves." Ionic and Corinthian, he says, are like women in that they were produced by nature to ornament and beautify the world. Together, male and female orders should encompass the whole variety of humanity, and all its qualities from robustness to grace and from ugliness to beauty.

Scamozzi repeats much of what Lomazzo had said about the individual roles of the orders in a facade. But he departs from Lomazzo and his other predecessors in one important respect: he calls the Composite the "Roman" order, crowns its capital with oak leaves, and endows it with what he calls a heroic cornice. Lomazzo's idea of the Composite as an upper range of nymphs or nymph-surrogates is thus abandoned. Scamozzi's Corinthian, meanwhile, which wears an olive crown, stands above the Roman and is in fact the highest and most perfect of the orders. Scamozzi's change is a logical adjustment of Lomazzo's idea that each of the orders represents a historic people, and that together, in superimposed ranks, they make a choir or hermetic army: hence the need for a Roman rather than a Composite category. Scamozzi then continues:

All five orders, superimposed and regulated as we have done, come together in a proportionate hierarchy [scandentia], beginning with the solidity of the Tuscan and the strength of the Doric, passing on to the gravity of the Ionic, to the beauty of the Roman and in the end arriving at the grace of the Corinthian, which is above all the others. And at the same time, compared together, one after another, they create a grand concert so that the ensemble delights the eye of whoever looks [2.104].

We perceive the orders as an angelic choir, a concert of beings sounding together. So perceived, the column-performers, with their structural analogies to poetry and music, are a kind of hermetic taxonomy in architectural form.

This many-affinitied grid, the Scamozzi facade, is governed by number and constitutes a set of Pythagorean hierarchies. Scamozzi supposes a range from the slave-like Tuscan to the free Corinthian—a range that is narrower than Lomazzo's, and which instead of the latter's simple height sequences (6, 7, 8, 9, and 10) has the more complicated 7$\frac{1}{2}$, 8$\frac{1}{2}$, 8$\frac{3}{4}$, 9$\frac{3}{4}$, and then the "most perfect" 10. But the latter hierarchy is no random one. As Scamozzi points out, 7$\frac{1}{2}$ is three-fourths of 10, that is, 7$\frac{1}{2}$:10::3:4, or as sesquialter is to duple (2.4). And 8$\frac{3}{4}$ is halfway between 7$\frac{1}{2}$ and 10. He gives no comparable justification for 9$\frac{3}{4}$, but in fact the five heights comprise the following duity:

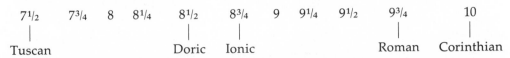

7$\frac{1}{2}$ 7$\frac{3}{4}$ 8   8$\frac{1}{4}$ 8$\frac{1}{2}$ 8$\frac{3}{4}$ 9   9$\frac{1}{4}$ 9$\frac{1}{2}$ 9$\frac{3}{4}$ 10

Tuscan   Doric   Ionic   Roman   Corinthian

Each of these values, furthermore, progresses towards 10 in its own way. And 10, the "most perfect" number, both perfect and cubic in fact, is the summa figuratio whose columnar/human form is Corinthian. Hence a facade with its orders so arranged rises from the imperfect to the perfect, from Earth to Heaven.

Number also links the orders and their human physiques to the geometry of the square. Indeed Scamozzi's greatest originality lies in his making this connection. He takes from Lomazzo the idea that the orders are more than columns and entablatures, that they are instead components in a scalalike grid encompassing a metempsychosis. Scamozzi then goes on to create specific rectangular areas of wall, including columns and entablatures, but also including pedestals, balconies, niches, attics, arches, and spandrels. These clearly bounded fields he calls "kingdoms" (Book VI). Each kingdom is populated by apposite sculptures of heads, plants, and istorie. Thus for the first time in architectural theory, Scamozzi gives us not only the Ionic column, for example, but the Ionic column as ruler or dictator of dimensions, distributions, and proportions. And the Ionic column thus rules, first within a temple front (Fig. 3.18), and then a loggia (Fig. 3.19), an arch (Fig. 3.20), and a portal (Fig. 3.21). The column is the prescriber, governor, or king of various rectangular countries. These countries or facade-tesserae are column-procreated number-forms. They are hence the end result of the principle that a column-figure fathers geometric surfaces.

Looking back to Lomazzo, we may conclude that he pushed the anthropomorphic side of architectural thought in two directions. He developed the idea of the orders as social strata or populations and applied this to their origins among different ancient peoples. And with his detailed account of the human characteristics of the orders he enriched the concept of column-as-character. More than any earlier writer, too, he simplified the numerical sequences of pedestal planes so as to accord with a Pythagorean sequence. In the final picture, the Tuscan progenitor creates upper, later races—races that imitate, ornament, and feminize themselves.

Scamozzi's man-in-square-and-circle performs all the functions of his predecessors plus procreating a wider family of forms. The architect himself is both a father

3.18 Ionic temple front, from Scamozzi

3.19 Ionic loggia, from Scamozzi

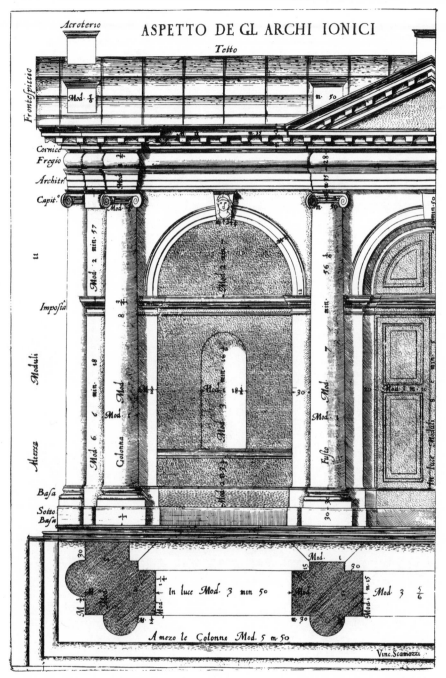

3.20 Ionic arch, from Scamozzi

3.21 Ionic portal, from Scamozzi

and a mother of buildings. Scamozzi also greatly extended the image of the palace as a creature, detailing the organic functions of rooms and openings, of dress and nudity. Even a palace's stones speak, eat, drink, and sweat. They can be noble or base. And though the palace is now very much a creature and a society of creatures or monsters, in Scamozzi's system the orders are more human and divine than ever. When properly distributed they represent generations of the human race and the range of a population's appearance. A columnar facade can be a concert of angels, rising from the imperfect Tuscan to the "most perfect" Corinthian; a hermetic ascending scala. Each column or group of columns reigns over its own kingdom on the facade, governing seen geometries through unseen numbers and partly seen human forms: a royal summa figuratio befitting our own ascent, in this chapter, from Vitruvius' man-in-square-and-circle.

4. Solid: The Corpo Transparente

4.1 Constructing See-Through Solids. So far we have discussed the cube in three ways: as a point-source, as a genealogical principle involving invisible guidelines or influences, and as a set of planes procreated by an imagined being. The next step is to discuss it in its Pythagorean fulfillment—as a transparent solid.

The cubic solid or corpo transparente is a form that encases or pervades a harmonious building, quantifying or measuring that building's relationship to number and Idea. As with linee occulte, Serlio is our phrasemaker; and again he describes a phenomenon that had existed earlier but without that name. Speaking of solids drawn in perspective (Fig. 2.17), he writes: "Enough has been said about the octagonal transparent body [corpo transparente] which it is necessary to know how to form before one comes to form the opaque body, . . . nor is there any more difference between a transparent body and an opaque one, than there is in seeing the bone structure of a corpse without its flesh, and seeing a similar body, alive, with its flesh, which covers that bone structure" (2.25r). In architecture and perspective the "hidden parts" are geometrical solids, and the "outer flesh" is the material building. Serlio also refers to the corpo transparente as the skeleton of the "corpo solido" (2.25v). Hence a corpo transparente is an exercise in three-dimensional architectural geometry—a volume; and a volume that he introduces, interestingly enough in view of Chapter 3 above, through the metaphor of the sectioned human physique.

However, one can also think of the corpo transparente not in terms of a physique but in terms of a glass or mica geometric model, for example, the 26-sided solid in the well-known Capodimonte portrait of Fra Luca Pacioli (Fig. 4.1). There are also the frequent intarsia representations of geometrical forms skeletally composed of wooden struts. For a classical and architectural prototype there is Nero's Temple of Fortuna Seia, said to have been made of a single transparent stone, which stood in the rotunda or "sala maggiore" of his Golden House. A visitor, says Cataneo, "being inside it, with the doors shut, was visible just as if he had been outside" (47r). Neither the idea of a transparent geometric model, then, nor that of transpar-

4.1 *Fra Luca Pacioli and Pupil*, by Jacopo de' Barbari [?], Capodimonte, Naples (Alinari)

ent buildings was particularly new at the time Serlio was writing about corpi transparenti.

But the use to which Serlio put his notion did not have many precedents. This use involved erecting a mental, "transparent" model on a drawn plan. The process was a little like what happened in Figure 2.14 B when I derived a horizontal axial section from Francesco di Giorgio's town hall plan. Or to put it differently, just as the architect was supposed to begin designing by drawing out lineamenta on the basis of pre-existing number ratios, and then was to construct surfaces from these lines, so now he was to imagine volumes from the surfaces.

To trace the development of the corpo transparente let us glance back at Manetti. He has told us that Brunelleschi measured the foundations of ruins with full-scale grids. If Brunelleschi also estimated heights from column spacings, wall thicknesses, and the like, he was creating a sort of practical corpo transparente by means of these measured values. The values were translated into numbers which appeared on a coded grid, and the three-dimensional building then "rose," in accordance with the code and the numbers, from the gridded plan. (Even earlier, with Vitruvius, the temple formulas and their idéae might be called corpi transparenti, that is, three-dimensional images constructed out of gridded planes.) But Manetti has something else to say on the subject. Talking about the building of Santo Spirito he says: "Filippo made a drawing on which were the foundations, only, of the edifice. And with this drawing he showed [the building committee] verbally how it would be when it was put into three dimensions [rilevato]. As this pleased them, they commissioned him to make, or have made, a wooden model [in] little braccia" (125). Once again, a three-dimensional building, now verbal rather than mental, is derived from a two-dimensional drawn plan.

4.2   The Limiting Body. But these developments are only inklings of what's to come. With Alberti we make real progress. He shows how the squares and canonical rectangles of the plan can determine volumes. He derives the interior volumes of his building from the cube, and at the same time sets cubical limits to the outer form of the whole. In large square buildings, for example, built with ceilings rather than vaults, the height of the whole must not be greater than the length of one side (799). And since in such a building the length of the sides is equal, the allowable volume, up to which the material shell may move, is the cube of the plan. Within the house, meanwhile, Alberti pictures a courtyard-heart. This is a large hollow parallelepiped defined by layered screens—the surrounding arcades and rooms—regularly penetrated by sight-line lattices, circulation space, and the like. Alberti posits a mental container for each of these elements, a container that acts therefore as a limiting body. There are ranges of possible atria, possible "tinelli," and so forth, always defined volumetrically. It is not that the rooms *must* fill up these invisible forms; they simply must not go beyond them. The least noble rooms are on the periphery and in the attics or basement. They make simple and flexible geometric demands. And they act as an interface between the noble form of the whole outer cube and the inner courtyard with its surrounding privileged spaces (417). The more noble a room is, the more limited these parameters. We have seen this same sort of limitation and hierarchy in planning, that is, in the surface articulation of linee occulte in Francesco di Giorgio and in Cesariano. But here is Alberti, a generation or more earlier, making equivalent demands. And doing so, moreover, not simply in terms of planes like his two successors, but in terms of volumes—in terms of limiting corpi transparenti.

This, as we might expect, leads Alberti to provide a greater variety of room proportions than Vitruvius. And the form in which Alberti cites these permissible ratios is also interesting. He says that in a palace the length of the atrium (in this case he means a courtyard) can be either ³/₂, ⁵/₃, or ⁷/₅ of its width. The height meanwhile remains ⁴/₃ of the length (797). By presenting the formulas in this fashion Alberti makes it clear that he is starting off with a square. Having established the width of the courtyard with this square, he makes the length a function of the width. As his terms also make clear, the first courtyard plan is a sesquialter and the second a superbipartiens. Drawing out the three formulas we get Figure 4.2. Note that in each case the walls can be divided into horizontal halves, using this same module of "width-thirds" or "width-fifths." In the first two examples, indeed, these fractions become cubic modules for the volumes of the courtyard, which respectively have proportions of 4:3:2 and 5:4:3. And in all three cases the height is derived from a plan module or dimension. Alberti's use of top-heavy fractions, ⁵/₃, ⁷/₅, and the like, shows that he thought of elevations as modular functions of the plans. For if he had said that the wall height in courtyard B should be 1¹/₃ of its length instead of ⁴/₃, he would have been stating a mere fractional ratio. The expression ⁴/₃, like the expression "superbipartiens," is "square-modular," so to speak. It preserves a geometrical dimensioning unit. The "width-thirds" do not disappear as soon as they add up to 1.

But Alberti is not consistent here or elsewhere when he prescribes volumes. In general he advocates arithmetical, geometric, and harmonic ratios; and yet of the three formulas in Figure 4.2 only A and B are so (arithmetical). C on the other hand

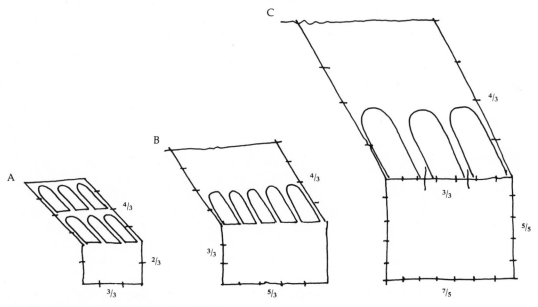

4.2 Courtyard volume formulas, after Alberti

involves incommensurables. Thirds and fifths are used together to plot out the volume, so that in the very process of being three-dimensionalized the single plan-module disappears. The conception of a *corpo transparente* that can be measured uniformly and universally in cubical tesserae is present in Alberti, but it is not by any means his only way of designing.

Alberti also gives formulas for the openings in walls. In his directions for distributing and sizing windows, for example, he says that for a wall with three windows the length of the wall must be divided into five parts at least and seven at most. Windows are then inserted in three alternating parts (Fig. 4.3 A, B). The height of the windows will then be either $7/4$ *or* $9/5$ of its base (801). With this information, as the illustration shows, we can construct elevations that provide everything but the height of the sills. (We would get the wall height independently from one of Alberti's room-volume formulas.)

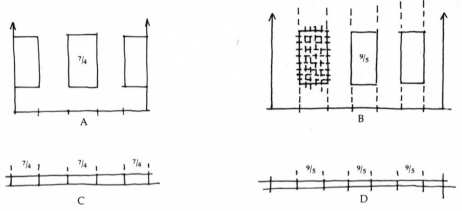

4.3 Wall and window formulas, after Alberti

We can now make a mental or graphic elevation on the basis of Alberti's formula. In other words we have a measured "transparent room." But equally well we can telescope this same information back into a "two-dimensional" plan (Fig. 4.3 C, D). This eliminates the necessity of applying arbitrary heights to the sill as in Figure 4.3 A and B. And once the craftsman knows the heights and widths of the windows from this plan, he can start making their frames. If, for example, the plan shows that $1/5$ of the sill equals one palm, the workman knows that the frame's light will measure 9 x 5 palms. In Figure 4.3 B, I have indicated the *linee occulte* that would mark out the wall grid in "parts," and within that the subgrid of one of the windows measured in palms.

4.3 Doric, Ionic, and Corinthian Volumes. Alberti's concept of the *corpo transparente* is a little cold and mathematical. Filarete's, though, has human interest.

The "piccol huomini" who populate his pages not only provide scale in the literal sense, they use the buildings actively and hence volumetrically. As described and illustrated, these people survey sites, mark out grids, and mount the stairs of the Palace of Vice and Virtue. There are hunts and rustic banquets. And on one occasion we see primitive men constructing the first houses (Fig. 4.4). In fact the latter scene illustrates nothing less than the erection of a visibly framed corpo transparente. The process begins as the poles are cut to the right dimension, via number, and brought to the site (right); then they are set into the ground as uprights, that is, as "lines." Other lines, the crosspieces, are added, making a three-dimensional parallelepiped-frame (left). Finally in the background we see panels of woven matting being placed in the walls (5v). Consciously or unconsciously Filarete's illustration embodies the familiar sequence, point (that is, number), line, plane, solid. It is a sequence that also involves the transformation of a framed (i.e., linear), transparent solid into an opaque, material one.

4.4 Men building primitive huts, from Filarete (Courtesy Yale University Press)

In a similar way Filarete deals with transparent, hidden, or implied columns. As noted in Chapter 3, he says that the orders can be expressed metonymically via moldings or rectangles (62v). Once this happens the order is in principle divested of its column. Or rather it now has an invisible column, a "colonna occulta." A palace can thus have a "Doric" plan or a "Doric" portal even when it lacks pilasters, columns, or even entablature (84r). Often Filarete shows such a portal elevationally on his plans. And sometimes the shape of the portal or of all the doors in the palace will be derived from the shape of the plan's perimeter.

An example is the Gentleman's Palace (Figs. 4.5–4.8). Filarete writes:

I took 200 br of length and 100 of width which I divided thus as can be seen in the design [Fig. 4.7 A]. First, in the front where the facade must be: in the middle there has to be the door, which will be 4 br wide and 8 br high, and thus all its members will be proportioned

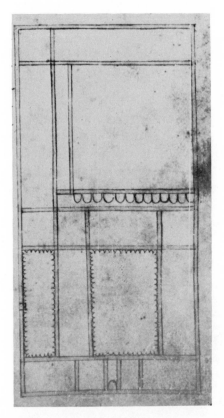

4.5 Plan of Doric palace, from Filarete (Courtesy Yale University Press)

4.6 Elevation of Doric palace, from Filarete (Courtesy Yale University Press)

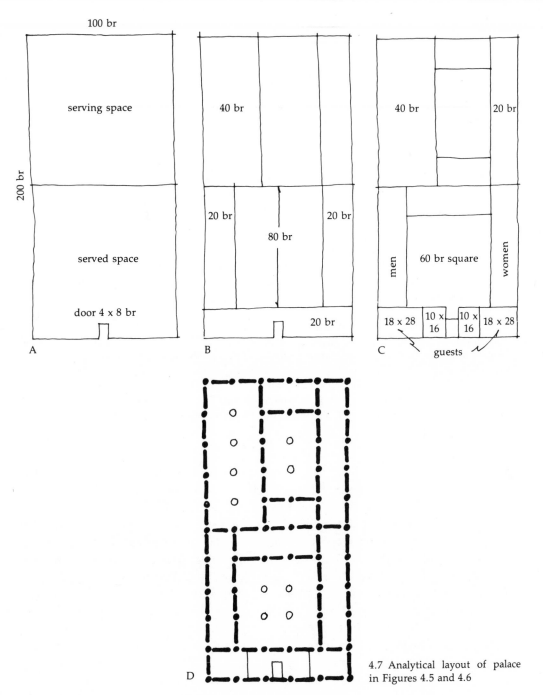

4.7 Analytical layout of palace in Figures 4.5 and 4.6

to this measurement. That is, all the other doors will be two squares, and of the Doric proportion and quality. This I did because the rank of those who are to possess this house, according to the universal numbering of persons, is among the great. Buildings ought to accord with their inhabitants, and for this reason I provide the form and rank of structure here laid out.

As its ground floor is seen drawn out . . . . I first subdivide it in the manner given above, that is into two main squares. The first of these I use for residential quarters, the second as a loading station and for horse stalls.

This is divided again, as shown—that is, I take 20 br from the front part and the same again from the sides. And on one side a wall is set in so that 80 br remain [Fig. 4.7 B]. Thus the front is 100 br and the residential part is set in 20 br all around [Fig. 4.7 C].

What is left over in the residential quarters is a central courtyard 40 [recte 60?] br on each side. Or you could say it consists of 100 br minus 40 for actual living space, and 60 br on a side remaining. I am offsetting the [rear] courtyard—that is, it is 20 br on one side and 40 on the other. This courtyard will house the mechanical equipment necessary to the house, and its entrance will be wide enough to let all such things through, e.g. firewood, wine, wheat, and all necessary supplies. Also the family servant quarters, kitchens, grain bins, and servants' rooms will be built around this courtyard.

The front section will contain the master's quarters. Opposite them, across the courtyard, will be the women's quarters whose measurements and compartmentation will equal [the men's; Fig. 4.7 C].

But, you see, for this first, ground-floor plan, as I said, at the entrance in front as you enter the doorway, there will be on each side a room 10 br wide and 16 long, so that just these two dimensions are subtracted, counting also the width of the entranceway running into the courtyard or cloister. The remainder, running down to the end of each side, left and right, makes 30 br of space on each side. From these spaces will be made two rooms, 18 x 28 br. These will be guest chambers. They are at the groundfloor entrance. . . . The height of these quarters on the ground floor will be 12 br [84r–84v; paragraphing added].

Despite the most careful attempts I have not been able to see how Filarete's figures check out. And my diagrams in Figure 4.7 necessarily differ from the original in Figure 4.5. But whatever Filarete's, or his scribe's, or his illustrator's, or my errors, there is a clear basic method. Filarete begins with number: 100 and 200. He turns number into line and into area: a double square. The double square generates a miniature of itself, of 4 x 8 br, which is repeated throughout the palace. This double-square numberform accords with the social "numbering" of the client. Further subdivisions work out to 20-br surface modules. After the layout is completed the volumes of the whole can be calculated from the uniform altitude of 12 br.

Meanwhile, as a hypostyle the palace occupies a 5-x-10-square grid of 50 bays, or of 6 x 11 columns (Fig. 4.7 D). So presented, only 10 of the hypostyle columns are "invisible." Filarete's values are furthermore all cubic.

These numerical and geometrical characteristics are comparable to what Francesco di Giorgio achieved twenty years later with his town hall. Bur Francesco's scheme was to be conceived entirely in terms of two dimensions. Here already, Filarete, if rather tentatively, is truly thinking in terms of volume. Openings, that is, elevational elements, are direct functions of the plan-shape and of the orders. And in fact Filarete's 12-br ceiling height creates a total of 30 visible tesserae and 15 invisible ones (Fig. 4.8). Only the guest-entrance complex (the "foreigners' quarters") is "loose" in that it does not abide by the three-dimensional grid. Finally, Filarete's perspective rendering of the Gentleman's Palace (Fig. 4.6) is not merely a straight cubic version of the plan. In the Magliabecchiana manuscript (Biblioteca Nazionale Centrale, Florence) at any rate, it is inscribed on the reverse of the sheet containing the plan, over the lower, residential square of that plan as the plan shows through; a neat practical variation on the idea of the corpo transparente.

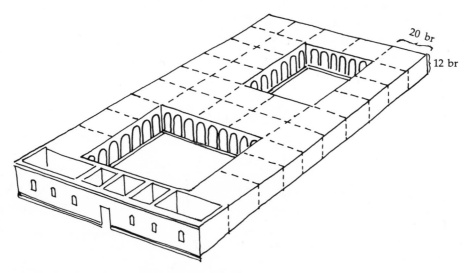

4.8 Ground-floor view of Doric palace, after Filarete

4.4 Volumetric Linee Occulte. Francesco di Giorgio was concerned with volume in a different way. He dealt with the problem of deriving room volumes from plans on an individual basis. And he improved on Alberti in this respect. Alberti's height parameters were too generous, and did not always conform to the mathematical ratios he advocated. On the other hand Filarete was too reductive. We have just seen him prescribing a uniform height for all rooms regardless of their shape. Francesco's system does away with both flaws. He evolved a continuously adjustable formula for height, width, and length. It reconciled, or as he put it "tempered," incommensurables within a cubic system and even allowed for irrational values. It also allowed for a hierarchy of room heights that would closely follow any hierarchy of room areas, a thing impossible in either Alberti's or Filarete's systems.

In introducing his scheme Francesco first discusses, then later on dismisses, the use of the diagonal as a way of establishing height. "The height [of a room] . . . is arrived at by squaring the width and dividing it by a diagonal from corner to corner, and letting that diagonal be the height" (2.345). But this could produce a value incommensurable with the width and length of the room. The resulting volume would not, in such cases, be integrally modular or "symmetrical." The system does have the advantage, though, of making heights vary consistently with areas so as to create volume variations.

Nonetheless, a better solution, says Francesco, is this: "Make a double square of two equal and connected squares, through which from one extremity to the other, E to P, is drawn a semicircular line [Fig. 4.9 A]. Then draw a diagonal line from Q to P [Fig. 4.9 B]. Then another line, SM, intersecting this latter," that is, bisecting QP at R and the arc QP at T (Fig. 4.9 C). TR, Francesco goes on, will equal about 1/5 of SM, the proposed height of the room, and also about 1/7 of EP, which is double the room's width. The diagonal SM is then swept to an upright position, G (Fig. 4.9 D). Thus TR is a seven-part planimetric value along EP and a five-part height measure on GS (2.349).

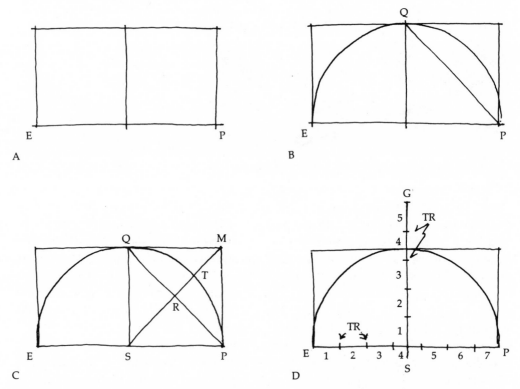

4.9 Method of establishing a "tempered incommensurable" volume module, after Francesco di Giorgio

del modulo E f. Et latezza delmnore quadrato A B C D Saria parti 5 ½ Et alatezza
di parti 4 ¼ fieri. La hnea O P inmezo della quale Siponghe ilcentro pigliando
La circumferenzia dallo P. Q questa fiea Lasoma alteza di ricto iltempio
Et Se Circulazione di tolo. Si questa adfici non debban paffare lefue dricttt linee
La Somita del magior quadrato trcando lafua proporzional volta paltcza quanto
rictrcha il Suo diamitzo. Et lapiramide del putaho ad beneplacito dellartefice
Et cofi iltempio con ragione. Et latezza Et lolarghezza feranno commenfurate
Si come pla figura Et difegnuo fimanifesta .ʔ.

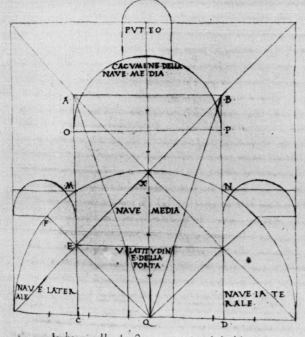

la iltempio oblongho facciato o tondo p darli debita altezza et che alla
Larghezza poportionabil ment abbi conrifpondenza formefi inprimo
uno quadrato di parci lati ilquale Sia quadripartito Dipoi fieri due linee

4.10 Volumes of a church, from Francesco di Giorgio (Courtesy Edizioni Il Polifilo)

Let us give dimensions to this formula. If we say that ES, the room's width, equals 10 br, then GS, the height, will be 14 (rounded off) and TR will thus be 2.8. And 2.8 br will equal $1/7$ of EP (that is, $2/7$ of ES) and $1/5$ of GS. Meanwhile, ES, which contains $3^1/2$ TRs, as it were, is also 3.5 x 2.8 [TR], or just under 10 br. Then 5x2.8=14. The difference between 3.5 and 5 is 1.5, and 5+1.5=6.5. And 6.5x2.8=18.2. Round off the 0.2. The length of the room, expressed in a series, is then 18 br in the sequence 10:14:18. This is an arithmetical series. The linear module, TR (procreated by a square married to a semicircle, be it noted), when endowed at the beginning with a cubic value, 10, produces all-cubic offspring.

Francesco's system is the main predecessor of Palladio's volume formulas. It allows rooms to reflect, individually, their numerical, geometrical, and social status. In Book IV of the second treatise, on churches, Francesco has a similar, more elaborate system which procreates *all* altitudes, including dome and vault profiles and door shapes, from squares (Fig. 4.10).

Francesco also has a second improvement on his predecessors, this time in the domestic realm. We noted that Alberti had decreed certain rules for window placement but that the rules were independent of wall and sill height. Now instead of vertical parts Francesco calls for horizontal ones. The wall (for example on the ground floor) is divided into fifths, and door heights are $2^2/3$ of these fifths (Fig. 4.11 A). The width of the opening is half the door's height, or $1^1/3$ of these "parts" or fifths. On the second floor, for windows we again deploy five horizontal "parts," while the windows are $2^1/3$ parts high and the sills are $1/5$ the height of the story, so that above the window there is $1^2/3$ fifths remaining. The width of these windows is one-half their height, or $1^1/6$ parts (Fig. 4.11 B). The windows are separated by distances equalling at least $1^1/2$ times their own width (2.330). All this relates the size and placement of openings in a palace to a room's wall height; thus is Francesco's system "volumetric" in this new sense: he crisscrosses his scala of volumes with sight-line and circulation grids.

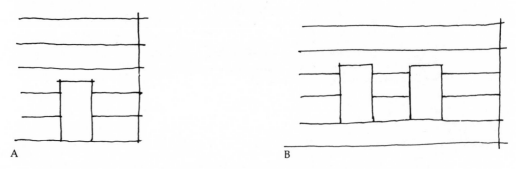

A   B

4.11 Wall (A) and window formulas (B), after Francesco di Giorgio

4.5   Volume Conventions on Plans. So far in this chapter we have looked mainly at formulas and diagrams in treatises. Quattrocento architectural sketchbooks provide a more fragmentary yet still enlightening picture. In sketchbooks such as Giuliano da Sangallo's Vatican "Libro," for example, one notes that many pages are not unlike the layouts in an illustrated architectural treatise. Sometimes they record information about ancient ruins, sometimes they present new designs, sometimes both. One often has the sense that the draftsmen are addressing an audience, that these elaborately lettered presentations are more than mere *aides-mémoires*, though they obviously have that function too.

Many of the Sangallo layouts consist of one or more ground plans surrounded by ornamental details and capitals, written information, dimensions or scale, and sometimes allusions to prototypes. I believe that in many cases the patron or builder was expected to combine this information with formulas in his head or in a contract and thus create a more complete design.

A possible example is folio 11r in the Vatican "Libro" (Fig. 4.12). Here are two vast cubic grid-plan palace projects, apparently designed for the younger Lorenzo de'Medici. But the original sheet (which has pasted-on extensions) also contains details at much larger scale. These show among other things two entablatures from the Pantheon measured in Florentine braccia, a pilaster capital from the Castel Sant'Angelo in Rome, and a profile of a storiated console. These details probably were intended to complement the plans. One would thus, as a potential client, choose one of the Francesco-like diagrammatic palaces and then construct the volumes of its rooms and courts. As a next step one would assign the illustrated entablatures to different parts of the building and extrapolate the positions of the columns from the plan. Knowing formulas for the orders one could then make a cost estimate, order materials, and tell craftsmen fairly accurately the number of running feet of entablature, and the number of capitals, shafts, and bases, and so forth, they were to make bids on.

Let us interpret a related project in the same book in more detail. This is the plan by Giuliano for the unbuilt 1488 Tribunali Palace in Naples (Fig. 4.13). This vast structure is laid out in roughly 50- and 75-br squares (Fig. 4.14). The main courtyard including seats is a 75-x-150-br double square, and the area immediately behind this is a 75-br square. The perimeter is a rectangle 230 x 280 br. An interface of office suites, living quarters, council halls, and the like occupies the areas between the perimeter and the central courts.

In Figure 4.15 A, I have made a sketch of the re-entered inner angle of the main courtyard arcade. This shows the two types of compartments called for in this arcade, X and Y, which alternate all the way around except that at every corner there are doublings of X. We can interpret the larger support bases, marked 1, as piers.

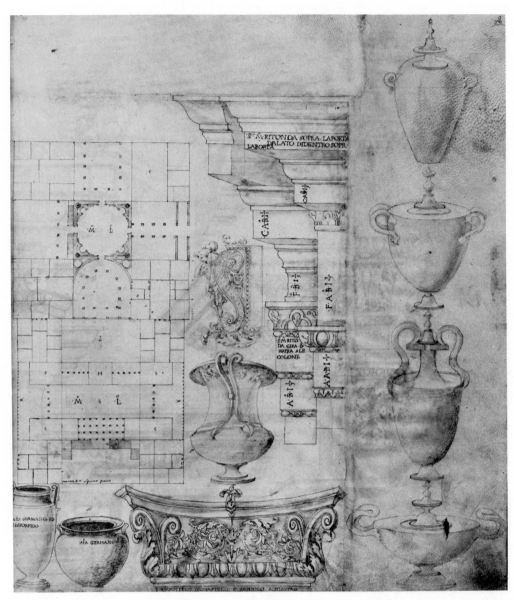

4.12 Plans and details of palaces and antiquities, from the "Libro di Giuliano da Sangallo" (Courtesy Vatican Library)

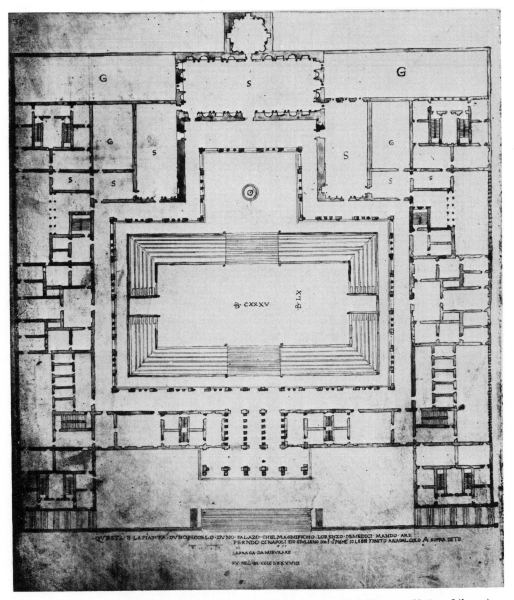

4.13 Plan of palace for Naples, from the "Libro di Giuliano da Sangallo" (Courtesy Vatican Library)

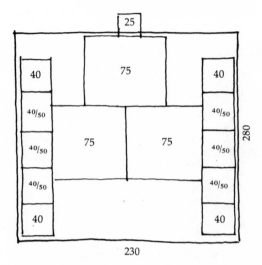

4.14 Modular layout of Naples palace

The smaller squares, marked 2, are antae, or else bases for columns addorsed to the piers. The small circles, 3, would be the bases of smaller columns. According to the dimensions in the plan these compartments are about 10-br wide from pier center to pier center. In such a case the piers, 1, would have to support lintels, and the antae or columns, 2, would then probably support arches inserted in each compartment of the X type (Fig. 4.15 B). The Y compartments could have either triple arches, triple trabeated openings, or perhaps some sort of Palladian window arrangement.

There is other volume information in the plan. Let's say that the contract calls for Doric piers in the courtyard at 1, Corinthian columns at 2, and Composite ones at 3. The craftsmen who are to make these things are told that they will have respective heights of 7, 9, and 10 diameters. They are also told that the entablatures are to be

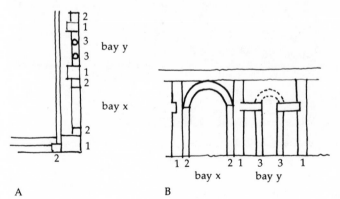

4.15 Detail of courtyard corner from Figure 4.13

respectively one-fourth, (for the Doric piers) and one-fifth (for the other two orders) of the column heights. We can even roughly measure these diameters from the bases shown on the plan. The craftsmen could then be told to seek out the details of each order from other drawings in the book. So now both builder and client know with fair accuracy the nature and cost of the whole courtyard wall. By doing the same for the exterior of the palace, and then by estimating the room volumes via formulas such as those given earlier in this chapter, we could build up a fairly precise and fairly complete corpo transparente on Giuliano's floor plan.

4.6 The Perspective Cross Section. Leonardo and Bramante made a different use of the notion of the corpo transparente. Leonardo in fact created drawings that have been described as the earliest perspective and elevational cross sections in the history of art. The invention of this type of drawing has also been linked to Leonardo's section drawings of human anatomy; and it is certainly true that quite often architectural and anatomical sections will appear on the same sheet, if not always in perspective (Fig. 4.16). The body and the building are both sliced open and a view of their interiors is drawn in chiaroscuro. One thinks also of Serlio, who was to make this same parallel in actually describing the corpo transparente, while more generally the notion is linked to the anthropomorphism discussed in the last chapter.

But another way of seeing the phenomenon is to say that Leonardo was rendering the cutaway parts of the building transparent, and showing the reminder in

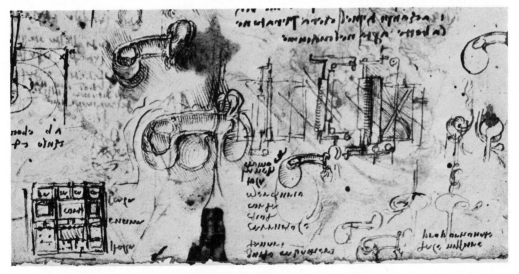

4.16 Cross sections in perspective, from Leonardo, Windsor 19106v (Courtesy Royal Library, Windsor, reproduced by gracious permission of Her Majesty the Queen)

perspective. In this sense the cutaway perspective rendering is a variation of the corpo transparente.

In any event, Leonardo cannot actually be credited with *inventing* the perspective cross section. And Filarete, who can, tells us that he thought of the building as having become partially transparent in this sense. Filarete's illustration of the Palace of Vice and Virtue (Fig. 4.17) is first of all clearly a perspective cross section. And he says of it: "One cannot demonstrate [the staircase] in a drawing unless one first has had [it] removed, as was necessarily done, with the result shown here. Hence it is necessary *to envisage the mode and form of the removed section in the mind*" (144r and v). The phrase I have italicized is Filarete's way of saying he saw the "removed" section as an imagined transparent half of the building which allows us to see the staircase. Meanwhile the corpo transparente's plan remains, as a literal vestige, at the base.

4.17 Cutaway perspective of Palace of Vice and Virtue, from Filarete (Courtesy Yale University Press)

Despite Filarete's precedence, however, Leonardo did more than any other early draftsman to develop the cutaway architectural perspective. And he did it by applying and extending Filarete's notion of the partial corpo transparente. The famous Manuscript B palace drawing (Fig. 4.18) is important because it reveals its uniform cubic corpo transparente in a way that no plan or elevation could do. The scheme consists of a complex of palaces set on roadways and canals. The whole is composed on dimensions of 6 and 20 br (Leonardo 741). The roads are 20 br wide, the upper set being 6 br higher than the lower. The arches that form the street arcades, and

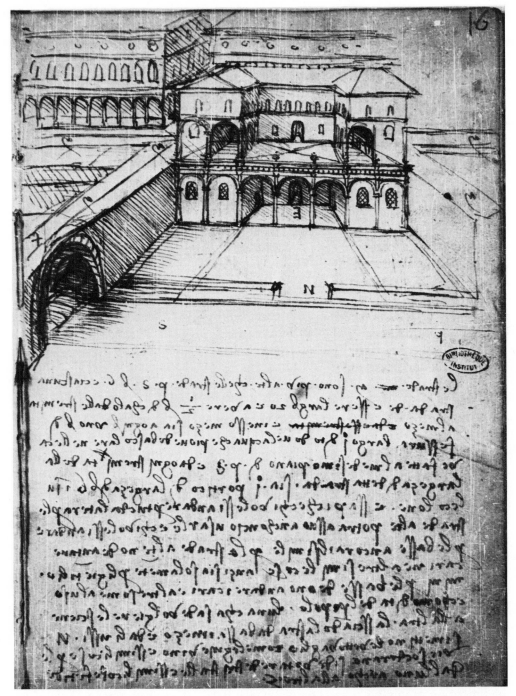

4.18 Cutaway perspective of palace, from Leonardo, Manuscript B (Courtesy Bibliothèque nationale, Paris)

the arched bays of the palaces themselves, are also 6 br wide, and 12 high. The palace in the foreground is rendered as if it were half transparent but with the plan remaining, exactly as in Filarete. Altogether, therefore, we now know that the urban sector Leonardo has drawn is based on two modules, a double-cube one of 6 x 12 br and a linear one of 20. Vertical double cubes create all three floors of the foreground palace. In width this palace is seven bays across, dually arranged as 2 3 2, and ten bays deep. What is to fill the courtyard area marked N we do not know. Not only has Leonardo indicated the mental or transparent part of the palace, he has incorporated a whole urban quarter with standardized roads and canals and (judging from internal evidence) a uniform cornice into a continuous three-dimensional grid.

Leonardo's sketch also involves a spatial hierarchy. The upper streets, set one module above the lower ones, are for gentlefolk. The lower streets are for all others and for vehicles. Elsewhere Leonardo specifically advocates a uniform cornice height, varying with street width (746). And he says that "a building always wants to be detached all around so as to demonstrate its true form" (753). A combination of uniform cornice heights, modular street widths, and detached buildings (or at any rate buildings that "want" to be detached) suggests a truly cubic city with voids and solids obeying a continuous, partly visible, partly invisible, social/geometric hierarchical lattice.

The sketch on Windsor 12585v (Fig. 4.19), which is also built out of a three-dimensional grid, again expresses the notion of a corpo transparente. The use of cubic dimensions and distributions is even clearer than in the Manuscript B drawing. Leonardo says: "The courtyard must have its walls be in height one-half their length, that is if the courtyard is 40 br long the house [wing] should be 20 br high in the walls of that courtyard. And that courtyard must be half as wide as the facade" (760). Thus the outer facade of the palace will be 80 br long, the courtyard 40, and the structure around the court 20 br high, or in terms of numberforms one could say $2:2^2:2^3$. Furthermore, unless it has different dimensions in the other direction, the building is also based on a 20-br modular cube, this time composed of four bays (Fig. 4.20). The palace itself, furthermore, being 80 br square by 20 high, is a quarter-cube. And the courtyard, 40 br square by 20 high, is a half-cube, while each wing around the courtyard, measuring inside, is 20 x 20 x 40, a double cube. The plan shows more: a square layout with two courtyards, also square, that recalls Filarete's Doric Gentleman's Palace (Fig. 4.8).

Leonardo's type of perspective rendering depends on creating, in the viewer's mind, that part of the scene which is implied but not seen because of the viewpoint and frame of the picture. The seen part of the picture need not be schematic as in the preceding examples. It can have immense detail. The corpo transparente of an elaborate perspective interior is far more than the erection of an Ionic arcade

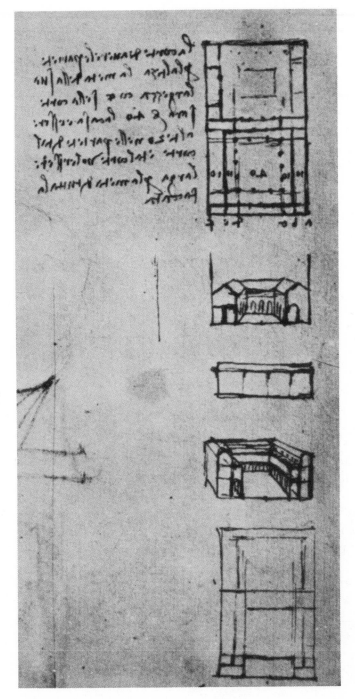

4.19 Sketch of palace, from Leonardo, Windsor 12585v (Courtesy Royal Library, Windsor, reproduced by gracious permission of Her Majesty the Queen)

around a courtyard or the calculation of room volumes. It is not simply a cost estimation device; it is a virtuoso exercise in what Lomazzo would later call vista interna.

A modern instance of this process can be seen in Arnaldo Bruschi's treatment of the so-called Prevedari Print (1481) attributed to Bramante (Fig. 4.21). Bruschi derives from this perspective interior a plan and section (Figs. 4.22, 4.23), though as he admits he has had to "true up" the original a bit. The pictured interior reveals itself in plan and section as a cubical structure based on a nine-square quincunx with three different modules: A, the large central square which appears once; B, the four corner squares, slightly smaller than A; and C, the sesquitertial offspring of A and B, forming the interfaces between A and B. Hence Bruschi, playing the Renaissance man of "virtù," has "incarnated" unseen architecture via the geometrical analysis of seen architecture (150–70, 745–50). His task has been made immeasurably simpler by the fact that the Prevedari interior is a cubic structure.

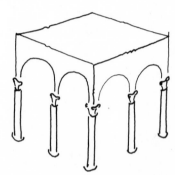

4.20 20-br cubic module from Figure 4.19

4.7 Prospettiva Transparente. Bruschi's basic technique had been described much earlier by Serlio. Serlio after all had used and perhaps coined the term "corpo transparente." And Serlio had literally built his whole architectural system out of three-dimensional perspective. In Book II he gives a series of exercises in the creation of architectural volumes. All distances are measured with the tesserae of a cubic lattice. For Serlio perspective is no mere trick to suggest depth. It is a measuring and surveying system, a bit like Cesariano's man-in-square-and-circle. Serlio posits four retreating squared-off planes (Fig. 4.24), each treated as a surface inscribed with lineamenta. He adds:

All things are born of the plane: three things in particular; lengths, i.e. the whole facade, of so many feet; widths, i.e. of doors, windows, shops and suchlike; heights, i.e. doors, windows, balconies, cornices, roofs, columns, . . . the thickness of walls, columns, and some pilasters. The lengths are taken from the foreshortened volumes, and also their widths, and so too the pilastrades [or archivolts] which are also widths, as was said. The heights are

4.21 Prevedari Print, attributed to Bramante (Courtesy British Museum)

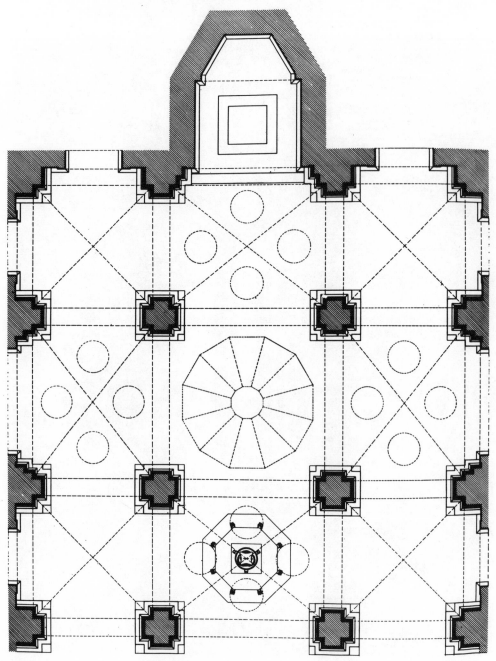

4.22 Plan extrapolated from Prevedari Print, from Arnaldo Bruschi, *Bramante architetto* (Bari and Rome: Laterza, 1968)

4.23 Section extrapolated from Prevedari Print, from Arnaldo Bruschi, *Bramante architetto* (Bari and Rome: Laterza, 1968)

taken from the transverse squares, so that the door is ten feet high and will be measured from the corner nearest us, along the line from the corner of the picture, rising straight up. And then you take five squares and measure that distance upward and that will be the height. And . . . so on with everything else (2.35v).

In other words, each of the 2-foot cube sides in Figure 4.24 exists as a frame of linee occulte until it is clothed by some architectural element. The "unseeable" parts of the buildings—the archivolts facing away from the observer, for example—are all drawn. Then their outlines are erased, leaving only seeable solids. This part is different from what Bruschi did with the Prevedari Print, for Serlio is actually drawing the whole structure as a transparent building seen in perspective, rather like the temple of Fortuna Seia in Nero's palace, and then causing the occult parts to vanish.

The importance of perspective in architectural design continues with Cataneo. In 1554 he is more convinced even than Serlio that it is one of the most important of the architect's "eruditioni." He is willing to throw out a whole quartet of other

4.24 Arcade in perspective, from Serlio

preparatory disciplines—philosophy, astrology, music, and law—to make room for it. Through perspective, he says, the architect can derive every sort of elevation and view from a given plan. More than a model, even, a perspective rendering shows what a building will look like:

[Perspective teaches] us what sort of thing light is, what shadow, what interval, and finds the causes of the visible which are discerned by means of its apparent distances. It discovers or searches out the breaking of the rays by one or more highlights on various figures or bodies, and the total configuration of shadows and highlights, and of the accidents of sight, of the object, and of the medium through which they are seen. One can therefore easily consider each part of the well-finished design one by one, and one avoids the expense of a model which at times is not small. If the architect is not a perspectivist he will never be able to gain honors in this way, nor show his conception via a drawing no matter how excellent a draftsman he is. And in his own mind he will acknowledge the great disadvantage of not being a good practitioner of perspective [1r].

Perspective rendering is thus the highest sort of architectural virtuosity. Such drawing provides important information on the behavior of light on the finished building, and on the order of objects in the scene as apprehended from a specific viewpoint and as seen through a medium. The apparent, tapered tesserae of perspective predict, when translated into the true cubes of real space, what will happen when the building is built. A perspective view thus *simultaneously* measures and displays or prophesies. The corpo transparente ceases to be abstractly mental and becomes pictorial. But the earlier notions connected with the corpo transparente, of skill and honor and even to some extent of privileged information, are still present in Cataneo's conception.

4.8   Hierarchical Volumes. Cataneo's successor, Palladio, says little about perspective; but he says a good deal about volume and about the ideal relationships of room height to plan, depending on size, function, and location. His work shows how flat surfaces, plans, and elevations can procreate families or societies of volumes. Palladio's flexible formulas, indeed, produce something like that continuous change in size that perspective also provides. But he gives us guidance also as to the proper hierarchies of these three-dimensional voids:

Rooms are built either vaulted or ceiled. If they are ceiled the height from floor to beams will be the same as the width [Method 1]. And the rooms on the floor above will be one-sixth lower than those below. If the rooms are vaulted (as is usually the case with the first story [order] because such rooms are more beautiful and less apt to catch fire) the height of the vaults in square rooms will be one-and-one-third of the width [Method 2]. But in rooms longer than they are wide, it will be necessary to determine the height from the proportions of length to width [Method 3, Fig. 4.25 A]. This height is calculated by putting the length next to the width, and dividing the whole into two equal parts. One of these halves becomes the height of the vault. For example [in room cabd] the width ac is added to the length ab

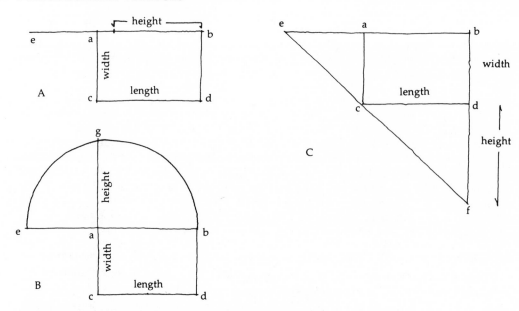

4.25 Three methods of establishing room volumes, after Palladio

and the line eb results. This line is divided into two equal parts atf, and fb will be the height of the room. If, in other words, the room to be vaulted is 12 feet long and 6 feet wide, 6+12=18. Half of 18 is 9; hence the vault will be 9 feet high [53].

This volume, 6:9:12, is an arithmetical progression. A fourth method in Palladio is to swing a semicircle on f from e to b (Fig. 4.25 B), then extending ac until it meets the perimeter of the semicircle at g. The distance ag will be the room's height. Palladio also advocates the formula, height:width::length:height. This method, his fifth, puts the three values into geometrical progression. A sixth method is to multiply the width by the length and take the square root of the result. A seventh method (Fig. 4.25 C) is to continue ab to e, as in Method 3, but then to project a diagonal from e to c and then onward till it meets a downward continuation of bd. The height of the room will be equal to this downward continuation, df.

Thus Palladio gives us a range of seven possible ways to establish room height, one method for ceiled rooms and six for vaulted. And the three "geometrical" methods, that is, those illustrated in Figure 4.25, are all based on the notion of the corpo transparente. They are geometrical projections, or invisible controlling numberforms that are larger than the rooms themselves, and that determine and contain the volumes of those rooms.

Palladio's rules for window placement emphasize the need for dominant uniform sight-line lattices throughout the palace. He says that there are no "certain and determined" rules for the heights and widths of openings. He sends us back to Vitruvius 4.6 for formulas, adding that doors should not be more than 3 x 6½ feet or less than 2 x 5. Windows should not be wider than one-fourth of a room's width nor narrower than one-fifth. Windows can also be designed 2¹/₆ squares high. But these rules are all subject to the necessity of having uniform windows throughout a floor. And the noble rooms establish the rules for the ignoble rooms around them. For example, take a room whose length is two-thirds greater than its width, that is, with a width of 18 feet and a length of 30. Palladio divides the width into 4½ parts. The windows are then made one part wide and 2¹/₆ high, or 4 x 8²/₃ feet. Windows of this size are then built willy-nilly throughout the floor. This will be true only of the main floor of the house. The floor above, we remember, will be one-sixth lower, and the window heights are lowered by the same proportion. As for doors between rooms (and this goes for pilastered windows as well) the pilasters should not be less than one-sixth of the opening nor more than one-fifth. Needless to say, axial symmetry in the modern sense prevails throughout, with all openings on axis, disposed in duities, both on the interior and on the exterior.

Palladio seems to have observed these formulas in several of the palaces in Book II of his treatise. Thus in 2.3, a house for Floriano Antonini in Udine (Figs. 4.26, 4.27), the multistory sala rises in the center to the roof, 32 feet square. The foremost flanking rooms are 17 x 28, the next pair 17 x 24. There are "piutosto ignobili" rooms next to the stairs, and a rear loggia 17 x 32 flanked by 17-foot-square rooms at its "heads" or narrow ends (though Palladio's engraver has not shown them as square).

According to Method 1 for square, ceiled rooms, this four-columned "tetrastyle" or main sala will have to be 32 feet high (Fig. 4.27). The vaulted, front 17 x 28 flanking rooms could variously have heights of 22½' (Method 3); 22' and 21' (Methods 4 and 5); 21½' (Method 6); and 28' (Method 7). By the same token the 17 x 24 rooms could either be 20½', 19'10", 22', about 20', 25', or 24'. The 17 x 17 rooms would follow the rule for vaulted squares and be 22'8" high.

Which of these heights fit the elevations? Checking Figure 4.26 we note that from the main floor to the beginning of the entablature is a distance of 19 feet. Then comes a 3³/₄-foot area of entablature plus attic. We do not know the exact placement of the floors behind this part of the facade, but main-floor heights of 20½', 21½', and 22'8" would all easily fit behind it.

These heights derived from Palladio's systems would all be cubic. The main sala itself is a pure cube. The volumes of the 17 x 28 rooms, if 22½' high, and those of the 17 x 24 rooms, if 20½' high, would form arithmetical series. The 17 x 17 x 22'8" rooms would not be in one of the canonical ratios, but they would be sesquitertial parallelepipeds. Cubism prevails everywhere—in Palladio's methods of calculation, in the resulting shapes, and in their distribution. On the other hand cubic *dimensions* are relatively uncommon, not only in the values supplied by me but in those

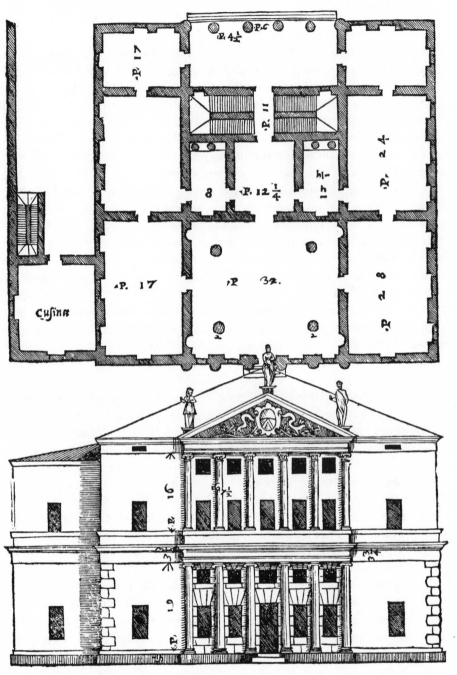

4.26 Palace for Floriano Antonini, Udine, from Palladio

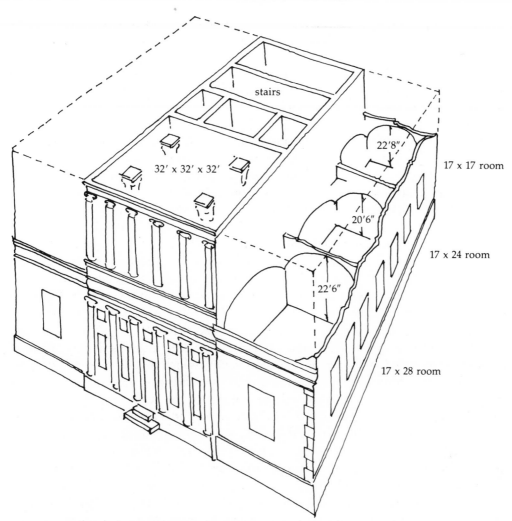

stairs

32' x 32' x 32'

22'8"

17 x 17 room

20'6"

17 x 24 room

22'6"

17 x 28 room

4.27 Cutaway perspective view of Antonini Palace

Palladio himself gives. One can, in a pinch, argue that upper floors are one-sixth lower than those below, their openings being correspondingly lower as well; and in the Antonini house some dimensions of the second-floor rooms are one-sixth greater in plan because the walls on the second floor are thinner. Thus the reciprocal of the "cubo expressissimo," 6, determines the status of the upper rooms. But beyond this it is hard to go. Palladio's cubism is not involved with values in themselves but is a product of his ideas about volume ratios—that is, corpi transparenti.

As we saw in Chapter 3, Palladio subscribes to the idea of a social hierarchy of rooms. In the Antonini house the central sala, 32 x 32 x 32, is clearly nobler than its surrounding rooms, and those flanking rooms have an order among themselves too, since the larger rooms, nearer the front, are mathematically proportioned and the rear rooms are not. One could put all this information into a table like Table 11, but at this point it is hardly necessary.

4.9   Inner and Outer Volume Hierarchies. Scamozzi enlarges Palladio's application, which is only partial, of mathematical series to room volumes. In speaking of ancient practice (1.298-306) he emphasizes the "perfection" of the volumes of the main rooms in Greek and Roman houses. The triclinium was 2:1 in area and had a height one-half its length plus its width (1.237; for example, if length = 4 and width = 2, the height will be 3, an arithmetical progression.) A similar rule affected Corinthian salottos, four-columned halls or tetrastyles, Egyptian halls, and indeed all rooms of rectangular plan. On the other hand exedras or reception rooms, painting galleries, and salottos other than Corinthian, were half-cubes. Scamozzi's formulas are often derived from Vitruvius but he gets them as well from authors like Suetonius and Palladio. Elsewhere (1.308–9) he gives fuller treatment to volume formulas from Vitruvius but finds them unsatisfactory. While Vitruvius' room shapes are all cubic parallelepipeds, Scamozzi implies that Vitruvius does not take enough account of the different shapes of roofs and vaults, which modify a room's proportions. Scamozzi solves the vault problem by measuring to the springing point rather than to the crest. Thus the curved volume of the vault proper is detached from the proportional system. On this basis Scamozzi advocates for principal rooms a height derived from "the perfect square of the width," plus not less than 16 feet and not more than 20 to accomodate the bed of the vault. Alternatives to the square are the sesquialter, the square-and-three-quarters, and the double square. Extreme dimensions, as usual, are advised only for loggias, vestibules, and the like.

But the main novelty is Scamozzi's suggestion that "great" rooms should be "served" by set groups of satellite rooms. And these satellite hierarchies reverse the usual cubic ascent from parallelepiped to cube:

Smaller rooms will be as high as they are wide, or perfect cubes. The next [largest] will be one-eighth higher than wide, the middle-sized rooms a quarter more, and the penultimate three-eighths more. The largest rooms will be one-and-one-half times higher than their width. And since these proportions are means between the length and width of rooms, they are also means in their forms [i.e. numberform means]. Whence, standing at one end of a room, you see from top to bottom at a single glance without moving the eye [ibid.].

Thus room heights, as well as room areas, can have more variety with Scamozzi's rules than with Palladio's, and the Ficinian concept of the observer and his viewpoint is brought in. In the process, however, Scamozzi rules out Palladio's climactic cubic salas.

Scamozzi gives rules for windows and doors, deriving their height and placement from the room volumes and distinguishing between main exterior doors and interior ones (1.318-19). Main exterior doors, like the windows of main facades, partake of the numerical and proportional character of the orders. We saw that Palladio had actually referred to stories *as* orders. And we also saw, in Chapter 3, that Scamozzi had prescribed facade "kingdoms" ruled by columns. Such order-derived compartmentation also has its place in the development of the corpo transparente. For these Tuscan, Doric, Ionic, Roman, and Corinthian surface compartments involve openings, and hence interior three-dimensional pervasions of the palace (Fig. 4.28). By incorporating these hierarchies of interior volumes and adjusting them to the outer hierarchies established by the "kingdoms," Scamozzi creates not only, let us say, an Ionic exterior loggia but an Ionic void behind it.

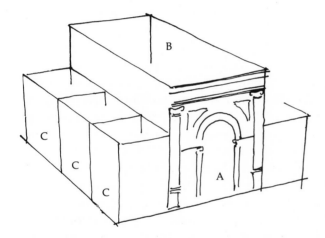

4.28 Ionic compartment and volume, after Scamozzi. Ionic facade compartment (A) dictates volume (B) which in turn dictates satellite volumes (C).

Scamozzi finally, and in view of all this logically, takes up Palladio's idea of the reciprocal relationship between exterior and interior (6.14 [36]). In Palladio this had only meant that windows and doors were to be arranged in a way that made sense both on the outer and on the inner facades. But Scamozzi claims that the whole framework of pilasters and columns, outside and inside, must match. It must be as if the walls were transparent, as if one could see the exterior orders from inside the building, as in an open hypostyle temple. The latter, for Scamozzi, is no longer a mere mental stage in the design process but a vision to be observed specifically from situations inside and outside the structure. And, Scamozzi adds, this reciprocity was not observed by the ancients; it is an achievement of his own age.

We have seen how the notion of the corpo transparente in Renaissance theory departs from classical ideas. For Vitruvius the mental building created from a drawn plan was an almost pure columnar formula. The Renaissance married this idea to one where proportional and cubic volumes had to be "symmetrical" or integrally measurable with the building's columnar dimensions and distributions. The Renaissance palace is thus a Vitruvian hypostyle—a columnar composition— but also a complex of astylar volumes. In this lies its principal "symmetry."

In the growth of this notion from Alberti through Scamozzi we first saw Alberti describing a palace's outer cube-jacket and at the same time creating parallelepipeds of volume inside it as rooms. In this sense the cube is the palace's goal, and the parallelepiped its tessera-source. Filarete's palaces were also procreated simultaneously in two directions—from the Doric outer perimeter and also from that perimeter's miniature, the portal. Francesco di Giorgio then developed Alberti's more latent notions about variations in ceiling height to accord with functional and distributional hierarchies. In Francesco's noble rooms, moreover, the proportions are mathematical while windows are set up along sight-line lattices that tied the volume patterns together.

This brings us to the 1480s. The next phase takes up the question of corpi transparenti and perspective—the envisaging of a three-dimensional form in two dimensions, using an omnidirectional isomorphic grid. Typical Renaissance palace ground plans can reveal a good deal of information about their corpi transparenti in this sense. The information comes from a double source: previous knowledge of the orders, and previous knowledge of volume formulas. Hence a palace is "symmetrical" when it can be integrally measured in various diameters, and also in intercolumniations, or "parts," "thirds," tesserae, or other modules.

At the same time, Leonardo, instead of slicing the palace off at ground-floor level, sliced it vertically (following Filarete) and revealed a cross section to correspond with an unseen or removed part which is mentally imaged. With this notion perspective became a vehicle for the corpo transparente—a mode not only of seeing but of designing, and of designing not just rooms and palaces but sections of cities. Cataneo, indeed, managed to see the perspective rendering as a corpo transparente, one that had been skillfully made visible by the architect-painter who "raised" it on a plan printed in a book.

Meanwhile, in the 1570s Palladio took up Francesco's ideas of volume hierarchies and established systems which made further use of mathematical ratios, while at the same time insisting on powerful sight-line lattices. In Palladio's palaces these lattices, plus the colossal geometric constructs that shape the noble rooms, are the "transparent bodies."

Scamozzi completes Palladio. Each noble room has a brood of satellites while at the same time being determined by the exterior orders of that part of the palace.

Major rooms in Scamozzi are also designed so as to be "seeable at a glance," that is in perspective, from a viewpoint. The palace as a whole is to be reciprocally integrated, inside and outside, in terms of its original hypostyle. Scamozzi's palace is a visible segment of an invisible paradimensional grid, a set of marriages between the moiety of numberforms and that of the orders.

5. Some Material Palaces, 1440–1500

5.1 Practical Problems. To illustrate the previous theoretical discussion, we will survey some of the material buildings that seem to embody Pythagorean principles. These principles can be discerned, at least in partial applications, in the most familiar monuments: the Medici Palace, the Rucellai Palace facade, the Piccolomini Palace in Pienza, the villas at Poggioreale and Poggio a Caiano, and the Strozzi Palace. This sequence matches that of our earlier treatise writers, for the architects include among others Brunelleschi's heir Michelozzo, Alberti, Alberti's follower Bernardo Rossellino, Francesco di Giorgio, and Giuliano da Sangallo. Their palaces can be analyzed as masonry numberforms. But after these buildings, cubism seems to disappear in practical architecture. In the Cinquecento, so far as I can determine, cubic theory remained primarily a mode of teaching, while in actual buildings newer and more complex forms of geometric-numerical structure prevailed.

Looked at in the cold light of practical building and deprived of its Neoplatonic aura, the cubic module is essentially a repeated volume. As such there is nothing new about it in the Renaissance. Any cellular building planned along right angles and straight lines can be seen as "cubic" in the broad sense, and its cells can equally well be cubic in dimensions, proportions, and distribution. Multistory churches, loggias, market halls, and other compartmented masonry and wooden constructions are cases in point. Modular volumes can even be a statical necessity: solid *must* go over solid, and void over void, if the building is to stay up.

But in this chapter I will be discussing buildings that had no such practical needs, and yet were formed of cubic grids. Italian palaces were usually not, until the Renaissance, built like multistory vaulted buildings, though they often contained vaulted rooms. Instead they were immensely overbuilt bearing-wall structures. The walls were very thick, and while the structural walls rose through several floors there was otherwise considerable freedom of room height and partitioning. Plans could be very irregular. This being so, an ordinary Italian palace with a ground floor devoted, say, to shops and storage, a main floor consisting of reception rooms and apartments, and with minor sleeping quarters on the upper floors, would normally have had a very different plan for each floor. So when we see, instead of this, a movement among builders toward cubic symmetry and arbitrary or unneeded regularity, we can say that we are witnessing a new Pythagorean sensibility in palace architecture.

A good example of a palace that is making this transition is the Medici by Michelozzo (begun about 1446). If one is permitted to judge on the basis of the earliest extant floor plans (Fig. 5.1)—and I am aware that these, dating from the 1650s, include remodelings—the ground floor (A) is relatively regular but the piano nobile (B) is from the Pythagorean viewpoint decidedly a warren. The same goes for the third floor (C). Yet as I shall show, the ground floor of the Medici Palace has in it the germs of cubical planning. Indeed, as a whole the building originally had a cube-

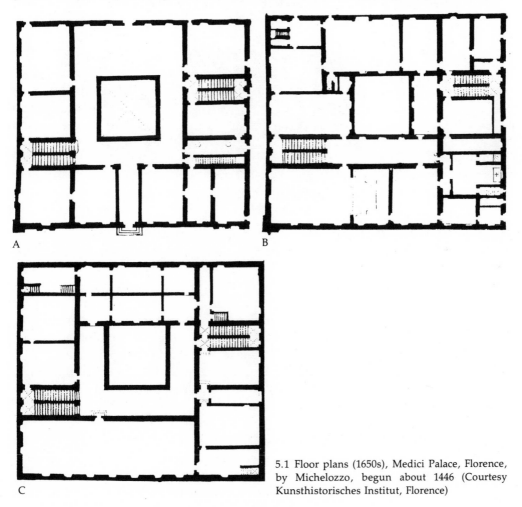

A

B

C

5.1 Floor plans (1650s), Medici Palace, Florence, by Michelozzo, begun about 1446 (Courtesy Kunsthistorisches Institut, Florence)

5.2 Post-1512 view of Medici Palace, from Del Migliore, *Firenze città nobilissima*

like exterior (Fig. 5.2). There were three ground-floor arches on the Via Cavour front and two rows of ten windows each on the two visible upper facades. This ground floor is a lot more regular than it appears to be even in Figure 5.1. And when in later palaces we move from this moderate and partial regularity to much greater regularity; when opening goes over opening, void over void, and solid over solid in accordance with the ideas of duity and modular symmetry rather than for the sake of statical necessity; and when we see isomorphic inner and outer volume compartments—then we have the right to speak of Pythagorean architecture.

Nonetheless a number of ambiguities crop up when we turn to actual buildings. There is the problem of wall thickness. We have seen that the clearest diagrams are linear; what is to be done with actual palaces and their thick walls? Are these thicknesses included, excluded, or split by the linee occulte? Are we speaking of true voids or what might be called capsules? This contradiction is resolved via the hypostyle metaphor, as I shall show. A second problem is that the buildings I discuss have not always been accurately measured or these findings accurately published. Some drawings I have worked with have proven ambiguous, and it could well be that others which I have trusted are in fact wrong. Then too, the original buildings have settled and have been remodeled; whatever ideal geometry they ever had is compromised. Finally, the original builders seldom worked to fine tolerances.

All these things interfere with the Pythagorean analysis of material buildings. But at the same time they help justify the Renaissance belief that a material form is the corruption of a mental one. In the strict sense, indeed, modern measured drawings are often too large and detailed to be accurate, or at any rate to be historistic. By being at larger scale than the drawings from which the palace was built, they endow its existing dimensions with a gratuitous precision. They fail to round off, or as Francesco would say "temper," the intended values. And when these modern drawings give dimensions in meters they lose these original values entirely. When one learns, say, from the Stegmann-Geymüller drawings that the original Medici Palace was 40.24 meters along the Via Cavour front, 37.36 meters deep along the Via Gori, and 23.99 meters high to the top of the main cornice, one merely has information about the building's size. But when one learns that as built it measured respectively 72, 64, and 40 braccia, one more easily understands that the palace was a parallelepiped based on three numbers of a five-number arithmetical progression derived from 8, the first true cube. Over and over again in my investigations, I have found that measurements in the original units yield mathematical relationships, symmetries, and duities that are hidden or even destroyed by modern measurements.

In this sense the following analyses will restore something to the buildings that has been lost. But not everything can be restored. While in their treatises architects like Francesco di Giorgio tell us the purpose of each room so that we can collate functions with proportions and distributions and so forth, in most existing buildings these original functions and names are not available. Hence the whole question of function/form hierarchies has to be left aside.

5.2   The Medici Palace. As originally built the Medici Palace rose from a corner site, a parallelepiped with a giant cornice but no frieze or architrave. Other Medici buildings were joined to it but did not read from the street as part of the same structure (Fig. 5.2, right). At first sight the main facade looks utterly symmetrical in the modern sense, and I have just mentioned some of its cubic propensities. This, so to speak, is one Medici Palace—the outer envelope. But pervading this envelope is a second Medici Palace. This second building is suggested by the visible cornice, which is the metonym for an invisible architrave, frieze, and columns—let us call it the unseen remainder of the order procreated by the cornice (Fig. 5.3). This more classical, semi-invisible building has an order not easily assimilated to the visible structure, at least when we use the formulas of contemporary treatise writers. Thus

5.3 Metonymic column, architrave, and frieze for Medici facade

Francesco di Giorgio states (1.387 and pl. 227) that the width of the architrave ought to equal the width of the column just at the capital base. He illustrates an entablature whose cornice is close to the Medici's, in which the width of the architrave is the same as that of the frieze. Both together, architrave and frieze, equal the height of the cornice. Hence, at least in the eyes of this slightly later contemporary of the architect's, the diameter of the columns supporting such a cornice ought to be one-half the cornice height, or about three braccia. Francesco also says that a Corinthian/Composite column should be nine diameters high. Hence, at Medici Palace scale, we wind up with a colonna occulta whose diameter is 3 br and whose height is 27, including capital. This brings us down to about the level of the architraves of the Michelangelo edicules at the building's corner. But that is no place to stop; it is too high for a proper pedestal and too low for a proper basement.

That is a flaw, though it is one mainly in the light of post-Michelozzo criticism. But even the primary visible Medici Palace has flaws, and these would have been visible, I should think, to the generation that built it. First of all, the Via Cavour facade is not quite symmetrical as a whole, for the three lower openings are not on axis with the upper windows (Fig. 5.3). The ground floor of the Via Gori facade has no regularity whatever. In fact the Medici Palace is less symmetrical, in the modern sense, than such earlier, "medieval" buildings as the nearby Davanzati Palace. The real novelties of the Medici exterior are thus the paired or corresponding facades, the large scale of the rustication, and the massive cornice with its implied columnar system.

These novelties are important. As Figure 5.3 tells us, the large cornice anticipates the colossal orders of the sixteenth century, where columns or pilasters rise from basement to attic. Meanwhile the apparent symmetry (in the modern sense) of the Medici facade will lead in later buildings to true modern symmetry. And the notion of the double facades, most important of all, will lead to the double paired facades of Palladio and others. Even the large-scale rustication prefigures the integration, in later palaces, of patterns of "quadroni" or large stones into the pilaster and window grids.

The Medici's inner hive also contains a prediction of things to come. The Via Cavour wall is thrust forward on the left (Fig. 5.4 front wall) so that the palace is not actually built around the square its plan suggests. Nor is the disposition of circulation space, for example stairwells, symmetrical in the modern sense, and we note that, as the facade suggests, the main axis of the whole is not centered through the vestibule and courtyard, though the lateral axis is on center.

And yet there is great order to this ground floor. We can reduce it to a hypostyle by extending the courtyard columns throughout as in Figure 5.4. The intercolumniations are uniform, 6 br each way. This transforms the palace into a 100-column hall with ten columns per side, making it a "hidden" specimen of Scamozzi's Adamic "portico quadrato di cento colonne." However, on the right, where the palace joins its neighbors, the system is out of phase and the last row of columns is separated from its neighbors by 9 br. But otherwise in all but a very few places the columns correspond to walls or room axes.

Figure 5.5 tells us that the module clusters created by the Medici hypostyle are practically all cubic, though some half-modules are used. And they are cubic both in distribution and dimensions. Thus there are ten bays across the far side of the

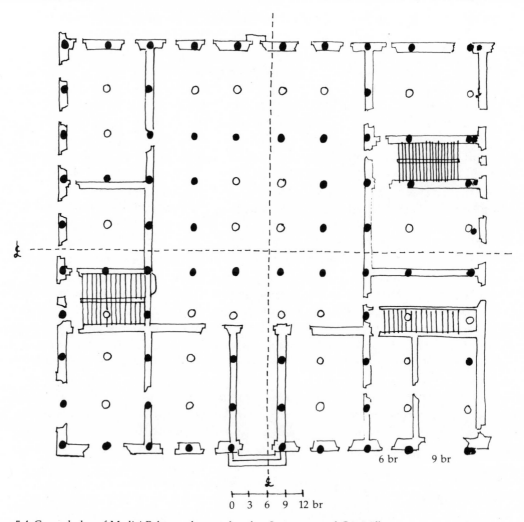

5.4 Ground plan of Medici Palace as hypostyle, after Stegmann and Geymüller

courtyard, four down the sides, three across the front, and nine in its center. Once again, the only ignoble or nonmodular spaces and rooms are those on the right where the palace joins its neighbors.

Figure 5.6 is a section through the main axis. Purely for demonstration I have interpreted this section as an 8 x 10 hypostyle with 6-br intercolumniations. Again, practically all the columns strike walls, ceilings, or axes. Thus despite its rough exterior the Medici Palace harbors a decent hypostyle skeleton.

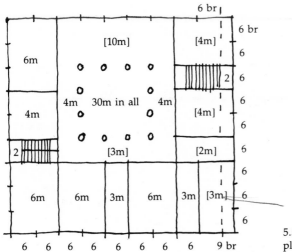

5.5 Modular analysis of Medici Palace ground plan (m = module)

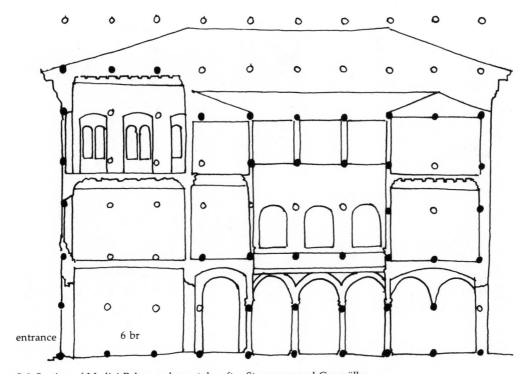

5.6 Section of Medici Palace as hypostyle, after Stegmann and Geymüller

5.7 Rucellai Palace, Florence, facade by Alberti, 1446 (Alinari)

5.3   The Rucellai Palace Facade. The great rival to the Medici Palace was of course the Rucellai, whose facade was designed by Alberti in 1446, just about the time the Medici Palace was begun. I shall analyze only the main facade, since only this part of the building is established as being Alberti's. It consists of three super-imposed stories: Doric, Corinthian, and Composite (Fig. 5.7). The bay system is borrowed from that of the Colosseum. You could even say that the Rucellai is a lineamenta version of the more plastic Roman original. I show the Rucellai as it is today and then illustrate it in an ideal form (Fig. 5.8). In this latter form the palace is fourteen bays long and has four portals. Another possibility is that it was intended to be eight bays long with two portals; or else an eleven-bay, three-portal setup could have been planned. These, unlike the present arrangement, would follow Alberti's rules for portal placement (85). I leave aside the question of whether Alberti obeyed his own rules in his buildings.

The present facade of the Rucellai, which is of course incomplete, is about 46 br long and 36 br high. The eight-bay version would be 52 x 36, or roughly a 4:3 rectangle. The eleven-bay version would be 78 br long, or 6 br more than a double square, and also 6 br longer than the original Medici facade.

Where the Medici can be interpreted as a single order with hidden columns, architrave, and frieze, the Rucellai has three orders, each with a full entablature. Furthermore the Rucellai seems to have been laid out on the basis of 1 br = 1 d, a simple way of achieving Renaissance symmetry. The ground-floor portal bays are

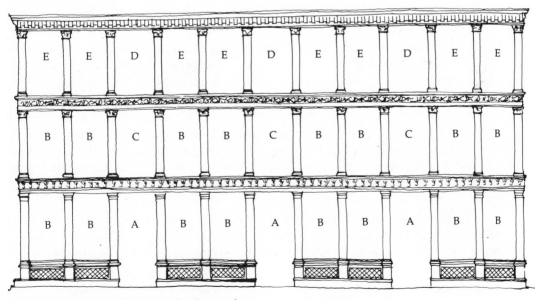

5.8 Rucellai facade idealized as 14-bay hypostyle

about $5^1/_3$ br, or diameters, wide, and the other ground-floor bays are about 5. The two lower orders are $8^1/_2$ d high and the upper story seems to have a height of $8^1/_4$. Unlike the Medici, then, the Rucellai is a visible and explicit, as opposed to an implicit, three-story hypostyle.

More than any earlier building, given its numerical variations, the Rucellai facade may be studied as an affinity table of numberforms, both as shown in Figure 5.8 and as shown in Table 15.

Table 15. The Rucellai facade compartments (idealized 14-bay structure)

Compartments				Orders*			
Type	Nearest canonical proportion	Distri-bution	Size (in br)	Name	Column height (in br)	Entablature height (in d)	Intercolum-niation (in d)
A	3:2	4	$5^1/_3 \times 8^1/_2$	Doric	$8^1/_2$	$2^3/_4$	$5^1/_3$
B	5:3	20	$5 \times 8^1/_2$	Doric	$8^1/_2$	$2^3/_4$ (first floor)	5
				Corinth.		$1^3/_4$ (second floor)	
C	3:2	4	$5^1/_3 \times 8^1/_2$	Corinth.	$8^1/_2$	$1^3/_4$	$5^1/_3$
D	3:2	4	$5^1/_3 \times 8^1/_4$	Comp.	$8^1/_4$	$2^1/_3$	$5^1/_3$
E	5:3	10	$5 \times 8^1/_4$	Comp.	$8^1/_4$	$2^1/_3$	5

* 1 br = 1 d, all pilasters 1 d wide

From this we know that there are two ascents in the Rucellai facade, one through the wider portal bays (A, C, D) and the other through the window bays B and E. In each ascent the proportions go from the oblong at the bottom to the more nearly square at the top. From the point of view of Pythagorean geometry this is orthodox. But in integrating these progressions with the orders and with the social divisions of the palace, Alberti has had to compromise the latter two. The Doric pilasters are relatively tall instead of having the squatness called for by the shaft heights of those orders. And there is no distinction between ground floor, piano nobile, and bedroom story. Furthermore, one has to set down the universal one-braccia shaft diameter for all orders as something of a solecism. Nor do the entablature widths change in concert with the compartmentation. The middle entablature is the thinnest of the three.

Nonetheless, the Rucellai facade is of great significance. It *is* a scala, though not a very well-structured one. The numerical table of its relations coalesces with the appearance of the facade itself. Alberti's drastic modification of the rules for the orders can be set down as a bold innovation, later to be refined and corrected. Indeed, the actual facade (Fig. 5.7) contains not only superimposed grids of rectangles and the orders, but also grids of openings and even of rustication. All four grids are roughly compatible and exist hierarchically. The largest grid is the most regular and the smallest the least so.

5.4   The Piccolomini Palace, Pienza. Could the Medici-type interior grid unite with the Alberti-type facade grid? Yes. And the child procreated by the Medici-Rucellai liaison is the Piccolomini Palace in Pienza, built by Alberti's quondam assistant Bernardo Rossellino. This building, begun about 1459, is at first glance an unimpressive imitation of the Rucellai (Fig. 5.9). The bays look too squat and the pilasters diminish too pronouncedly in width from floor to floor. Nonetheless, these facades—there are three that concern us—yield interesting relationships.

The main façade (Fig. 5.10) including the podium is about $30^{1}/_{3}$ br by $60^{2}/_{3}$, a dou-

5.9 Piccolomini Palace, Pienza, by Bernardo Rossellino, begun about 1459 (Alinari)

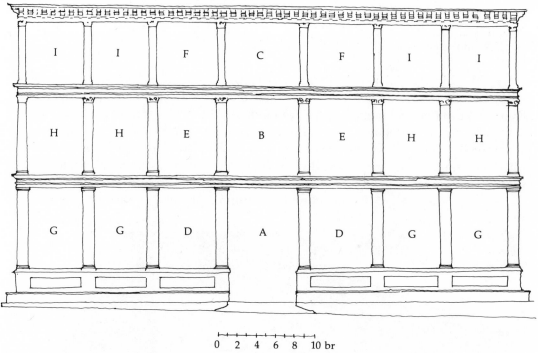

| I | I | F | C | F | I | I |

| H | H | E | B | E | H | H |

| G | G | D | A | D | G | G |

```
├──┼──┼──┼──┼──┼──┼──┼──┼──┼──┤
0    2    4    6    8   10 br
```

5.10 Piccolomini facade as hypostyle

ble square. This large form is echoed, Filarete-fashion, by the double square of the central door. The depth of the palace is 68 br (less the ell), which does not add up to a mathematical proportion, though of course 30, 60, and 68 are all cubic values. Otherwise the facade is divided into three orders—Doric, Corninthian, Composite—like the Rucellai. Again like the Rucellai these dimensions lend themselves to expression in diameters as well as braccia. However, where in the Rucellai all diameters were the same, here, as noted, they differ greatly from one floor to the next. As a result there are many more different-sized compartments. In other words, where the Rucellai orders were assimilated to strictly filiated rectangles, with A and B procreating C, D, and E without outside interference (Table 15), in the Piccolomini the rectangles of the compartments are strongly modified by the changing widths of the pilasters (Table 16). I have lettered the Piccolomini compartments in a different sequence than those of the Rucellai. This is because in Alberti's facade there is essentially a series of upward and downward movements within each stack of bays. In the Piccolomini facade there are two types of movement—the vertical ascent and descent within the bay-stacks, and also a duity movement from the sides, culminating in the central bay.

Table 16. The Piccolomini facade compartments

	Compartments			Order				
Type	Nearest canonical proportion	Distri-bution	Size (in br)	Name	Shaft width (in br)	Column height (in d)	Entab-lature height (in d)	Inter-colum-niation (in d)
A	7:8	1	7×8	Doric	1¼	7	1	6⅓
B	1:1	1	7¼ × 7¼	Corinth.	1	7½	1¼	6
C	4:5	1	7½×6	Comp.	¾	8⅓	2¼	8
D	4:5	2	6⅓×8	Doric	1¼	7	1	5¾
E	1:1	2	6½ × 7½	Corinth.	1	7½	1¼	6¼
F	6:7	2	6¾×6	Comp.	¾	8⅓	2¼	9
G	3:4	4	5¾×8	Doric	1¼	7	1	5¼
H	6:7	4	6×7½	Corinth.	1	7½	1¼	6
I	1:1	4	6¼ × 6	Comp.	¾	8⅓	2¼	8

The Piccolomini has nine different compartment types as opposed to five in the Rucellai. Both of the Piccolomini's movements go toward the square. A, B, C; D, E, F; and G, H, I all ascend to (and in the first instance go beyond the square. The sequences G, G, D, A; H, H, E, B; and I, I, F, C also move towards the square (in the latter case, the goal is overshot). B, the compartment directly over the main portal, *is* a square and consequently the summa figuratio of both movements.

Furthermore, the vertical ascents of the compartments *match* those of their orders, as was not the case with the Rucellai. Doric moves to Corinthian to Composite; and as we saw earlier, in this period the Corinthian was held to be nobler than the Composite. Hence the piano nobile, the only floor to possess a perfect square, possesses also the noblest order. The increases in column height, entablature height, and intercolumniation (except for the portal) as we ascend, *match* the decrease in shaft width. As to distribution, there is a strong duity relationship between the wide *unique* portal compartments, A, B, C; the *pair* of portal-flanking compartments, D, E, F; and the *quartet* of outer, narrowest compartments, G, H, I.

Among the compartment proportions there is the portal stack itself, which rises from 7:8 to the perfect 1:1 and recedes to 4:5. The portal-flanking pair take up where the central group left off, at 4:5, moves on to a rough 1:1 and then to 6:7 on the upper floor. And in the outer quartet we go upward from 3:4 to about 6:7 to almost 1:1. Thus each type of stack has three types of proportion: perfect (1:1), orthodox (4:5, sesquiquartal; 3:4, sesquitertial), and unorthodox (7:8, 6:7). In terms of the duity relationship they can be stated as follows:

	Axis	*Pair*	*Quartet*
	unorthodox	orthodox	orthodox
	↓	↓	↓
	perfect	perfect	unorthodox
	↑	↑	↓
	orthodox	unorthodox	perfect

One must concede that this is an eminently more well-knit scheme than Alberti's. But nonetheless it derives directly from him, and the achievement entails certain losses. The visual effect of Rossellino's facades is poor compared to that of the Rucellai. In the Piccolomini Palace the upper cornice is too heavy for its own order. And I have already mentioned the too-abrupt change in shaft widths and the general squatness of the compartmentation. Also, the fact that C is a horizontal rectangle, and the only one in the facade, is unfortunate.

There are other interesting things about this palace. The main facade scala appears, with modifications, on three sides of the building rather than only on one as in the Rucellai. The fourth facade at Pienza, the so-called "theatrum" overlooking the garden and Mount Amiata, consists of a set of three superimposed arcades, as if

5.11 Theatrum, Piccolomini Palace (Alinari)

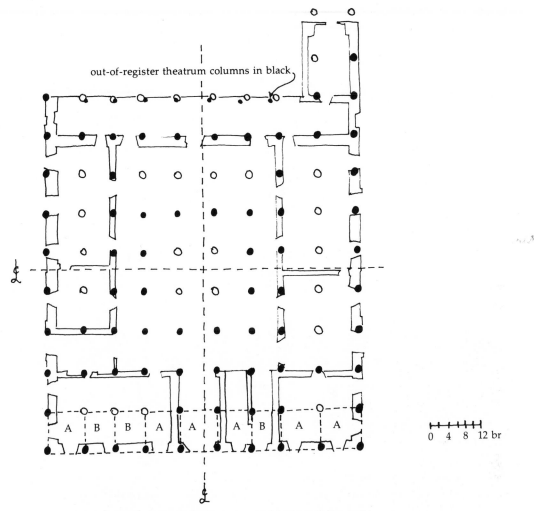

out-of-register theatrum columns in black

A ┊ B ┊ B ┊ A ┊ A ┊ A ┊ B ┊ A ┊ A

0   4   8   12 br

5.12 Plan of Piccolomini Palace as hypostyle, after Stegmann and Geymüller

it were a three-dimensional version of the other three closed facades (Fig. 5.11). The whole is thus a solid block penetrated by a rational scheme of plane and volume tesserae on all sides, not unlike Cesariano's sectioned cube, or his Greek forum.

The same can be said of the plan (Fig. 5.12). This is a 9-x-9-bay columnar grid. There are two modules, A which occurs 54 times on the ground floor, and B which occurs 27 times. A is an 8-br square and B a rectangle 6 x 8 br. Thus as in the Medici we have a 100-column hypostyle. But the distribution is less regular. The Medici was marred only by the right-hand file of wider bays. The Piccolomini has a more internal irregularity: ABBAAABAA. Once again, the center of the whole is not aligned with the main portal, vestibule, and courtyard. The Piccolomini is often called the first axially symmetrical—in the modern sense—civic building of the Renaissance. Yet here we learn that in some ways it is even less symmetrical than the Medici. Nonetheless, aside from the irregular module distribution, the correspondence between columns and walls is more nearly perfect than in the Medici. There is no lack of alignment whatever on the first floor, except for the small partitions halfway up the sides, and more significantly the theatrum arcade columns.

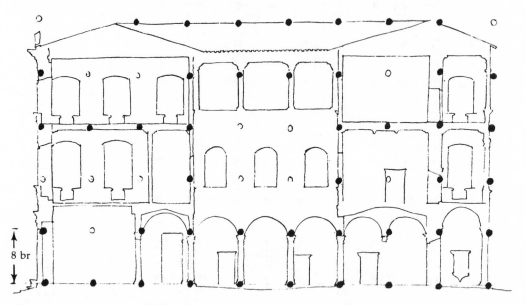

5.13 Section of Piccolomini Palace as hypostyle, after Stegmann and Geymüller

On the other hand the Piccolomini section view as a hypostyle (Fig. 5.13) seems to work less well than in the earlier structure. An 8-br uniform grid functions best but is not really right. This grid articulates the courtyard columns at base and capital, the third-floor level, third-floor courtyard capitals, the roof ridge, and a few other places. But the rest of the "columns" float, and not on linee occulte.

5.5 Poggioreale. The previous achievements all belong to the period before 1460 or so. Then (so far as I can tell without hunting down further specimens) there comes a pause. We wait more than twenty years, till the mid-1480s, for another period of activity. (The same lull, by the way, occurs in the composition and publication of treatises.) But then Francesco di Giorgio rewrites his book, Alberti and Vitruvius are printed, and Poggioreale and Poggio a Caiano are constructed, followed shortly by the Strozzi Palace. At least two Pythagorean churches, Santa Maria del

Calcinaio in Cortona and Santa Maria delle Carceri in Prato, also belong to this flurry.

One of the key monuments is Poggioreale. This villa was erected outside the eastern walls of Naples for Alfonso of Calabria around 1485–1489. The architect was Giuliano da Maiano, followed by Francesco di Giorgio. The plan of the palace can basically be reconstructed (Poggioreale itself no longer stands) from a much-published sketch made by Baldassare Peruzzi when he visited the villa in the early sixteenth century (Fig. 5.14). I have applied Peruzzi's sketch to a 6-x-6-bay grid (Fig. 5.15)—which does no essential injustice to the layout and proportions of the original sketch. The ground plan is a 10:11 rectangle, and a 72-column 8 x 9 hypostyle. There are two modules, a square and a sesquialter. The square, B, appears a total of 35 times as a whole module, and 7 times (across the center belt of Figure 5.15) as a half-module. A appears, always entire, 14 times; and 15 of B's appearances and 6 of A's are "invisible." This accounts for all volumes and articulations shown in, or deducible from, Peruzzi's sketch. Unfortunately, we do not know the size of the villa so that no dimensions or scale can be deduced. But we do know something about room functions: the four corner pavilions contained bedroom suites, one per floor, and the central courtyard, two stories high, was an open-air dining room.

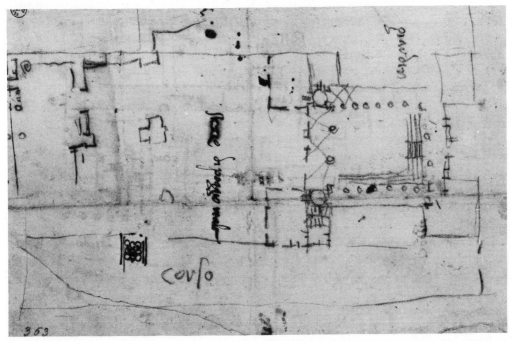

5.14 Sketch of villa at Poggioreale, Naples (no. 363A), by Baldassare Peruzzi (Courtesy Uffizi, Florence)

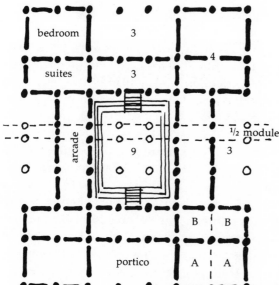

5.15 Peruzzi's sketch as hypostyle

Carlo Pedretti has recently identified a tiny Leonardo sketch (Fig. 5.16) as another plan of Poggioreale (*Leonardo at Romorantin* 42ff.). This can be dated to around 1506–1508. It is on one of the sheets of the Codex Atlanticus along with a project for a villa for Charles d'Amboise. (The latter, apparently, is set within a hypostyle loggia.) Again we have no idea of scale. But Leonardo has drawn his version of Poggioreale with corner pavilions whose own inner corners overlap the corners of the central rectangle. The basic idea, therefore, is of a quincunx whose central element is large and whose corner elements are smaller and identical to each other. This notion, which is very new at this time, will reappear again and again in the course of the sixteenth century. Also, Leonardo's sketch can neatly assimilate a grid that is slightly different from that shown in Figure 5.15: an 11-x-11-column arrangement with square bays (Fig. 5.17). The tristyle loggias on each front are unorthodox. Otherwise, as is not the case with the Peruzzi sketch, the bay distributions are cubic: 9 tesserae in each pavilion, 36 in the center courtyard, 8 in each portico area. At this point I cannot be sure if the Leonardo sketch actually portrays Poggioreale or not, and if it does, whether it corrects misinformation in the Peruzzi sketch. I will address these problems in another publication. But from what has been shown here, and from the literature on Poggioreale, we do know that it was the first of our palaces to boast two pairs of identical facades, a four-quarter plan—that is, a plan in which each quarter of the building is identical—and to have marked, true, central cross-axes.

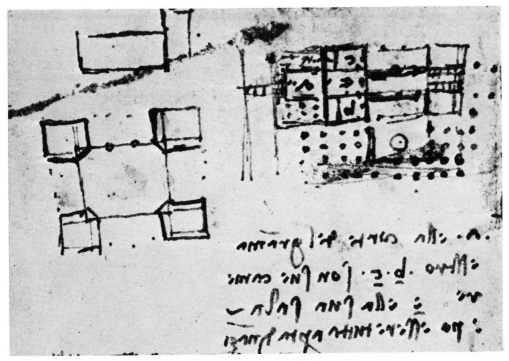

5.16 Plan of Poggioreale [?] and of villa for Charles d'Amboise (around 1506–1508), from Leonardo, Codex Atlanticus 231 2-b (Courtesy Biblioteca Ambrosiana, Milan)

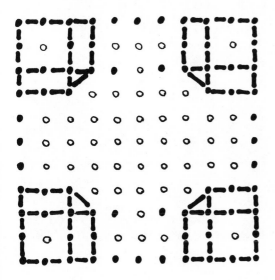

5.17 Leonardo's sketch as hypostyle

5.6 Poggio a Caiano. There is a tradition that Lorenzo himself designed Poggioreale. Perhaps, like Filarete's Duke, he dictated its numberforms to the architect-amanuensis. The same thing is said of the Neapolitan villa's contemporary, Poggio a Caiano, Lorenzo's own country palace outside Florence, begun about 1485 (Fig. 5.18). In this case the working architect was Giuliano da Sangallo. The building is set on a high arcaded terrace 90 br square. The main facade, not counting the terrace, is 72 x 24$\frac{1}{2}$ br. There are no cubic values or sequences on the exterior of the palace.

The plan, however, does fit into our development (Fig. 5.19). It is a 6-x-6-bay square using three modules. A is 14 x 14 br and appears 16 times. B is 12 x 14 and appears 8 times. C is 11 x 14 and appears 12 times. Each corner block consists of 4 A's, arranged as a square. B, in pairs, form the vertical axis. The horizontal axis consists of pairs of C. There are "loose" or nonmodular walls in the rear, for rooms devoted to ignoble functions, naturally. That is proper. Less proper is the fact that the central portico is out of alignment. This is an Ionic tetrastyle temple front, in antis, with very wide intercolumniations (4 d). The jarring relationship between

5.18 Villa at Poggio a Caiano, outside Florence, by Giuliano da Sangallo and others, begun around 1485 (Alinari)

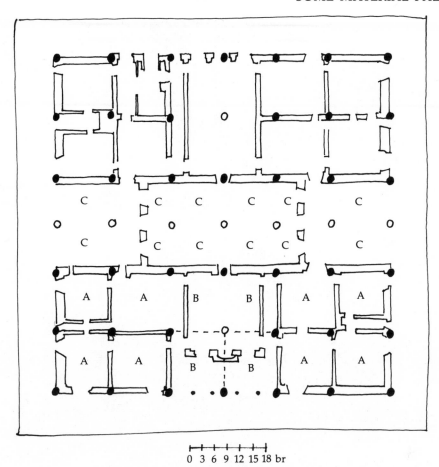

5.19 Plan of Poggio a Caiano as hypostyle, after Stegmann and Geymüller

this portico and its flanking windows, on the one hand, and the modular distribution of the building on the other, suggest that the portico may be an afterthought or
a later addition. Of the hypostyle columns, 40 are visible and 9 invisible. These latter mark out the open cross-axis of the whole (Fig. 5.19).

But the real importance of Poggio a Caiano is that, like Poggioreale, its plan is a
quincunx with four square modular clusters, that is, 4A at each corner, and an open
hall in the center, 4C plus flanking pairs of $\frac{1}{2}$C's. This disposition of interior volumes is reflected on the exterior (as was also the case with Poggioreale) in the form
of projecting wings (Fig. 5.20). So Poggio a Caiano, like Poggioreale, belongs to two
worlds, that of Quattrocento Pythagoreanism and that of the new quincunx plans
that were to be exploited in the High Renaissance.

5.20 Flank of Poggio a Caiano

5.7   The Strozzi Palace. The Strozzi Palace (Fig. 5.21) is attributed to Giuliano da Sangallo, Il Cronaca, and Benedetto, brother of Giuliano da Maiano. It was apparently begun in 1489, close on the heels of Poggio a Caiano. Of its three visible facades two are twins 9 bays wide. The main facade (on the right) is 13. All bays are completely regular; but otherwise the heavy rustication, the window and door trim, and the huge cornice (though now with a full entablature) recall the Medici Palace. The Strozzi, however, is much bigger, 92 br along the main front instead of 72.

The plan (Fig. 5.22) is an exact 4:3 rectangle. The courtyard plan is 5:3. The distribution of rooms, circulation spaces, and so forth, is bilaterally symmetrical in the modern sense with a few minor exceptions. The true axes of the block are consis-

5.21 Strozzi Palace, Florence, by Giuliano da Sangallo, Il Cronaca, and Benedetto da Maiano, begun 1488 (Alinari)

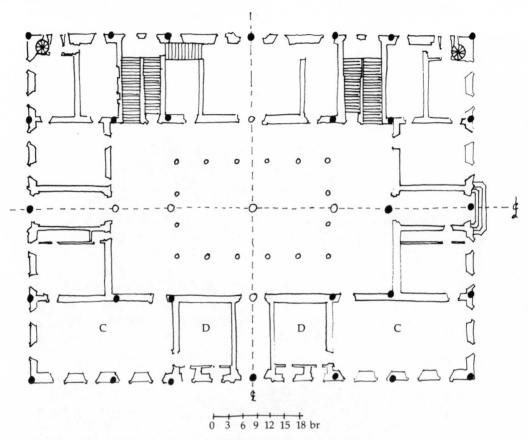

C   D   D   C

0   3   6   9   12   15   18 br

5.22 Plan of Strozzi Palace as hypostyle, after Stegmann and Geymüller

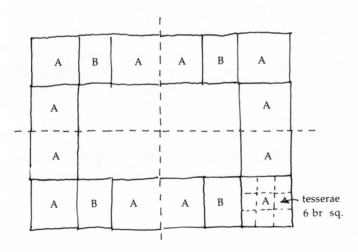

A	B	A	A	B	A
A					A
A					A
A	B	A	A	B	A

tesserae
6 br sq.

5.23 Modular analysis of ground floor of Strozzi Palace

tently articulated. And the block, whose complete measurements are 92 x 72 x 54 br high, is a harmonic series, cubic both in dimensions and proportions. There are two modules, A which is 18 br square and B which is 12 x 18 (Fig. 5.23). The pattern on the main facade is ABA, ABA. The large bays can be subdivided into small tesserae 6 br square. The tesserae meanwhile emphasize the imperfect assimilation of the courtyard columns. The grid of bays is 7 x 5 columns or 6 x 4 bays. The subgrid of smaller tesserae is 17 x 13 columns or 16 x 12 bays—221 columns and 192 bays in all. As at Poggio a Caiano the cross-axis is marked by invisible columns, this time 11 in number.

In the section (Fig. 5.24) the same spaces carry up through the third and fourth floors. And there is indeed a progression, from barrel- or cross-vaulted rooms on the ground floor, to the piano nobile which is cross-vaulted only, and then to the ceiled third and fourth floors. The crests of the cross vaults are about 12 br high, those of the barrel vaults 15. The distance from the parapets to the tops of the openings in the upper tiers of the courtyard is about 9 br. We thus have cubic heights for four cube-base modules throughout. The two rooms marked C in Figure 5.22 are 15 x 30 x 15 br high, or double cubes. The rooms marked D are 12 x 9 x 12 br high.

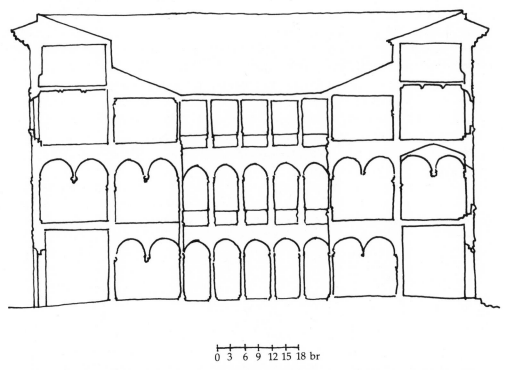

0 3   6 9 12 15 18 br

5.24 Section of Strozzi Palace, after Stegmann and Geymüller (barrel vaults on lower left and right)

The attic rooms (shown in Fig. 5.24) are $7^1/_2$ br high, and more ignoble in comparison.

The section view also makes clear the prominence, within the building, of the two regular rows of arched openings, openings that form vaults in the rooms and arcades in the courtyard. These arched openings are approximately all of the same dimensions, 12 br high by 6 wide (measuring intercolumniations or the equivalent). Seen in section they suggest an arcaded exterior facade or even recall Leonardo's sketch in Figure 4.18. One reads the outer, taller roomstacks as wings and the central arcaded areas as a frontispiece. Or we can compare the two lower floors of the Piccolomini facade (Figs. 5.9, 5.10). Such a comparison suggests that a facade can be the exterior reflex of a cutaway section, and that the cubical bays of the inner rooms and the arched components of the courtyard can be expressed as the outer walls of buildings, proclaiming a hypostyle matrix within, and suggesting how the outer arcuated shell is integrated with the interior vaults.

The development of cubic architecture in material buildings seems to cease with the Strozzi Palace. A new kind of planning, based as noted on the quincunx, on the colossal order and temple front, and on intraposed grids at different scales, appears in place of the Pythagoreanism I have discussed, with its more regular lattices and its exploitation of the cube. The scala, with its discrete articulations and subtle modulations toward the square, is abandoned. Symmetry in the modern sense replaces the earlier sort, at least in actual building practice. Instead of configurations like the one in Figure 5.25 (left) in other words, we get patterns, either of plan or elevation, like that in Figure 5.25 (right). And in a *built* building by Palladio, for example the Villa Rotonda at Vicenza, there are practically no cubic number values or sequences despite the central plan, four identical facades, and the derivation of the whole from the square. Nor does the Rotonda use the room-volume formulas Palladio expounds in his own book. On the other hand Palladio's unbuilt project, the Leonardo Mocenigo villa, is a perfectly Pythagorean palace. Thus the progress of cubism in material buildings is observable but neither uninterrupted nor longlasting. We do see in its brief material career, however, the full complement of

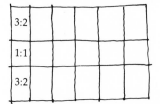 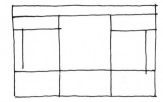

5.25 Cubic grid (left) versus quincunx grid (right)

cubic qualities—Pythagorean sequences, procreating numberforms, social/number-form hierarchies, mathematical ratios, scalae, at least one instance of metonymy, paired and corresponding facades, and of course hypostyle plans and sections. But beyond this, as the earlier chapters show, the mystical and speculative nature of Pythagorean architectural theory after Cesariano tends to push this whole body of thought and belief out of the realm of practice and into that of theory and instruction.

6. Summary

I began this book by linking three Vitruvian notions. The first was Vitruvius' belief that the cube was the source of all number and form. The second was his idea that an unseen, formative hypostyle pervades the Greek temple. The third was cubices rationes, the descriptive principles favored by classical poets. In line with these notions Vitruvius was able to "reduce" a Greek temple to an algorithm. Such algorithms compressed, stored, and transmitted the temples they described, making them reproducible across separations of time and space. One also infers that Vitruvius would have defined these algorithms as "signifieds," while the temples themselves were "signifiers." Hence a given temple's meaning is the algorithm describing it.

This notion, that the meaning of a work of art can consist of a verbal/numerical description of it, led to the further notion that describing (or designing) a building is a separate, higher activity from building one. The result, in the Renaissance, was a hierarchical concept of design and construction similar to the Pythagorean hierarchy; a hierarchy in which number ranked highest, and then respectively drawings, model, and material structure.

6.1 Point. The Renaissance reconstruction of this classical cubism began with Alberti. He revived the Pythagorean principles of duity and cube-as-source. Filarete then sacralized the design-construction hierarchy, while Ficino, going even further, held that buildings possessed magical powers and that their architects were demiurges. For Ficino, buildings, through their hierarchies of design, construction, and appearance, were explanatory models—that is, signifieds—of human thought and of the cosmos. The basic pattern of this explanation is the affinity table, a device that is reflected in grid plans and facades. These things are therefore visible fragments of the invisible, infinite grid or temple of the cosmos. And like that cosmic temple the architectural one is filled with beings, with humanlike numberforms which constantly procreate and populate within their geometrical frames, forcing reluctant matter back into the condition which it instinctively tries to escape from; forcing materiality back to Idea, and to the First of Cubes.

Francesco di Giorgio enlarged the square's family by adding to it genealogical

192

lines of temples or rooms. Cesariano decided that cubices rationes were embodied in the Sectioned Cube. This, with its inner and outer cubic goals, its interfaces, tessera components, and cubic distributions, was Cesariano's Vitruvian model for architectural description and design. Cesariano also prepared the way for Barbaro's version of compound proportions. And with Barbaro not only numbers but sensegenres are compounded: there are ratios of spaces to silences and of words and lines or chapters to numbers, surfaces, and solids. Numberforms engage in literary and musical actions. And where in Ficino their sexual actions had been purely mathematical, in Barbaro they are subject to desire and friendliness.

In equating the square with God, Serlio reaffirmed the cube-face as both source and destiny of material form and of number. On its way to and from this source a numberform may pass through discordant states that, via duity, ultimately balance out. Redemption—that is, being put back on the path to the First of Cubes—is possible even for the most irregular shapes. Lomazzo, following another of Serlio's ideas, described the Greek 100-column hall as the common ancestor of all good architecture, while Poggioreale was the re-founder, the new Adam, of this race. So firmly did Scamozzi the philosopher-architect believe in the hypostyle principle that he recreated a classical villa a priori on the basis of Pythagorean principles.

Not all the designs I have analyzed here obey all cubic criteria. And cubism is not all there is to the Pythagorean palace. It is merely its beginning and its end. And even if actual designs or material buildings fall into randomness, irrationality, and obliqueness, they can be rescued by those who divine the architect's intentions. Being possessed or occupied by correct invisible counterbuildings, material buildings can, as Pico della Mirandola might say, "pass into the nature of gods as if they themselves were gods." The critical as opposed to the creative aspect of the Pythagorean palace is just this ability to take visible chaos and "reduce" it to hidden symmetries and proportions, and thence to its cubic point-source.

6.2 Line. The tools for this procedure are duity, cubices rationes, linee occulte, Man the Beautiful, and the corpo transparente. The term cubices rationes varies in meaning. It can include the whole Pythagorean cult or else merely be the cubic signified (as with Cesariano)—that is, the properly phrased, numbered, and laid-out description. Linee occulte are the hidden lines that serve as axes, sightlines, or joints between visible building components. They are graphic ascents and descents, the rails of metempsychosis, the numberforms' bloodlines. Linee occulte are also the ruled guidelines or "ruling" unseen grids that animate designs and reveal their hypostyle underpinnings. As a visible building sheds its material husk in the observer's mind, and as his mind is filled with the structure's geometrical and numerical beauty—at first in admiration and then perhaps in Colonna-like ecstasy—the image thins into its occult lineaments and melts into Idea.

In this context we can think of Brunelleschi's parchment-strip grid with which he measured ruins as being both workaday and magical. It was a measuring contrivance; but in its miniature form drawn on paper, and with its letters and numbers "which Filippo alone understood," it was also a conjuring square for the duplication of the vanished structure, a hermetic signified. Brunelleschi's public computations can even be thought of as a nuptial performance, a magical coition between the architect and the ruin which resulted in the storage or gestation, and in the possible new birth or reproduction, of the dead temple. Alberti on the other hand eschewed diagrams. His lineamenta were mental and literary. But his is only a higher transformation than Brunelleschi's: the building in Alberti is a set not of graphic symbols but of verbal and numerical ones. It is thus aligned with, and in the closest possible relation to, general truths.

Filarete's "lines," meanwhile, are those of family and parenthood—marriage lines. And he describes in homely detail the architectural metempsychosis through linee occulte that Alberti had referred to in a more stately way. Filarete also combines Brunelleschi's full-scale lattice at the site with the notion of a drawn modular grid. Francesco di Giorgio, after restudying Vitruvius, integrated functional bloodlines and hierarchies into the kinship model. The module grid became a table of social organization. An annotated plan could be a true as well as a metaphorical affinity table. As such it was both the signified of the building and that of the building's users. Francesco employs duity, symmetry, and other cubic tools so as to enlarge the affinities between plan and function.

Serlio brings perspective into the picture. His linee occulte are invisible connections or influences between features within the building; but they are also invisible connections between the observer's eye and an actual or portrayed structure. Serlio's perspective grid is like Ficino's cosmic temple. Both equally develop from point (viewpoint) out to infinity and back to point (vanishing point). Traveling along those coordinates the image can be both infinitely large and infinitely small. Thus a perspective construction is a way of visualizing a metempsychosis. In this and other ways linee occulte are truly occult: they manifest or even create hidden links. Among these links are astrological influences and gravity, which for Barbaro is the architectural form of love.

6.3   Plane. The plane in Neoplatonism, while formed of lines, is also the child, lover, and parent of Man the Beautiful. This again goes back to Vitruvius. He had equated the column, the human physique, and the square and circle. The whole development which we looked at in Chapter 3 really only fills out this proposition. Surface reality is made of contiguous or overlapping squares and circles. These in turn are generated by the physiques of beings such as angels, intelligences and daemons—beings shaped like man but invisible, of different sizes, and magical or divine. In Ficino the continual coitions of these beings impose new flows of form on matter. They continually assimilate material chaos to the invisible geometric scala that rises to heaven. Such physiques pervade not only the cosmos but the worlds of our thoughts, books, and drawings. They constitute our letters, numbers, codes, algorithms. A printed page is an army of dancing daemons. A hypostyle hall is a forest of beings. An architectural plan is a group of gesticulating gods. Plans are also prone colossi; facades are upright ones. A multistory columnar facade is a scala of slaves or servants, men, matrons, virgins, and divinities. Such a facade is a population table, a racial history, and a genealogy.

And the architect is basically a procreator. Like Jupiter he scoops female matter out of earth to shape and give life to populations. He is matter's paramour. In Filarete, the architect, after coition with the patron, produces an infant, the model. The same sort of thing happens more complexly with Francesco di Giorgio. For him the city is a great prone god or goddess, the parent of smaller beings cavorting on it like genii or tributaries on a statue of Nilus. Francesco di Giorgio feminizes this architecture, and sees the female orders as superior, physically, morally, and stratigraphically, to the male. Leonardo meshes a human proportional system with these creaturely procreators. Thus once again number is the catalyst that turns a human body into a geometrical surface. And a "symmetrical" man is a complex of inches, hands, arms, feet, and heads that total out to what Vitruvius would call summae figurationes. In a more Ficinian way Colonna, the passionate calculator-speculator, loves and woos dreamed temples numberwise, and measures their seminal virtue. And just as Francesco establishes that the link between a town square and a church facade, or between a column and a compartment, is their use of a human and ideal, albeit variously scaled figure, so it is Leonardo's man, alone, who connects the square with the circle. And so too in the Piccolomini facades the different-sized, differently proportioned compartments are connected or blood-related only by the pilasters that have dictated their heights and widths in diameters, in braccia, and in proportions.

In his diagram of the man in square and circle Cesariano emphasizes these notions of a seminal virtue and nuptial numerology that integrate more and more territory through their extending grid. Earth itself can be thus measured. There are infinities of micro and macroworlds, and symmetries that go right down to our very veins and knuckles. "De immenso et innumerabilibus," as Giordano Bruno would put it. At the same time Cesariano's Persian captives suggest the metaphor of suffering in the anthropomorphized building. Consisting of patient immured creatures, this building rises tirelessly over us. Its motionlessness measures our freedom, if we have the eyes, the virtù, to do the measuring. Other sixteenth-century writers systematically connect various types of istorie—and these are of course further "petrified" activities—with these personification-orders and surfaces.

Serlio reinforces the orders' connection with the inhabitants of the palaces they guard and support. And he expands the expressive possibilities of the system by emphasizing the metonymic use of the orders. Now, not only may a part stand for a whole, but the parts of different orders, the rustic Tuscan and the girlish Corinthian, may "mix it" in some scene of strife or seduction. Serlio expands the social hierarchies that these actors belong to by introducing the bestial and bastard orders. The theater is itself a world, the auditorium being a set of concentric social spheres within a square, and the stage a reflecting world or society of buildings, of huts, houses or palaces, inhabited by actors in dramatized istorie. Thus do Serlio's viewers, at socially correct distances from the one perspective viewpoint, obliquely see that fragment of the cosmos-temple which it is proper for them to see.

A theater "palace" is a world of creatures. But a palace can also be one single creature. Palladio makes the parallel between the building and the creature, with rooms as organs, some ugly and some beautiful, some to be emphasized, others to be hidden. For him architecture is a robed and ornamented body. To Lomazzo, meanwhile, the palace facade is a world-creature. Not only whole beings but being-fragments—throats, heads, legs, ankles—pervade it. And within the single world-being is a world *of* beings: for the orders still speak of their allied gods, and they also rise layer on layer through the levels and races of man and woman to the freed superhuman statues of the rooftop, the "symblegmata," who have at last shuffled off their mortal column-coils at heaven's level.

Scamozzi humanizes further. He again sees the architect as father, mother, and lover. And he posits the family in its palace moving from room to room in accordance with seasons and weather, propelled by attraction and controlled by status. The Composite order is now the human Roman. Across the facade each column rules its kingdom, a surface zone dictated and measured by that column. Not only intercolumniations but the dimensions and distributions of windows, balconies, and niches obey the king.

6.4   Solid. I have defined the corpo transparente in two ways: first as a transparent solid that pervades, and shapes and contains, a material structure; second, as imagined volumes rising from a drawn plan. A corpo transparente is thus the cube and the fulfillment of a facade or a plan.

At first, with Brunelleschi, we may discern the notion of the corpo transparente in the edifice of words that is built up from a ground plan. Alberti went further: he established volume-parameters as a form of corpi transparenti for courtyards and outer blocks. The cruciform penetrations of these volumes by windows and doors were also controlled by mathematical formulas. They generated more invisible parallelepipeds, which now not only defined perimeters but linked walls. Francesco di Giorgio's individual volume formulas for each room vary the hierarchies of corpi transparenti. By using these formulas, and formulas for the orders, a sketchbook plan could be transformed into an invisible (though probably incomplete) building—a corpo transparente in my second sense. Leonardo's cutaway perspective sections continue the emphasis on cubic volume and cubic number, hierarchically arranged. And of course Serlio's perspective constructs, while made of linee occulte (and in part of linee visibili) always become transparent solids. Palladio, elaborating the volume-hierarchy idea, creates hierarchies within hierarchies, like Barbaro's ratios of ratios; hierarchies that descend from the pure cube through harmonic, geometric, and arithmetical ratios to random ones. With other writers, the perspective rendering, as a work of art and virtù, became the second kind of corpo transparente. The concept of symmetry was developed so that the internal and external hypostyles were to seem to coalesce, and so that exterior orders and their compartments would procreate interior volumes.

6.5   Material Palaces. The Medici Palace adumbrates cubic architecture. And soon after the Medici we see facade grids, composed of the orders, expressing real or unreal inner hypostyles. Horizontal and vertical ascents toward the square appeared, as did symmetries between pilaster diameters, braccia, proportions, and window and portal modules. Facades tended to pair off and procreate, and also to look like plans and sections. In Poggioreale we have the first structure in our series whose real axes were accurately articulated. With such buildings, and with the Strozzi where the facade grid is implicit but perfect, cubic architecture's materialization is complete.

But at this very moment Poggioreale and Poggio a Caiano forecast something new: the quincunx plan with overlapping modules. This begot a more intricate architecture that departed from cubic principles. But if the "material" Pythagorean palace was dead after about 1500—and further research may show that this was not completely the case—it had a long theoretical afterlife. Architects continued to learn to think in terms of the primacy of the cube when they read such writers as Serlio, Cesariano, Barbaro, Palladio, Lomazzo, and Scamozzi. And in a sense these writers, preaching Pythagoreanism purely as a learning device, and conceiving of these ideas as purely theoretical and hence "immaterial," most truly ennobled architecture.

Bibliography

I have omitted, in the works listed below, those already listed at the front of the book under Abbreviations for Works Cited. In general, I have emphasized writings that deal with the Pythagorean or anthropomorphic content of architecture.

The Bibliography is divided into four parts. The first deals with Pythagoreanism, Neoplatonism, and proportion; the second lists writings on and by the architects and architectural writers discussed in the text. Part 3 deals with related architecture in general, and the last part is a short listing of works on the buildings discussed in Chapter 5.

1. Pythagoreanism, Neoplatonism, and Proportion

Adam, James. *The Nuptial Number of Plato: Its Solution and Significance.* London: Clay, 1891. Adam fastens on the number 216 (i.e. $3^3 + 4^3 + 5^3$), though without citing Vitruvius. This number, with its factors, was considered by Plato a determinant of human gestation and growth. The world, in its own birth, growth, and decadence, was said to follow the same rhythm in a magnified version. On p. 41n Adam shows that Plato's original text is ambiguous as to whether, in nuptial copulation, couples were forbidden to beget children at the wrong time, or whether it was a question of the wrong couples copulating.

——. *The Republic of Plato.* 2 vols. Cambridge: Cambridge University Press, 1963. For a revised version of Adam's theory about the nuptial number see 2.545C and pp. 264–312 of the commentary.

Aulus Gellius. *Noctes atticae,* ed. P. K. Marshall. 2 vols. Oxford: Clarendon, 1969. See 1.20.3ff. for theories about the cube.

Baldi, Bernardino. *Cronica de matematici overo epitome dell'istoria delle vite loro.* Urbino: Monticello, 1707. A sixteenth-century view of the famous mathematicians, classical and Renaissance, including Vitruvius (pp. 40–41), Alberti (pp. 98–99), and Barbaro (p. 134).

Bell, Eric Temple. *Numerology.* Baltimore: Williams & Wilkins, 1933.

Belli, Silvio. *Quattro libri geometrici . . . il primo del misurare con la vista . . .* [1565]. Venice: Megietti, 1595. Printed in many editions, this treatise on the ocular estimation of size, distance, and proportion, is one of several that taught the virtù of mental geometry.

Bindel, Ernst. *Pythagoras: Leben und Lehre in Wirklichkeit und Legende.* [Stuttgart]: Freies Geistesleben, 1962. For the themes discussed in the present book, cf. Bindel, pp. 163ff. (number theory, the tetractys, factoring).

Bongus [Bungus], Petrus. *Numerorum mysteria ex abditis plurimarum disciplinarum fontibus hausta.* Paris: Chaudière, 1618. This book, first published in 1585, is one of the most elaborate Renaissance treatises on numerology. There is a chapter on each number in all its bearings.

Bousquet, Jean. *Le trésor de Cyrène à Delphes.* Paris: University of Paris, 1952. On pp. 77ff. the author deals with cubic theory in antiquity.

Brachert, Thomas. "Symmetria," *Jahresbericht und Jahrbuch der Schweizerisches Institutes für Kunstwissenschaft* (1967), 87ff.

Brumbaugh, Robert S. *Plato's Mathematical Imagination: The Mathematical Passages in the Dialogues and Their Interpretation.* Bloomington: Indiana University Press [1954]. For the nuptial number see pp. 107ff.

Burckert, Walter. *Lore and Science in Ancient Pythagoreanism,* trans. E. L. Minar. Cambridge: Harvard University Press, 1972. The purpose of this book is to disentangle ancient Pythagoreanism from Aristotle's and Plato's versions of it. A classic work with a full bibliography.

Cassirer, Ernst. *Individuum und Kosmos in der Philosophie der Renaissance* [1927]. Darmstadt: Wissenschaftliche Buchgesellschaft, 1963.

Cerrera Vera, Luis. *Libros del arquitecto Juan Bautista de Toledo.* El Escorial: Imp. del real monasterio, 1951. This architect owned a number of books on magic—12 out of a total of 41 by my count.

Conant, Levi Leonard. *The Number Concept: Its Origin and Development* [1896]. New York and London: Macmillan, 1931.

Cusanus, Nicolas [Nicholas of Cusa]. *De docta ignorantia,* in Cusanus, *Opera omnia,* ed. E. Hoffmann and E. Klibansky. Heidelberg: Meiner, 1932 et seq. For Cusanus' discussion of spheres see 2.103–10.

Della Porta, Giovanni Battista. *Magiae naturalis libri XX* [1589?]. Amsterdam: Weyerstraten, 1664. For number theory and sexual interpretations of the cosmos.

Denkinger, Marc. "L'énigme du nombre de Platon et la loi des dispositifs de M. Diès," *Revue des études grecques,* 68 (1955), 38–76.

deVogel, C. J. *Pythagoras and Early Pythagoreanism.* Assen: Van Gorcum, 1966. For ideal numbers see pp. 202–7.

Dickson, Leonard Eugene. *History of the Theory of Numbers.* 3 vols. Washington: Carnegie Institution, 1919–1923. For Pythagoreanism see 1.3–50, for figured numbers 2.1–39.

Edgerton, Samuel Y., Jr. "Florentine Interest in Ptolmaic Cartography as Background for Renaissance Painting," *Journal of the Society of Architectural Historians,* 33 (1974), 275–92. The modular grid in perspective design and in mensuration.

Favaro, Giuseppe. "Misure e proporzioni del corpo humano secondo Leonardo," *Atti del r. istituto veneto de scienze lettere ed arti,* 88 (1918–1919), 109–90. An extremely important article; see section 3.6 above.

Frank, Erich. *Plato und die sogenannten Pythagoreer.* Halle: Niemayer, 1923. Cf. particularly p. 3 and pp. 269ff. for the Duity Principle based on the musical theories of Philolaos.

Gafuri, Franchino. *Practica musicae sive musicae actiones in IV libris* [1496], ed. and trans. Clement A. Miller. N.p.: American Institute of Musicology, 1968. Book IV is devoted to the numerical proportions of intervals between canto and tenor.

——. *De harmonia musicorum instrumentorum opus.* Milan: Pontano, 1581. Discusses various planetary modes or scales—male, female and "promiscuous" (4.13).

Garin, Eugenio. *La cultura filosofica del rinascimento italiano.* Florence: Sansoni [1961].

———. "Le elezioni e il problema dell'astrologia in umanesimo e esoterismo," *Atti del V. convegno internazionale di studi umanistici* (1960), 17–37.

———. "Magia ed astrologia nella cultura del rinascimento," *Belfagor*, 5 (1950), 657–67. A good introductory essay.

———. *Studi sul platonismo medievale.* Florence: Le Monnier, 1958. For Platonism and especially the study of the *Timaeus* in the Middle Ages.

———. *Umanesimo e esoterismo.* Padua: CEDAM, 1960.

———. *L'umanesimo italiano: Filosofia e rita civile nel rinascimento.* Bari: Laterza, 1952.

Ghyka, Matila C. *Le nombre d'or.* 2 vols. Paris: Gallimard [1931]. The second volume deals, among other things, with the transmission of Pythagorean magic in architecture. Most of the examples are either Gothic or Baroque.

Gilbert, Neal. *Renaissance Concepts of Method.* New York: Columbia, 1960.

Giorgi, Francesco [also known as Francesco Giorgio and as Francesco Zorzi; not to be confused with the Sienese architect and writer Francesco di Giorgio Martini who is treated in this book]. *De harmonia mundi totius cantica tria* [1525]. Paris: Berthelin, 1544. The man-in-circle as the creation and manipulated artifact of the various gods, right down to the particular flare of the nostril, etc. Canticus 3, ch. 2; also Canticus 1, Tonus 6, ch. 2; and Canticus 6, ch. 23–30. But Giorgi seems mainly to be dealing with the medieval concept of the "homo-universus." On folio 100v of this edition is a table of human symmetries matched up with those of the city of Jerusalem the Golden.

Graf, Hermann. "Bibliographie zum Problem der Proportionen." Speyer: Landesbibliothek, 1958.

Heninger, S. K., Jr. "Some Renaissance Versions of the Pythagorean Tetrad," *Studies in the Renaissance,* 8 (1961), 7–35. A rather simple article but with a useful bibliography of that neglected subject of Renaissance Pythagoreanism. The author does not make it clear whether all the tetrads he cites were intended by their creators to be Pythagorean.

———. *Touches of Sweet Harmony: Pythagorean Cosmology and Renaissance Poetics.* San Marino, Cal.: Huntington Library, 1974.

Hermes Trismegistus [att. to]. *Corpus hermeticum,* ed. and trans. A. D. Nock and A.-J. Festugière. 4 vols. Paris: Belles-Lettres, 1945–1954. For the discussion of God and Nature each falling in love with Man, see the *Poimandre,* 1, tractati 1, 14, 15, 16. In the present book, however, I have used the translations in Ficino 2^2.1836–73.

Herrera, Juan de. *Tratado del cuerpo cúbico conforme a los principios y opiniones de "Arte" de Raimundo Lulio.* Madrid: Plutarco, 1935. Herrera tries to create a full-fledged knowledge taxonomy out of medieval cubic doctrines.

Hopper, Grace Murray. "The Unregenerated Seven as an Index to Pythagorean Number Theory," *American Mathematical Monthly,* 43 (1936), 409–13. A good bibliography of classical writers on numerology and a discussion of numbers' sex and virginity.

Hopper, Vincent F. *Medieval Number Symbolism* [1938]. New York: Cooper Square, 1969. A fine basic introduction. Pythagoreanism is discussed on pp. 33–49.

Kieskowski, Bohdan. *Studi sul platonismo del rinascimento in Italia.* Florence: Sansoni, 1936. See ch. 3 and 4 on Ficino, the Academy, etc.

Michel, Paul-Henri. "L'esthétique arithmétique du Quattrocento: Une application des médiétés pythagoriciennes à l'"esthétique architecturale," *Mélanges de philosophie, d'histoire, et de la littérature offerts à Henri Hauvette.* Paris: N.p., 1934. Deals mainly with Alberti.

Michel, Paul-Henri. *Les nombres figurés dans l'arithmétique pythagoricienne.* Paris: Conférances du Palais de la découverte, ser. D, no. 56 [1958].

———. *De Pythagore à Euclide: Contributions à l'histoire des mathématiques préeuclidiennes.* Paris: Belles-Lettres, 1950. This is the most complete modern work on the subject. For number forms see pp. 295ff. and for factoring pp. 329ff.

Pacioli [Paccioli], Luca. *De divina proportione* [1509]. Milan: Fontes ambrosianae, 1956. Pacioli castigates non-Pythagorean architects for being like tailors, i.e. mere craftsmen, rather than mathematicians.

Panofsky, Erwin. *Idea: Ein Beitrag zur Begriffsgeschichte der älteren Kunsttheorie* [1924]. Berlin: Hesslin, 1960.

———. "The History of the Theory of Human Proportions as a Reflection of the History of Styles," in Panofsky, *Meaning in the Visual Arts.* Garden City: Doubleday [1955], pp. 55–107.

———; Klibansky, Raymond; and Saxl, Fritz. *Saturn and Melancholy.* New York: Basic Books, 1964.

Pythagoras [att. to]. *I versi aurei di Pitagora,* ed. Antonio Farina. Naples: Libreria scientifica [1962]. The Greek text and Italian translation. An excellent bibliography. For the tetrad see p. 40n.

Robb, Nesca A. *Neoplatonism of the Italian Renaissance.* London: Allen & Unwin [1935].

Rose, Paul L. "Humanist Culture and Renaissance Mathematics: The Italian Libraries of the Quattrocento," *Studies in the Renaissance,* 20 (1973), 46–105.

Scholfield, P. H. *The Theory of Proportion in Architecture.* Cambridge: Cambridge University Press, 1958. An overcited, cranky, narrow book.

Shumaker, Wayne. *The Occult Sciences in the Renaissance: A Study of Intellectual Patterns.* Berkeley: University of California Press, 1972. Good but hostile to the subject. Ficino is discussed in the chapter on Hermetism.

Steinetz, Kate T. "A Pageant of Proportion in Illustrated Books of the Fifteenth and Sixteenth Centuries in the Elmer Belt Library of Vinciana," *Centarus,* 1 (1951), 309–33. Interesting illustrations from an English translation of Lomazzo's treatise, and anthropomorphic alphabets from Geoffroy Tory, *L'art et science de la vraye proportion des lettres.* Paris: V. Gaultherot, 1549.

Taylor, Alfred E. *A Commentary on Plato's Timaeus.* Oxford: Clarendon Press, 1928. Very full.

Warburg, Aby. *La rinascita del paganesimo antico,* ed. Gertrud Bing. Florence: Nuova Italia [1966].

Wittkower, Rudolf. *Architectural Principles in the age of Humanism* [1949]. London: Tiranti, 1967. See the bibliography in the preface and in appendix II. For the man-in-square-and-circle see pp. 14–16, for Pythagoreanism and the cube p. 103, and for volume formulas pp. 107–13, 128–30. For Barbaro on proportion see pp. 137–42.

———. "The Changing Concept of Proportion," *Daedalus,* 89 (1960),199–215.

———. "Systems of Proportion," *Architects' Year Book,* 5 (1953), 9–18.

Young, Grace C. "On the Solution of a Pair of Simultaneous Diophantine Equations Connected with the Nuptial Number of Plato," *Proceedings of the London Mathematical Society,* ser. 2, vol. 23 (1925), 27–44.

2. Architects and Architectural Writers

Alberti

Alberti, Leone Battista. *Opere volgari,* ed. Cecil Grayson. 3 vols. Bari: Laterza, 1960 et seq. See 2:299–300 for Pythagorean precepts and 3:135 for ocular surveying.

Behn, Irene. *Leone Battista Alberti als Kunstphilosoph.* Strassburg: Heitz, 1911. Still one of the best books on Alberti. For his Pythagoreanism see p. 32 (symmetry and unity), pp. 94–106 (numbers, proportions, point/line/plane/solid, etc.), and pp. 132–37 (domestic architecture).

Gengaro, Maria Luisa. *Leon Battista Alberti: Teorico e architetto del rinascimento.* Milan: Hoepli, 1939. A good solid but abstract (and unillustrated) book.

Gadol, Joan. *Leon Battista Alberti: Universal Man of the Renaissance.* Chicago: University of Chicago Press [1969]. See p. 109 for the perfect number 6.

Grayson, Cecil. Biographical article in *Dizionario biografico degli italiani.*

Klotz, Heinrich. "L. B. Albertis 'De re aedificatoria' in Theorie und Praxis," *Zeitschrift für Kunstgeschichte,* 32 (1969),93–103. This article makes excellent new parallels, based on new readings of Alberti's text, between the treatise and the executed buildings.

Krautheimer, Richard. "Alberti and Vitruvius," *Studies in Western Art: Acts of the XX International Congress of the History of Art.* Vol. 2, *The Renaissance and Mannerism.* Princeton: Princeton University Press, 1963, pp. 42–52.

——. "Alberti's Templum Etruscum," *Münchner Jahrbuch der bildenden Kunst,* ser. 3, vol. 12 (1961), 65–72.

——. "Alberti's Templum Hetruscum," *Kunstchronik,* 13 (1960), 364–66, and the discussion by members of the audience who heard this lecture, pp. 367–68. One objection to Krautheimer's reconstruction was that he applied unwarranted semicircular apses to the building.

Lang, Susi. " 'De lineamentis': L. B. Alberti's Use of a Technical Term," *Journal of the Warburg and Courtauld Institutes,* 28 (1965), 331–35. Lang defines lineamenta primarily as ground plans that generate the essentials of the elevations. She does not, however, consider the term in a Pythagorean context.

Mancini, Girolamo. *Vita di Leon Battista Alberti.* 2nd ed. Florence: Carnesecchi, 1911. Still the best book on Alberti's life and work as a whole. Mancini emphasizes on p. 285 how in the *Ludi matematici* Alberti sought to teach ocular measurement of distance and proportion. For the Palazzo Rucellai and the document asserting that it was planned to be fourteen bays wide see pp. 418–28.

Westfall, Carroll William. *In This Most Perfect Paradise: Alberti, Nicholas V, and the Invention of Conscious Urban Planning in Rome, 1447–55.* University Park, Pa.: Pennsylvania State University Press, 1974.

Barbaro

Alberigo, Giuseppe. Biographical article in *Dizionario biografico degli italiani.* With a good bibliography

Zoubov, V. P.; Venediktov, A. I.; and Petrovsky, Th. A., eds. *Desiat knig ob arkhitectouré Vitrouvia s commentariem Daniele Barbaro.* Moscow: n.p., 1938. Text based on the Italian edition of 1556 but with the main additions and variants of the second Italian and of the Latin editions, and with a full bibliography.

Brunelleschi

Benevolo, Leonardo; Chieffi, Stefano; and Mezzetti, Giulio. "Indagine sul S. Spirito di Brunelleschi," *Quaderni dell'Istituto di storia dell'architettura*, ser. 16 (1968), 1–52. A model article
on modular analysis.

Heydenreich, Ludwig H. "Spätwerk Brunelleschis," *Jahrbuch der preussischen Kunstsammlungen*, 52 (1931), 1–28. For Brunelleschi in Rome see pp. 8–9.

Horster, Marita. "Brunelleschi und Alberti in ihrer Stellung zur römischen Antike," *Mitteilungen des Kunsthistorisches Instituts zu Florenz*, 17 (1973), 29–64. A detailed rundown on
each man's probable or possible knowledge of ancient Roman monuments.

Nyberg, Dorothea. "Brunelleschi's Use of Proportion in the Pazzi Chapel," *Marsyas*, 7
(1954–1957), 1–7. An interesting attempt to demonstrate Brunelleschi's use of various mathematical ratios including the double Golden Section. However the author seems insecure
mathematically, for example, quoting two-number sequences as "arithmetical" and "geometric" ratios, and using the term "harmonic" where she might less misleadingly have
said "harmonious."

Wittkower, Rudolf. "Brunelleschi and Proportion in Perspective," *Journal of the Warburg and
Courtauld Institutes*, 16 (1953), 275–91. This article discusses the ratios by which objects
diminish in perspective, and thus can be linked up with Renaissance thought on man-as-
microcosm/macrocosm-as-man.

Cataneo

Berti, Elena. "Un manoscritto di Pietro Cataneo agli Uffizi e un codice di Francesco di
Giorgio Martini," *Belvedere*, 7 (Jan.–July 1925); 100–103. Further proof that Francesco's
ideas were known in the High Renaissance.

Cesariano

Caporali, Gianbatista. *Architettura. Con il suo commento et figure. Vetruvio in volgar lingua
raportato*. Perugia: Bigazzini, 1536. This includes only the first five books and is directly
lifted from Cesariano.

Leoni, Francesca. "Il Cesariano e l'architettura del rinascimento in Lombardia," *Arte lombarda*, 1 (1955), 90–97, with some earlier bibliography and an interesting discussion of
symmetry.

Colonna

Casella, Maria Teresa, and Pozzi, Giovanni. *Francesco Colonna: Biografia e opere*. 2 vols.
Padua: Antenor, 1959. Proves beyond doubt that Colonna was the author of the *Hypnerotomachia*, thus superseding a great deal of earlier writing.

Colonna, Francesco. *Hypnerotomachia Poliphili*. Critical edition edited by Giovanni Pozzi and
Lucia A. Ciapponi. 2 vols. Padua: Antenor, 1964. The notes contain fascinating analyses
of the architecture mentioned by Colonna, including a grid analysis of the gate I discuss
above in section 3.8. I do not quote from this edition, however, because it is so hard to
come by.

Croce, Benedetto. "La 'Hypnerotomachia Poliphili,' " *Quaderni della critica*, 6 (1950), 46–54.
Reprinted in Croce, *Poeti e scrittori del pieno e del tardo rinascimento*. 3 vols. Bari: Laterza,
1952, 3.42–52. Stresses Poliphilus' erotic attachments to buildings.

Gnoli, Domenico. "Il sogno di Polifilo," *La bibliografia*, 1 (1899–1900), 189–212, 266–83. A
brilliant, complete discussion of structure, sources, and language.

Ilg, Albert. *Über den kunsthistorischen Werth der Hypnerotomachia Poliphili: Ein Beitrag zur Geschichte der Kunstliteratur in der Renaissance.* Vienna: Braunmüller, 1872.

Praz, Mario. "La 'Hypnerotomachia Poliphili,' " *Paragone letteratura,* vol. 1, no. 6 (1950), 11–16. On Poliphilus' passion for architecture and hieroglyphs which makes him "adhere amorously to the contours of things."

Schneider, René. "Note sur l'influence artistique du songe de Poliphile," *Etudes italiennes,* 2 (1920), 1–16, 65–73. On copies and adaptations of the woodcuts in the 1499 edition.

Weiss, Roberto. "A New Francesco Colonna," *Italian Studies,* 16 (1961), 78–83. A useful review of Casella and Pozzi's work.

Ficino

Chastel, André. *Marsile Ficin et l'art.* Geneva and Lille: Droz-Giard, 1954. The standard work on this subject, full of illuminating points.

Gandillac, Maurice de. "Astres, anges et génies chez Marsile Ficin," in E. Garin, ed., *Umanesimo e esoterismo.* Padua: CEDAM, 1960, pp. 85–109.

Ivanov, N. "La beauté dans la philosophie de Marsile Ficin et de Léon Hébreu," *Humanisme et Renaissance,* 3 (1936), 12–21. Shows that for these Neoplatonists corporal beauty was the simulacrum of heavenly beauty; and that there are correspondences between sight, light, and intelligence on the one hand, and hearing, harmony, and the soul on the other.

Kristeller, Paul Oskar. "Ficino and Pomponazzi on the Place of Man in the Universe," *Journal of the History of Ideas,* 5 (1944), 220–42.

——. *Il pensiero filosofico di Marsilio Ficino.* Florence: Sansoni [1953].

——. *Supplementum ficinianum.* 2 vols. Florence: Olschki, 1937. Previously unpublished letters and minor writings.

——. "Unità del mondo nella filosofia di Marsilio Ficino," *Giornale critico della filosofia italiana,* 15 (1934), 395–423. An interesting article on attributes, graduations, symbols, and things symbolized.

Marcel, Raymond. *Marsile Ficin.* Paris: Belles-Lettres, 1958. An excellent biography written from an orthodox Roman Catholic viewpoint.

Saitta, Giuseppe. *Marsilio Ficino e la filosofia dell'umanesimo.* 3d ed. Bologna: Fiammenghi & Nanni [1954]. More of a textbook than a monograph.

Schiavone, Michele. *Problemi filosofici in Marsilio Ficino.* Milan: Marzorati, 1957.

Toffanin, Giuseppe. *Storia dell'umanesimo dal XIII al XIV secolo.* 3d ed. Bologna: Zanichelli, 1947. See pp. 251–72, which discuss Ficino and the arts.

Filarete

Filarete [real name Antonio Averlino]. *Trattato di architettura,* ed. A. M. Finoli and L. Grassi. 2 vols. Milan: Polifilo, 1972. This is now the standard edition, though I have used the earlier John Spencer edition in the text since I had begun my research with it.

Lazzaroni, Michele, and Muñoz, Antonio. *Filarete: Scultore e architetto del secolo XV.* Rome: Modes, 1908. Still the best biography.

Onians, John. "Alberti and ΦΙΛΑΡΕΤΗ: A Study in their Sources," *Journal of the Warburg and Courtauld Institutes,* 34 (1971), 96–114. Deals with Filarete's Golden Book and his Hellenism versus Alberti's Ciceronianism.

Saalman, Howard. "Early Renaissance Architectural Theory and Practice in Antonio Filarete's *Trattato di architettura,*" *Art Bulletin,* 41 (1959), 89–106.

Sinisi, Silvana. "Filarete nascosto," *Quaderni contemporanei.* Salerno: Università degli studi, vol. 5. Attempts to show Filarete's Hermetism.

——. "Il palazzo della memoria," *Arte lombarda,* 38–39 (1973), 150–60.

Spencer, John R. "La datazione del trattato del Filarete desunta dal suo esame interno," *Revista d'arte,* 31 (1956), 93–103.

——. "Filarete and Central Plan Architecture," *Journal of the Society of Architectural Historians,* 17 (1958), 10–18.

Tigler, Peter. *Die Architekturtheorie des Filarete.* Berlin: De Gruyter, 1963. A curiously ineffectual book though with some good things in it.

Leonardo

Förster, Otto. *Bramante.* Vienna: Schroll, 1956. See pp. 135–37 for Leonardo's and Bramante's mathematical interests.

Garin, Eugenio. "La cultura fiorentina nell'età di Leonardo," *Belfagor,* 7 (1952), 272–89. On Leonardo's empiricism.

Hellmann, Günter. "Die Zeichnung Leonardos zu Vitruv," in *Mouseion: Studien aus Kunst und Geschichte für Otto H. Förster.* Cologne: DuMont Schauberg [1960], pp. 96–98.

Heydenreich, Ludwig H. *Leonardo da Vinci.* 2 vols. New York: Macmillan; Basel: Holbein [1954]. On p. 80 Heydenreich claims that Leonardo demonstrated for the first time "the basic forms for plans and perspectival architectural drawings of the Renaissance," which includes "the fully developed cross-section done in perspective." But see above, section 4.6.

Metternich, Franz Graf von. "Der Kupferstich Bernardos de Prevedari aus Mailand von 1481," *Römisches Jahrbuch für Kunstgeschichte,* 11 (1967–1968), 1–108. Metternich arrives at a slightly different reconstruction than Bruschi. See above, section 4.6.

Panofsky, Erwin. *The Codex Huygens and Leonardo da Vinci's Art Theory.* London: Warburg Institute, 1940. See especially pp. 19–30, 35–58, 100–126, this last including a discussion of the man-in-circle-and-square.

Pedretti, Carlo. *A Chronology of Leonardo da Vinci's Architectural Studies after 1500.* Geneva: Droz, 1962. See especially pp. 37–48.

——. *Leonardo: The Royal Palace at Romorantin.* Cambridge: Harvard University Press, 1972. Important discussions of Poggioreale and of Leonardo's geometric planning.

Solmi, Edmondo. "Le fonti dei manoscritti di Leonardo da Vinci," *Giornale storico della letteratura italiana,* 10–11 (1907–1908), Supp. p. 231. Leonardo and the cube-as-earth, disagreeing with Ficino.

Toni, G. B. de. "Intorno un codice di Luca Pacioli nella Biblioteca di Ginevra e i disegni geometrici dell'opera 'De divina proportione' attribuiti a Leonardo da Vinci," in *Per il IV. centenario della morte di Leonardo da Vinci.* Bergamo: Instituto di studi vinciani in Roma, 1929, pp. 1–64.

Lomazzo

Barelli, E. S. "Il Lomazzo o il ruolo delle personalità psichologiche nella estetica dell'ultimo manierismo lombardo," *Arte lombarda,* vol. 3, no. 2 (1958), 119ff.

Casati, Carlo. *Leone Leoni d'Arezzo scultore e Giovanni Paolo Lomazzo.* Milan: Hoepli, 1884.

Klein, Robert. "Les sept gouverneurs de l'art selon Lomazzo," *Arte lombarda,* vol. 4, no. 2 (1959), 277ff.

Paris, Annamaria. "Sistema e giudizi nell'*Idea* del Lomazzo," *Annali della scuola normale superiore di Pisa* (1953), 187–96.

Martini, Francesco di Giorgio

Berti, Elena. "Un manoscritto di Pietro Cataneo agli Uffizi e una codice di Francesco di Giorgio Martini," *Belvedere*, 7 (1925), 100–103.

Betts, Richard J. "The Architectural Theories of Francesco di Giorgio." Diss., Princeton University, 1971.

Brinton, Selwyn. *Francesco di Giorgio Martini of Siena.* 2 vols. London: Besant, 1934–1935.

Eisler, J. "Remarks on Some Aspects of Francesco di Giorgio's Trattato," *Acta historiae artium academiae scientiarum hungaricae*, vol. 18, nos. 3–4 (1972), 133–231. Discusses grids, anthropomorphic columns, and the like, but in a random and ill-informed manner.

Fehring, Günter. "Studien über die Kirchenbauten des Francesco di Giorgio." Diss., University of Würzburg, 1956.

Hellmann, Günter. "Proportionsverfahren des Francesco di Giorgio Martini." *Miscellanea bibliothecae hertzianae*, 16 (1961), 157–66. On Francesco's use of "quadratura"; while Hellmann's diagrams work in terms of the plans he analyzes (which are from the treatises), he doesn't show that quadratura is necessary in order to create the plans, or that Francesco advocated quadratura in his writings.

Lotz, Wolfgang. "Ein Dinokratesdarstellung des Francesco di Giorgio," *Mitteilungen des Kunsthistorisches Institutes in Florènz*, 5 (1937–1940), 428–33.

Lowic, Larry. "Francesco di Giorgio on the Design of Churches." Diss., Yale University, 1976.

Millon, Henry. "The Architectural Theory of Francesco di Giorgio," *Art Bulletin*, 40 (1958), 257–61. A key article which shows that one of Francesco's man-generated plans and facades can be superimposed over the plan and facade of a building attributed to Francesco (Santa Maria del Calcinaio, Cortona). However a number of possible objections remain. The Codex Magliabecchiana drawing Millon reproduces (my Fig. 3.5 above) has an aspect ratio of 5:3. Millon's redrawing of this, fitted to the church facade, has a different proportion, 3:2. Secondly, the vertical grid Millon fits over the plan matches it inconsistently—that is, sometimes fitting outsides of walls, sometimes their interiors, and not in accordance with any regular scheme.

Papini, Roberto. *Francesco di Giorgio architetto.* 3 vols. Florence: Electa, 1946. See especially 1.201–7 for the town halls and palaces in the treatises that I discuss.

Reti, Ladislao. "Francesco di Giorgio Martini's Treatise on Engineering and Its Plagiarists," *Technology and Culture*, 4 (1963), 287–98. Shows that copies of Francesco's drawings of machines were made by other treatise writers throughout the sixteenth and seventeenth centuries.

Scaglia, Gustina. Review of Maltese edition of Francesco's treatises, *Art Bulletin*, 52 (1970), 439–42. Discusses the attribution of drawings to Francesco and his debt to the Sienese engineer Taccola. Scaglia is also the author of an important forthcoming study on the Vitruvius manuscripts utilized by Francesco.

Palladio

Ackerman, James S. *Palladio's Villas.* Locust Valley, N.Y.: J. J. Augustin [1967]. A charming general introduction with some substance in the footnotes.

Burger, Fritz. *Die Villen des Andrea Palladio: Ein Beitrag zur Entwicklungsgeschichte der Renaissance-Architektur*. Leipzig: Klinkhardt & Biermann [1909]. Still the best, most analytical, and most well-knit study of this subject.

Forssmann, Erik. *Palladios Lehrgebäude: Studien über den Zusammenhang von Architektur und Architekturtheorie bei Andrea Palladio*. Stockholm: Almqvist & Wiksell [1965]. A good chapter on Palladio's theories and on Palladio and Vitruvius.

——. *Visible Harmony: Palladio's Villa Foscari at Malcontenta*. N.p.: Sveriges arkitektur-museum, 1973. This booklet shows that Malcontenta was built in exact obedience to the dimensions published for it by Palladio in the *Quattro libri*.

Pane, Roberto. *Andrea Palladio*. Turin: Einaudi, 1961. The most critically sensitive book on Palladio.

Pée, Herbert. *Die Palastbauten des Andrea Palladio*. Würzburg, 1939. Still valuable.

Puppi, Leonello. *Palladio*. Boston: New York Graphic Society, 1973. The most complete, best-illustrated monograph-catalogue.

Rosci, Marco. "Rassegna degli studi palladiani 1959–69," *L'arte*, n.s. 10 (1970),114–24. This well-annotated bibliography brings out the current quarrel between the "Wittkowerians" and the "Panians" over the interpretation of Palladio's buildings.

Scamozzi

Barbieri, Franco. *Vincenzo Scamozzi*. Vicenza: Cassa di risparmio di Verona, Vicenza, e Belluno, 1952.

——. "Vincenzo Scamozzi studioso ed artista," *Critica d'arte*, 8 (1949–1950), 222–30, 300–313.

Jannaco, Carmine. "Barocco e razionalismo nel trattato d'architettura di Vincenzo Scamozzi (1615)," *Studi secenteschi*, 2 (1961), 47–60.

Pallucchini, Rodolfo. "Profilo di Scamozzi," *Bollettino del centro internazionale Andrea Palladio*, 3 (1961), with bibliography.

——. "Vincenzo Scamozzi e l'architettura veneta," *L'arte*, 7 (Jan. 1936), 3–30.

Puppi, Lionello. "Sulle relazioni culturali de Vincenzo Scamozzi," *Ateneo veneto* (1969), 49–66.

Scamozzi, Vincenzo. *Taccuino di viaggio da Parigi a Venezia, 14 marzo–11 maggio 1600*, ed. Franco Barbieri. Venezia: Istituto per la collaborazione culturale [1959].

Zorzi, Giangiorgio. "Rivendicazione di alcuni scritte giovanili di Vincenzo Scamozzi," *Atti del'istituto veneto di scienze lettere ed arti: Classe di scienze morali e lettere*, 113 (1955), 139–208.

Serlio

Colombier, Pierre du, and d'Espezel, Pierre. "L'habitation au xvie siècle, d'après le sixième livre de Serlio," *Humanisme et Renaissance*, 1 [1934?], 31–49. A good early article on Serlio's middle-class housing, bringing out his hierarchical tendencies.

Dinsmoor, William B. "The Literary Remains of Sebastiano Serlio," *Art Bulletin*, 24 (1942), 55–91, 115–54. The classic article on Serlio bibliography and on the then-unpublished manuscripts of the so-called Sixth Book in Munich and New York.

Huber, Martin R. "Sebastiano Serlio: Sur une architecture civile 'alla parisiana'; ses idées sur le 'gusto francese e italiano,' sa contribution à l'évolution vers le classicisme français," *L'information de l'histoire de l'art*, vol. 10, no. 1 (Jan.–Feb. 1965), 9–17.

Rosci, Marco. *Il trattato di architettura di Sebastiano Serlio*. Milan: ITEC, 1966. The strongest study of Serlio so far, with much earlier bibliography, though perhaps in his analysis of Serlio's sources Rosci neglects Francesco di Giorgio.

Rosenfeld, Myra Nan. "Sebastiano Serlio's Late Style in the Avery Library Version of the Sixth Book on Domestic Architecture," *Journal of the Society of Architectural Historians,* 28 (1969), 155–72.

——. "Sebastiano Serlio's Drawings in the Nationalbibliothek in Vienna for his *Seventh Book on Architecture*," *Art Bulletin,* 56 (1974), 400–409.

Serlio, Sebastiano. *Sesto libro delle habitationi di tutte li gradi degli uomini* [facsimile of Munich ms], ed. Marco Rosci. Milan: ITEC, 1966.

Tafuri, Manfredo. "Il mito naturalistico nell'architettura del '500," *L'arte,* n.s. 1 (1968), 7–36. A fascinating discussion of ideas like those mentioned above in section 3.8.

Vitruvius

Baldi, Bernardino. *De verborum vitruvianorum significatione.* . . . Augustae vindelicorum: n.p., 1612. A nearly contemporary glossary; symmetry is discussed on p. 169, the definitions matching the one I give having been taken from Philander and from Vitruvius himself.

Ciapponi, Lucia A. "Il 'De architectura' di Vitruvio nel primo umanesimo," *Italia medioevale e umanistica,* 3 (1960), 59–99. A full, excellent study. It deals not only with editions and commentaries but with quotations from and references to Vitruvius. The article shows that, despite the oft-repeated myth of Poggio Bracciolini's "discovery" of the Vitruvius ms at Montecassino in 1414 (which in any case occurred in 1416 at St. Gall), Vitruvius' entire text was well known in Italy from the days of Petrarch.

Ebhardt, Bodo. *Die zehn Bücher der Architektur des Vitruv und ihre Herausgeber (seit 1484)* [1918]. Ossining, N.Y.: Saltock, 1962. A well-illustrated gathering of major Vitruvius texts up to 1915 with a catalogue of editions.

Fontana, P. "Osservazioni intorno ai rapporti di Vitruvio colla teorica dell'architettura del rinascimento," in *Miscellanea di storia dell'arte in onore di I. B. Supino.* Florence: Olschki, 1933, pp. 305–22.

Koch, Herbert. *Vom Nachleben des Vitruv.* Baden-Baden: Verlag für Kunst und Wissenchaft, 1951.

Krinsky, Carole Herselle. "Seventy-Eight Vitruvius Manuscripts," *Journal of the Warburg and Courtauld Institutes,* 30 (1967), 36–70.

Mortet, V. "Recherches critiques sur Vitruve et son oeuvre. VI. Le canon des proportions du corps humain," *Revue archéologique,* ser. 4, vol. 13 (1909), 57–77.

Zoubov, Vassili Pavlovitch. "Vitruve et ses commentateurs au xvie siècle," in *La science au seizième siècle: Colloque international de Royaumont, 1957.* Paris: Hermann, 1960, pp. 67–90. Brings out the extreme number orientation of the period very well.

3. Related Architecture in General

Ammanati, Bartolomeo. *La città: Appunti per un trattato,* ed. Mazzino Fossi. Rome: Officina, 1970.

Bandmann, Günter. "Ikonologie des Ornaments und der Dekoration," *Jahrbuch für Ästhetik und allgemeine Kunstwissenschaft,* 4 (1959), 232–58. An important discussion of anthropomorphic and zoomorphic architecture.

Biermann, Hartmut. "Das Palastmodell Giuliano da Sangallos für Ferdinand I. König von Neapel," *Wiener Jahrbuch für Kunstgeschichte,* 23 (1970), 154–95. A curiously sullen article, with good things in it but far too many comparisons.

Chastel, André. *Art et humanisme à Florence au temps de Laurent le Magnifique.* Paris: Presses universitares, 1959. This book ends with the author's own interesting attempt at an affinity table alla Lomazzo (p. 487):

Raphael	Eros	Glory
Leonardo	Hermes	Grandeur
Michelangelo	Saturn	Tragedy

Chierici, Gino. *Il palazzo italiano dal secolo xi al secolo xix* [1957]. New ed. Milan: Vallardi [1964].

Del Migliore, Ferdinando L. *Firenze, città nobilissima*. . . . Florence: Stella, 1684.

Fiocco, Giuseppe. *Alvise Cornaro: Il suo tempo e le sue opere*. Vicenza: Pozza, 1965. For Cornaro's architectural treatises see pp. 155ff.

Forssmann, Erik. *Dorisch, jonisch, korinthisch: Studien über den Gebrauch der Säulenordnungen in der Architektur des 16.–18. Jahrhunderts*. Stockholm: Almqvist & Wiksell [1961]. A charming book that would have been better with a short introduction on Quattrocento developments. Also, the richer, more fantastic ideas, even of the authors Forssmann does consider (e.g. Serlio), are scanted.

Goldthwaite, Richard A. "The Florentine Palace Considered as Domestic Architecture," *American Historical Review*, 77 (1972), 977–1012.

Lotz, Wolfgang. "Der Raumbild in der italienischen Architektur-zeichnung der Renaissance," *Mitteilungen des Kunsthistorischen Institutes in Florenz*, 7 (1956), 193–226. Discusses the development of the perspective cross section and Filarete's Temple of Vice and Virtue.

Marchini, Giuseppe. *Giuliano da Sangallo*. Florence: Sansoni, 1942. Contains a full bibliography.

Mazzanti, Riccardo and Enrico, and del Lungo, Torquato. *Raccolta delle migliori fabbriche antiche e moderne di Firenze*. 2 vols. Florence: Feroni [1876].

Patzak, Bernhard. *Palast und Villa in Toscana*. Leipzig: Klinkhardt & Biermann, 1912–1913.

Rowe, Colin. "Mathematics of the Ideal Villa," *Architectural Review*, 101 (Mar. 1947), 101–4. A clever article making comparative grid analyses of the plans of a Palladio and a LeCorbusier villa.

Rusconi, Giovantonio. *Della architettura*. Venice: Gioliti, 1590. Profusely illustrated with specimens of Vitruvius' temple plans, the Persian Portico, etc.

Sambin, Hughes. *Oeuvre de la diversité des termes*. Lyon: Durant, 1572. This book contains a hierarchical "world" of columns and terms, which are shown as humanoid statues. They first emerge from primeval rock formations as Tuscan peasants, and then pass through successively more civilized stages into a superhuman and supernatural state, the Composite.

Schiapparelli, Attilio. *La casa fiorentina e i suoi arredi nei secoli xiv e xv*. Florence: Sansoni, 1908. An indispensable study with rich yields from contemporary inventories; no plans, however.

Shute, John. *The First and Chief Groundes of Architecture* [1563]. London: Country Life, 1912. Like Sambin's book, noted above, this elaborates the analogy of the column and the human type, adding classical gods as well.

Sindona, Enio. "Introduzione alla poetica di Paolo Uccello," *L'arte*, 17 (1972), 7–100. On rational three-dimensional cubic space as a form of Neoplatonism.

Soergel, Gerda. "Untersuchingen über den theoretischen Architekturentwurf von 1450–1550 in Italien." Diss., University of Cologne, 1958.

Stegmann, Carl von, and Geymüller, Heinrich von. *Die Architektur der Renaissance in Toscana*. 12 vols. Munich: Brückmann, 1885–1907. The Medici, Rucellai, and Piccolomini Palaces are all in vol. 2, though no full elevations are given—on the assumption perhaps that the facade bays are all the same. As to the Rucellai (2.5), slightly different widths than mine are given for the pilasters (see above, section 5.3). Where my measurement of the ground-floor shafts came to exactly 1 br, Stegmann and Geymüller give 0.53m or $^9/_{10}$ br for these shafts, and for those of the piano nobile 0.557 or just under 1 br.

Stein, Otto. "Die Architekturtheoretiker der italienischen Renaissance." Diss., University of Karlsruhe, 1914. A summary work which omits Barbaro.

Tafuri, Manfredo. *L'architettura del manierismo nel '500 europeo.* Rome: Officina, 1966. An excellent book by the most original mind now engaged in Renaissance architectural research. Much discussion of magic—Bruno, Paracelsus, etc.

Vasari, Giorgio, the Younger. *La città ideale,* ed. Virginia Stefanelli. Rome: Officina, 1970. Many grid plans.

Vignola, Giacomo Barozzio. *Regole delli cinque ordini* [1562]. Rome: De Rossi [166?].

Weber, Henny. "Achsialität und Symmetrie im Grundriss des italienischen Profanbaus von der Frührenaissance bis zum Frühbarock." Diss., University of Berlin, 1937. An important book.

Weise, Georg. "Vitalisomo, animismo, e panpsichismo, e la decorazione nel '500 e nel '600," *Critica d'arte,* vol. 6, no. 36 (1959), 375–98; vol. 7, no. 38 (1960), 85–96. Shows how "stemmi" and other devices of architectural decoration become more and more anthropomorphic and creaturely due to hermetic influence.

4. Buildings Discussed in Chapter 5

Stegmann and Geymüller (see Part 3 above) give plans and elevations for all the material palaces except Piccolomini. Mario Bucci, *Palazzi di Firenze,* 3 vols. (Florence: Vallecchi, 1973), discusses only those in Florence. It is not particularly accurate but does bring together material not easily available elsewhere.

Medici Palace

Bombe, Walter. "Der Palazzo Medici-Riccardi und seine Wiederherstellung," *Monatshefte für Kunstwissenschaft,* 5 (1912), 216–23.

Bulst, Wolfgang. "Die ursprüngliche innere Aufteilung des Palazzo Medici in Florenz," *Mitteilungen des Kunsthistorischen Institutes in Florenz,* 14 (1969–1970), 369–92.

Fabriczy, Cornel von. "Michelozzo di Bartolommeo," *Jahrbuch der preussischen Kunstsammlungen,* 25 (1904), app. pp. 34–117. See pp. 38 and 41 for the dating of the Medici Palace.

Hatfield, Rab. "Some Unknown Descriptions of the Medici Palace in 1459," *Art Bulletin,* 52 (1970), 232–49.

Hyman, Isabelle. "Notes and Speculations on San Lorenzo, Palazzo Medici, and an Urban Project by Brunelleschi," *Journal of the Society of Architectural Historians,* 34 (1975), 98–120. Shows from archival entries that the Medici data is not 1444 but "closer to" 1446.

Morisani, Ottavio. *Michelozzo architetto.* Turin: Einaudi, 1951, pp. 51–56.

Warburg, Aby. "Die Baubeginn des Palazzo Medici," in Warburg, *Gesammelte Schriften.* 2 vols. Leipzig and Berlin: Teubner, 1932, 1.165–68.

Piccolomini Palace, Pienza

Carli Enzo. *Pienza: La città di Pio II.* Rome: Editalia [1966].

Heydenreich, Ludwig H. "Pius II. als Bauherr von Pienza," *Zeitschrift für Kunstgeschichte,* 6 (1937), 105–46.

Poggio a Caiano

Chastel, André. *Art et humanisme à Florence au temps de Laurent le Magnifique*. Paris: Presses universitaires, 1959. Interesting essays on the Etruscan Revival, Poggio a Caiano (pp. 151–57), perspective, Leonardo, and Neoplatonism.

Foster, Philip. "Lorenzo de' Medici's Villa at Poggio a Caiano." Diss., Yale University, 1974.

Hamberg, Per G. "The Villa of Lorenzo the Magnificent at Poggio a Caiano and the Origin of Palladianism," *Figura*, n.s. 1 (1959), 76–87.

Poggioreale

Frommel, Christoph L. *Die Farnesina und Peruzzis architektonisches Frühwerk*. Berlin: De Gruyter, 1961, pp. 90–97.

Hersey, George L. *Alfonso II and the Artistic Renewal of Naples, 1485–1495*. New Haven: Yale University Press, 1969, pp. 58–70, with earlier bibliography.

——. "Poggioreale: Notes on a Reconstruction, and an Early Replication." *Architectura*, 1 (1973), 13–21.

Rucellai Palace

Dezzi Bardeschi, Marco. "Il complesso monumentale di S. Pancrazio a Firenze ed il suo restauro," *Quaderni dell'Istituto di storia dell'architettura*, ser. 12, fascs. 73–78 (1966), 1–66. For the Rucellai see pp. 15–19. New documents date the palace to 1450/51.

Kent, F. W. "The Rucellai Family and Its Loggia," *Journal of the Warburg and Courtauld Institutes*, 35 (1972), 397–401.

Mancini, Girolamo. *Vita di Alberti* (see above, Part 2, under "Alberti").

Perosa, Alessandro, ed. *Giovanni Rucellai e il suo zibaldone*. Vol. 1, *Il zibaldone quaresimale*. London: Warburg Institute, 1960. For the palace see pp. 143–44, which show that the present structure was built out of eight earlier houses.

Sanpaolesi, Piero. "Precisazioni sul Palazzo Rucellai," *Palladio*, n.s. 13 (1963), 61–66.

Strozzi Palace

Goldthwaite, Richard A. "The Florentine Palace" (see above, part 3).

——. "The Building of the Strozzi Palace: The Construction Industry in Renaissance Florence," *Studies in Medieval and Renaissance History*, 10 (1973), 99–194.

Pampaloni, Guido. *Palazzo Strozzi*. Rome: Istituto nazionale delle assicurazioni, 1963.

Warburg, Aby. "Francesco Sassetti's letzwillige Verfügung," in Warburg, *Gesammelte Schriften*. 2 vols. Leipzig and Berlin: Teubner, 1932, 1.147ff.

Index

Buildings are listed under their locations.

PYTHAGOREAN PALACES

Designed by R. E. Rosenbaum.
Composed by Vail-Ballou Press, Inc., in 10 point VIP Palatino, 3 points leaded, with display
   lines in Palatino.
Printed offset by Vail-Ballou Press on P & S Offset, 60 pound basis.
Bound by Vail-Ballou Press in Joanna book cloth and stamped in All Purpose foil.

Library of Congress Cataloging in Publication Data
(For library cataloging purposes only)

Hersey, George L
   Pythagorean palaces : magic and architecture in the Italian Renaissance.

  Bibliography: p.
  Includes index.
  1. Palaces—Italy. 2. Architecture, Renaissance—Italy. 3. Architecture
—Composition, proportion, etc. 4. Pythagoras and Pythagorean school.
I. Title.
NA7755.H47   728.8'2'0945   76-13661
ISBN 0-8014-0998-5